John Churton Collins

Bolingbroke, a Historical Study, and Voltaire in England

John Churton Collins

Bolingbroke, a Historical Study, and Voltaire in England

ISBN/EAN: 9783744715805

Printed in Europe, USA, Canada, Australia, Japan

Cover: Foto ©ninafisch / pixelio.de

More available books at **www.hansebooks.com**

BOLINGBROKE

A HISTORICAL STUDY

AND

VOLTAIRE IN ENGLAND

BY
JOHN CHURTON COLLINS

NEW YORK
HARPER & BROTHERS, FRANKLIN SQUARE
1886

PREFACE.

THE Essays comprised in this volume were originally contributed to the *Quarterly Review* and to the *Cornhill Magazine*, and the Author has to thank Mr. Murray for permission to reprint the papers on Bolingbroke, and Messrs. Smith and Elder for permission to reprint the papers on Voltaire in England. Both series of Essays have been carefully revised; to both series, but particularly to the second, considerable additions have been made. They have been collected in a volume not because the Author attaches undue importance to them, but because he ventures to think that they throw light on two singularly interesting episodes in the political and literary history of the eighteenth century, and because he is willing to believe that, as they are the result of more research than will perhaps appear upon the surface, they may be of some use to future biographers of Bolingbroke and Voltaire.

CONTENTS.

THE POLITICAL LIFE OF LORD BOLINGBROKE.

Introduction	3, 4
The Biographers	4, 5
Characteristics of Bolingbroke	6–13
His Influence on English Literature	14
On the Course of Public Thought both in England and Abroad	14, 15
Ancestry and Early Education	15–21
His Youth: Licentiousness	22, 23
Continental Travels	23–25
Marriage	26
Entrance into Public Life	27
State of Parties on the Accession of Queen Anne	27–30
Character of Robert Harley	30–32
St. John's Political Attitude	32
State of Public Affairs, Prospect and Retrospect	33–35
Character of Godolphin: his Policy	35, 36
St. John rapidly rises into Distinction: his Appointment to the Secretaryship of War	37–39
The Whigs come into Power	39
Duplicity of Harley, shared in by St. John	39, 40
Fall of Harley	41
Retirement of St. John	41, 42
Overthrow of the Godolphin Administration: Causes of same: its Splendid Services	42–46
Administration of Harley and St. John	45–47
Difficulties of Harley's Position	47–49
Party Writers: Swift and his Services	50, 51
Marlborough	52
Dissensions among the Tory Party	52, 53

CONTENTS.

	PAGE
Harley rising into Undeserved Popularity through Guiscard's Unsuccessful Attempt on his Life	53–56
Secret Negotiations with France	56, 57
Resentment of the Whig Party: Crisis in Parliament	58, 59
St. John Victorious	59
Tactics of the Tories	59–61
Preliminaries of the Treaty of Utrecht: St. John's Negotiation with France	61, 62
His Promotion to the Peerage	62, 63
His Diplomatic Mission to Paris	63, 64
Treaty of Utrecht Concluded	65, 66
Reflections on the Treaty, and on Bolingbroke's Conduct	66–68
Dissensions between Bolingbroke and Oxford	68–70
Bolingbroke Determined to bring Matters to a Crisis	71–73
Oxford is Removed	73
Bolingbroke Prime-minister: his Intrigues with the Jacobites	73, 74
The Earl of Shrewsbury Secedes	75
The Queen Dies, and the Tory Party Collapses	75, 76

BOLINGBROKE IN EXILE.

Importance of this Period	79, 80
Retrospect at the Close of Bolingbroke's Political Career	81
Bolingbroke's Schemes	82, 83
His Advances not Encouraged by the Elector	84
Arrival of the King in England	84
The Whigs come into Power, their Proceedings against the late Government	84–86
Bolingbroke's Attempt at Self-justification Unsuccessful	86
Threatening Prospects	86, 87
Flight of Bolingbroke	87, 88
Imprudence of this Step	88–90
His Arrival in Paris: Interview with Berwick and Stair	90
Impeached by Walpole: Considerations thereon	90–92
Declared an Outlaw	93
The Pretender, his Character: Reasons which guided Bolingbroke in Espousing his Cause	93–97

	PAGE
Bolingbroke Organizes the Jacobite Movement in Paris: Disappointments and Trials	97, 98
Circumstances Favorable to the Cause	99, 100
Negotiations of Bolingbroke	100–102
Inauspicious Events: Death of Louis XIV., Flight of Ormond	102–104
Declining Prospects of the Jacobite Cause: its Collapse	104, 105
Bolingbroke's Services to the Pretender: is Dismissed	105–108
News Arrives in London	108
Bolingbroke Attempts to come to Terms with the English Government	108, 109
His Retirement and Private Studies	109–112
Connection with the Marquise de Villette and Subsequent Marriage	113, 114
Literary Pursuits	114–116
Friendship with Voltaire	116–120
His Desire to Return to England repeatedly Thwarted: at last Acceded to	121
His Interview with Walpole and Carteret	121–124
His Offer of Intercession at the French Court Declined by Walpole	124, 125
Walpole Averse to Bolingbroke's Restoration: at last Forced to Consent to it by the King	126, 127
Bolingbroke's Double Life	127, 128

LITERARY LIFE OF LORD BOLINGBROKE.

Bolingbroke as an Opponent of the Ministry: his Position and Influence in the Political Contest	131, 132
State of Parties: the Leaders of the Opposition	132–137
Organization of the Opposition: Publication of the *Craftsman*	137, 138
Bolingbroke one of its Chief Contributors	138
His Interview with the King	139, 140
Death of the King	141
Critical Aspect of Affairs	141
Walpole Restored to Power	142
Factions in Parliament, Venality of Office-holders	142–144

CONTENTS.

Tactics of the Opposition	144–147
Nearly Successful	147
The Excise Bill	147–149
Review of Bolingbroke's Contributions to the *Craftsman* from 1727 until 1734	150
His "Remarks on the History of England"	151–153
His "Dissertation upon Parties"	153–155
Bolingbroke as a Writer on Philosophical and Metaphysical Subjects: his Life at Dawley	155, 156
His Friends	157, 158
Bolingbroke's Friendship with Pope	158
His Influence on Pope's Mind and Studies	159–163
Departure from England: Reasons for same	163–165
His Residence in France: Inquiries	165
His "Letters on the Study of History"	166, 167
His "Letter on the Spirit of Patriotism"	168
Character of the Prince of Wales	169–171
Bolingbroke Attempts to Ingratiate himself with the Prince	171, 172
The "Patriot King:" Considerations thereon	172–175
Walpole's Influence Declines: his Resignation	175, 176
Bolingbroke Arrives too Late from France: his Last Chance Lost	176
Retrospect of Bolingbroke's Literary Career	176, 177
His Unworthy Conduct towards Pope	177–180
Last Days of Bolingbroke	180
Afflictions of Age	181
Death of Lady Bolingbroke	181
Death of Bolingbroke	181
Publication of his Philosophical Works	181
Review of his Philosophical Works	181
Summary of his Philosophy	185–187
Epilogue	187

VOLTAIRE IN ENGLAND.

SECTION I.

Voltaire's Stay in England: an Unwritten Chapter in his Biography	191, 192

Date of his Arrival.................................. 193, 194
First Impressions................................... 195, 196
The Friends he makes in England: Bubb Dodington, Sir
    Everard Falkener............................... 197, 198
Interview with Pope.................................. 200–202
Reverses of Fortune: Family Afflictions.............. 202, 203
At Eastbury: meets Young............................ 205, 206
His Views on Men and Manners........................ 206–208
Lady Hervey: Voltaire's English Verses..............   209
His Double-dealing in Politics...................... 210–212
His Effusiveness as a Critic........................   212
Studies of English Life............................. 213–216
Visit to France.....................................   216

SECTION II.

Scrap-book of Voltaire: a Clew to his Familiarity with English
    Life... 216, 217
His Study of Newton's Works, of Locke's, of Bacon's, and
    of Berkeley's.................................. 217–219
Sympathy with the Free-thought Movement as Inaugurated
    by Collins and Woolston........................   220
His Literary Productions in the English Language.... 221–224
Preparations for the Publication of the "Henriade".. 224–226
Issue of the Work...................................   226
Its Immense Success................................. 227, 228
Piratical Publishers................................ 228, 229
Domestic Troubles...................................   230
Alterations of the Manuscript.......................   231
Comments of the Press............................... 231, 232
Untoward Incident: Voltaire's Clever Escape.........   233
British National Self-complacency strikingly Illustrated... 233, 234

SECTION III.

Voltaire's Different Literary Undertakings from April,
    1728, until March, 1729........................ 234–236
His Growing Familiarity with English Literature..... 236, 237
His Indebtedness to English Men of Letters.......... 237–240

Retrospect at the Close of his Stay in England............ 240, 241
His Respect for the English.......................... 242
Calumnious Statements Circulated as to the Cause of his
    Departure from England......................... 243, 244
Last Interview with Pope............................ 244
Voltaire's Return to France.......................... 245

POLITICAL LIFE OF BOLINGBROKE.

SUMMARY.

Introduction, p. 3, 4—The Biographers, p. 4–6—Characteristics of Bolingbroke, p. 6-14—His influence on English literature, p. 14—On the course of public thought both in England and abroad, p. 15—Ancestry and early education, p. 16-22—His youth: licentiousness, p. 22, 23—Continental Travels, p. 23, 24—Marriage, p. 26—Entrance into public life, p. 27—State of Parties on the accession of Queen Anne, p. 27-29—Harley, the Speaker of the House of Commons: his character, p. 30-32—St. John's political attitude, p. 32, 33—State of public affairs, prospect and retrospect, p. 33-35—Character of Godolphin: his policy, p. 35-37—St. John rapidly rises into distinction: his appointment to the Secretaryship of War, p. 38, 39—The Whigs come into power, p. 39—Duplicity of Harley, shared in by St. John, p. 40—Downfall of Harley, p. 41—Retirement of St. John, p. 41, 42—Overthrow of the Godolphin Administration: causes of same, p. 43-46—Its splendid services, p. 42, 43—Administration of Harley and St. John, p. 46, 47—Difficulties of Harley's position, p. 47-49—Party writers: Swift's services, p. 50, 51—Marlborough, p. 51, 52—Dissensions among the Tory party, p. 52, 53—Harley rising into undeserved popularity through Guiscard's unsuccessful attempt on his life, p. 53-56—Secret negotiations carried on with France, p. 56-58—Resentment of the Whig party: climax in Parliament, p. 58, 59—St. John victorious, p. 59—Tactics of the Tories, p. 59-62—Preliminaries of the Treaty of Utrecht: activity of St. John in preparing same: his promotion to the peerage, p. 62, 63—His diplomatic mission to Paris, p. 63, 64—Treaty of Utrecht concluded: Treaty discussed, p. 65-67—Reflection on the treaty, and on Bolingbroke's conduct, p. 68—Dissensions between Bolingbroke and Oxford, p. 68-71—Bolingbroke determined to bring matters to a crisis, p. 71-73—Oxford is removed, p. 73—Bolingbroke Prime-minister: Jacobite intrigues, p. 74—The Earl of Shrewsbury secedes, p. 75—The Queen dies, and the Tory party collapses, p. 75, 76.

ESSAYS.

THE POLITICAL LIFE OF BOLINGBROKE.*

WE have little respect for the public conduct of Bolingbroke; we have no liking for his personal character; we regard his political writings with suspicion, and his metaphysical writings with contempt; but we cannot transcribe these title-pages without strong feelings of regret. It was, as he once bitterly observed, his lot during life to suffer more at the hands of his friends than at the hands of his enemies; and what was his lot in life, has been by a rare refinement of misfortune his lot ever since. The edition of his works by Mallet is, if we except the type and paper, one of the worst editions of an English author that ever issued from the press. It is frequently disfigured by misprints; it swarms with errors in punctuation; its text, as a very cursory collation with the original manuscripts will suffice to show, is not always to be depended on. It was hurried into the world with indecent haste, without one word of preface, without any attempt at arrangement, with

* "The Works of the late Right Honorable Henry St. John Lord Viscount Bolingbroke," published by David Mallet.
"Memoirs of Lord Bolingbroke," by George Wingrove Cooke.
"The Life of Henry St. John Viscount Bolingbroke," by Thomas Macknight.

scarcely a line of annotation. The result is that nine-tenths of the political papers must be as unintelligible to a reader who is not minutely acquainted with the parliamentary controversies which raged round Walpole, as the "Letters of Junius" would be to a reader who was similarly ignorant of the career of Wilkes, or of the administration of Grafton. And what applies to these papers will apply, with scarcely less propriety, to the more important works on which Bolingbroke's literary fame must rest—to the "Letter to Wyndham," to the "Dissertation on Parties," to the "Remarks on the History of England." It would, in truth, be difficult to name a writer of equal merit, who is more dependent on a judicious editor for those little services which so often turn the scale between popular recognition and oblivion. But a hundred and twenty years have rolled away without this useful functionary making his appearance, and the works of one of the greatest masters of our tongue are confined almost exclusively to the perusal of readers who can dispense with illustrative assistance.

In his biographers and apologists he has been equally unlucky. The "Memoirs of his Ministerial Life," which appeared in 1752, the "Life and History," which appeared in 1754, the "Biography," by Goldsmith, the "Mémoires Secrètes," the "Essai Historique," by Grimoard, have followed one another in rapid succession into oblivion, and into an oblivion which, we are bound to add, they justly merited. Nor can we speak very favorably of the more elaborate biographies at the head of this article. The work of Mr. Wingrove Cooke, though skilfully executed, is, like his "History of Parties," too superficial and too inaccurate to be ever likely to attain a permanent place in literature. Indeed, the "Life" by Mr. Macknight has already superseded it. Mr. Macknight's volume is fairly entitled to the praise of diligence and impartiality. He has carefully consulted all obvious sources of information; he has availed himself to the full of the work of his predecessor; he has studied with care the bulky correspondence in which Bolingbroke loved to pour himself out, and he has produced in consequence a work of some pretension. But his style is slipshod, and his grasp is feeble. Of proportion and perspective in the disposition of his material he has no idea. He is continually expanding where he ought to retrench; he is continually retrenching where he ought to expand. He gives us, for example, a long and tedious dissertation on the Treaty of Utrecht, but he despatches in a few pages one of the most curiously interesting periods in his hero's career—the period between 1733 and 1736. He enters at length into all the questions which embroiled the Opposition with Walpole; but of Bolingbroke's influence on literature and philosophy he says scarcely one word, of his character, nothing. His acquaintance, moreover, with the literary and political history of the eighteenth century is not sufficiently extensive to prevent him from habitually blundering when the course of his narrative obliges him to touch on such topics, and such topics are, unfortunately, of the essence of his task. In a word, Mr. Macknight has produced a work which is beyond question the best biography of Bolingbroke, but he has not produced a work which students can consult with satisfaction, or to which the general reader will be likely to turn for amusement. He is neither a Coxe nor a Southey. Of M. Rémusat's Essay we shall content ourselves with saying that it is a sober and patient study, eminently suggestive, luminous and animated. As a biography it is necessarily defective; as a critique it is admirable.

Bolingbroke belongs to a class of men whose peculiarities both of intellect and temper are sufficiently unmistakable. The course of his public life, though often tortuous and perplexing, presents on the whole few ambiguities. The details of his private life may still be collected with singular fulness from innumerable sources. For nearly half a century he lived among shrewd and observant men of the world, and of these some of the shrewdest and most observant have recorded their impressions of him. His speeches have perished, but his writings and his correspondence remain; and both his writings and his correspondence are eminently characteristic.

Seldom has it been the lot even of the great leaders of mankind to unite in the same dazzling combination such an array of eminent qualities as met in this unhappy statesman. His intellect was of the highest and rarest order—keen, clear, logical, comprehensive, rapidly assimilative, inexhaustibly fertile. His memory was so prodigious that he complained, like Themistocles, of its indiscriminating tenacity; but the treasures of Bolingbroke's memory were at the ready call of a swift and lively intelligence. "His penetration," says Chesterfield, "resembled intuition." His imagination was warm and vivid, his judgment clear, his energy almost superhuman. While a mere youth he was distinguished alike by audacity and tact, by rare skill in debate, by rare talents for the practical duties of statesmanship. His powers of application were such as are not often found conjoined with parts so quick and with a temperament so naturally mercurial. "He would plod"—we are quoting Swift—"whole days and nights like the lowest clerk in an office;" and even in his latter years the unremitting intensity of his studies excited the wonder of younger students. His mind had early been enlarged by foreign travel and by an unusually wide experience. In the world of books and in the world of men he was equally interested, and he was equally at home. "He joined," writes Chesterfield, "all the politeness, the manners and the graces of a courtier to the solidity of a statesman and to the learning of a pedant." The most accomplished of his acquaintances have observed that there was scarcely any branch of human knowledge which had escaped his curious and discursive glance. His face and figure were such as sculptors love to dwell upon; and such as more than one of his contemporaries have paused to describe. His person was tall and commanding; his features were of classical beauty, but eager, mobile, animated; his forehead was high and intellectual, his lips indicated eloquence, his eyes were full of fire. Grace and dignity blended themselves in his deportment. The witchery of his manners has been acknowledged by the most malignant of his detractors, and his exquisite urbanity passed into a proverb. "To make St. John more polite," was the phrase employed by a poet of those times as a synonym for superfluous labor. "Lord Bolingbroke," says Aaron Hill, "was the finest gentleman I ever saw." From the multitude, indeed, he stood coldly and haughtily aloof, but his sympathy with men of genius and learning was quick, catholic, and generous. He rescued Fenton from the drudgery of a private school, and his patronage was extended not only to those poets and wits who have given him a place beside Mæcenas and Alphonso da Este, but to scholarship and to science. One of the most distinguished mathematicians of that century has recorded his gratitude to him, and even George Whitefield relates with pride how he once numbered Bolingbroke among the most attentive and eulogistic of his listeners. Long before his abilities had fully matured themselves, the gates of St. Stephen's were closed against him; but not before an audience familiar with the eloquence of Halifax and Somers had pronounced him to be the first orator of his age. "I would rather," said Pitt, "have a speech of Bolingbroke's than any of the lost treasures of antiquity." The charm of his conversation has been described by men whose judgment is without appeal, by Pope and Voltaire, by Swift, Orrery, and Chesterfield.

His character was, however, so unhappily constituted that these superb powers were seldom or never in harmonious co-operation. The virtues which balance and control, sobriety, moderation, consistency, had no part in his composition. His impetuosity and intemperance amounted to disease. To the end of his long life he was the slave not merely of every passion, but of every impulse; and what the capricious tyranny of emotion dictated had for the moment the power of completely transforming him. He exhibited by turns the traits peculiar to the most exalted and to the most debased of our species. His virtues and his vices, his reason and his passions, did not as in ordinary men blend themselves in a gradation of tints, but remained isolated in sudden and glaring contrast. His transitions were from extreme to extreme. He was sometimes all vice, he was sometimes all elevation. When his fine intellect was unclouded, his shrewdness and sagacity were a match for De Torcy; his dexterity and adroitness more than a match for Marlborough and Godolphin. When his intellect took the ply from his passions, there was little to distinguish him from the most hot-headed and hare-brained of his own tools. In his sublimer moments he out-Catoed Cato, in his less exalted moods he sank below Sandys and Dodington. When in retirement, he shut himself up with the "Tusculans" and the Enchiridion, he lived and talked as became a disciple of the Porch. When he reappeared among men, his debaucheries were the scandal of the two most profligate capitals in Europe. His actions were sometimes those of a high-minded and chivalrous gentleman, capable of making great sacrifices, and distinguished by a spirit of romantic generosity. A change of mood would suffice to transform him into the most callous, the most selfish, the most cynical of misanthropes. He was never, we believe, a deliberate hypocrite, but his emotions were so transient, his conduct so capricious, that he might have passed for Tartuffe himself. The fascination of his manners and the brilliancy of his parts naturally surrounded him with many friends. Friendship was, he said, indispensable to his being; it was the noblest of human instincts; it was sacred; it should be inviolable; it was in its purity the prerogative only of great and good men. His letters to Prior, to Swift, to Alari, and to Pope, abound in the most extravagant professions of attachment. His letters to Lord Hardwicke are sometimes almost fulsome. But what was the sequel? He quarrelled with Alari for presuming to advise him. He dropped Swift when the letters of Swift ceased to entertain him. He dropped Hardwicke from mere caprice. His perfidy to Pope is, we believe, literally without example in social treachery. He bore the most excruciating of human maladies with a placid fortitude which would have done honor to Stylites; but the slightest error on the part of his cook would send him into such paroxysms of rage that his friends were glad to be out of his house. His whole soul was tormented by an insatiable thirst for literary and political distinction; it would, we believe, be impossible to find in his voluminous correspondence half a dozen letters in which he does not express contempt both for the world and for the world's regard. His opinions were as wayward and as whimsical as his actions. He delighted to write of himself as the votary of a mild and tolerant philosophy which had taught him the vanity of ambition, and could be nourished only in that retirement which, thanks to his enemies, he was enabled to enjoy. Before the ink was dry he was ransacking our language for scurrilous epithets against those who had excluded him from public life. Resignation was, he said, the virtue on which he especially prided himself. His life was notoriously one long and fierce rebellion. He professed the greatest respect for prescription, and is one of the most revolutionary of writers; for the Church, and would have betrayed it; for Christianity, and was in the van of its most ferocious assailants. He delivered himself sometimes in rhodomontade redolent of the ethics of Seneca and of the Utopias of Plato and Xenophon, and sometimes in rhodomontade breathing the spirit of the Prince and of the Fable of the Bees. As the subject of Anne, he went as far as Filmer in his estimate of the royal prerogative; as the subject of George, he went beyond Paley in depreciating it. As the minister of Anne, he was the originator of the Stamp Act; as the subject of George, he was the loudest and most vehement of those demagogues who clamored for the absolute freedom of the press. In power he was the author of the Schism Act; out of power he taunted Walpole with deserting the Dissenters. The age he lived in he pronounced to be the Nadir of moral and political corruption; he proposed to purify it by a scheme which postulates the perfection of those whose vices are to be cured by it.

The truth is that, with quick sensibilities he had no depth of feeling, with much insight no convictions. What would in well-regulated minds have developed into principle, remained in him mere sentiment; and his sentiments were like the whims of a libertine, ardent, fanciful, and transitory. His head was hot, but his heart was cold.

In the latter part of his career he set himself up as the castigator of political immorality, and as the loftiest and most disinterested of patriots. His own public life had been such that each part of it seems elaborately designed to set off and heighten the turpitude of some other part. The shameless charlatanism of his career at the head of the extreme Tories might have passed perhaps for honest zeal—intemperate, indeed, but pure—had he not at the head of the extreme Whigs found it expedient to cover his former principles with ridicule. It was not till he became the hottest of factious incendiaries out of power that men realized the baseness of his despotic conservatism in power. It was not till he betrayed the interests of St. Germains that it was possible to estimate the extent of his treachery to the interests of Hanover. It was not till he became the teacher of Voltaire and the Apostle of Scepticism that his unscrupulousness in forcing on the Bill against Occasional Conformity and in originating the Schism Bill fully revealed itself.

Some of his biographers have indeed labored to explain away many of the inconsistencies of his public conduct. In other words, they have attempted to do for Bolingbroke what in ancient times Isocrates attempted to do for Busiris, and what in our own day Mr. Beesly has attempted to do for Catiline, and Mr. Christie for Shaftesbury. But the attempt has failed. The facts speak for themselves. There can be no doubt about Bolingbroke's repeatedly declaring the Revolution to be the guarantee of our civil and religious liberties, and that both before and after his fall he labored to set the Act of Settlement aside. There can be no doubt about his satisfying himself that if the Pretender ascended the throne without giving pledges for the security of our national faith there would be civil war, and that he moved heaven and earth to put the Pretender on the throne without insisting on any such pledges. It is certain that he defended the Treaty of Utrecht mainly on the ground of England's exhaustion being such that without repose paralysis was imminent; and that not long afterwards he was lamenting that he could not at the head of a French army violate his own Treaty, and plunge that country, of which he had boasted himself the savior, into the double horrors of foreign invasion and internecine strife. It is certain that he professed the principles of the moderate Tories, of the extreme Tories, of the Jacobites, of the Hanoverians, of the Whigs in office and of the Whigs in opposition, and it is equally certain that, with the exception of the last party, they all taunted him with perfidy.

It would, however, be a great mistake to confound Bolingbroke either with fribbles like the Second Villiers, whom he resembled in the infirmities of his temper, or with sycophants like Sunderland, whom he resembled in want of principle. His nature had, with all its flaws, been cast in no ignoble mould. The ambition which consumed him was the ambition which consumed Cæsar and Cicero, not the ambition which consumed Harley and Newcastle. For the mere baubles of power he cared nothing. Riches and their trappings he regarded with unaffected contempt. He entered office a man by no means wealthy, and with expensive habits; he quitted it with hands as clean as Pitt's. The vanity which feeds on adulation never touched his haughty spirit. His prey was not carrion. His vast and visionary ambition was bounded only by the highest pinnacles of human glory. He aspired to enroll himself among those great men who have shaped the fortunes and moulded the minds of mighty nations—with the demi-gods of Plutarch, with the sages of Diogenes. As a statesman he never rested till he stood without a rival on the summit of power. As a philosopher he sought a place beside Aristotle and Bacon, and the infirmities of age overtook him while meditating a work which was to class him with Guicciardini and Clarendon.

This was not to be. One faculty had indeed been granted him in a measure rarely conceded to the children of men—a faculty which is of all others most likely to mislead contemporaries, and least likely to deceive posterity—the faculty of eloquent expression. His style may be praised almost without reservation. It is distinguished by the union of those qualities which are in the estimation of critics sufficient to constitute perfection—by elevation, by rapidity, by picturesqueness, by perspicuity, by scrupulous chastity, by the charm of an ever-varying music. It combines, as no other English style has ever combined, the graces of colloquy with the graces of rhetoric. It is essentially eloquent, and it is an eloquence which is, to employ his own happy illustration, like a stream fed by an abundant spring—an eloquence which never flags, which is never inappropriate, which never palls. His fertility of expression is wonderful. Over all the resources of our noble and opulent language his mastery is at once exquisite and unlimited. Of effort and elaboration his style shows no traces. His ideas seem to clothe themselves spontaneously in their rich and varied garb. He had studied, as few Englishmen of that day had studied, the masterpieces of French literature, but no taint of Gallicism mars the transcendent purity of his English. His pages are a storehouse of fine and graceful images, of felicitous phrases, of new and striking combinations. As an essayist he is not inferior to his master, Seneca. As a political satirist he is second only to Junius. As a letter-writer he ranks with Pliny and Cicero, and we cannot but regret that so large a portion of his correspondence is still permitted to remain unpublished.

On English prose his influence was immediate and permanent. It would not indeed be too much to say that it owes more to Bolingbroke than to any other single writer. Hooker and Taylor had already lent it color and pomp; Dryden had given it verve, variety, flexibility; De Foe and Swift had brought it home to the vulgar; the Periodical Writers had learned from the pulpit to endow it with elegance and harmony; but it was reserved for Bolingbroke to be the Cicero of our tongue. He was, in truth, the founder of a great dynasty of stylists. On him Burke modelled his various and exuberant eloquence. From him Junius learned some of his most characteristic graces. The two Pitts made no secret of their obligations to him; and among his disciples are to be numbered Goldsmith,* Gibbon, Hume, and even Macaulay.

His genius was, it is true, too irregularly cultivated, his aspirations too multiform, his reason too essentially under the control of passion, to secure him any high place among the teachers of mankind, and yet few men have impressed themselves more definitely on the intellectual activity of

---

* For the influence of Bolingbroke's style on that of Goldsmith we would point especially to "The Present State of Polite Learning in Europe," and to the Dedication of the "Traveller." What Macaulay learned from him was, we think, the art of combining dignity with sprightliness, copiousness with scrupulous purity: many turns of expression, and the rhetorical effect both of the short sentence and of clause iteration.

their age. That great revolution in the study of history which found its first emphatic expression in Montesquieu is undoubtedly to be traced to him. There is scarcely a chapter in Gibbon's great work in which his influence is not discernible. By the philosophers of the Encyclopédie he was recognized as a leader. Voltaire's obligations to him are confessed by Condorcet. To Bolingbroke he owed his introduction to the works of Bacon, Newton, and Locke; much of his philosophy, many of his historical theories. Indeed, Voltaire appears to have regarded him with feelings approaching as nearly to reverence as it was perhaps possible for him to attain. Idolized by Pope, Bolingbroke suggested and inspired some of the most valuable of Pope's compositions—the Essay on Man, the Moral Essays, the Imitations of Horace. His influence on the academics of Italy is evident from the *Elogio* of Salvatore Canella. The spirit which he kindled during the administration of Walpole still burns in the epics and ballad of Glover, in the tragedies of Brooke, in the best of Akenside's compositions, in the stateliest of Thomson's verses, in the noblest of Collins's odes, in Goldsmith's fine philosophic poem, in the most spirited of Churchill's Satires. To the influence of his writings is to be attributed in no small degree that remarkable transformation which converted the Toryism of Rochester and Nottingham into the Toryism of Pitt and Mansfield. He annihilated the Jacobites. He turned the tide against Walpole, and he formulated the principles which afterwards developed into the creed of what is called in our own day Liberal Conservatism. It would in truth be scarcely possible to overestimate the extent of his influence on public opinion between 1725 and 1742.

He sprang from an ancient and honorable race, which

had, as early as the thirteenth century, mingled the blood of a noble Norman family with the blood of a Saxon family not less illustrious. William de St. John, a Norman knight, was quartermaster-general in the army of the Conqueror. The estates which rewarded the services of his son passed with other property into the hands of a female representative, who became the wife of Adam de Port, one of the wealthiest of the Saxon aristocracy. Their son William assuming the maiden name of his mother, the name De Port was merged in the name of St. John. The family grew and prospered. John St. John was one of the Council of Nine appointed after the battle of Lewes. The widow of his descendant Oliver became by her marriage with the Duke of Somerset the grandmother of Henry VII.; and a window in Battersea church, gorgeous with heraldic emblazonry, still commemorates this alliance with the Tudors. In the reign of Elizabeth the St. Johns became the Barons of Bletso; in the reign of James I. one of them was created Earl of Bolingbroke. Nor were the representatives of the younger line less eminent. The services of Oliver St. John as Lord Deputy of Ireland were rewarded with the Barony of Tregoze in Wiltshire. During the civil wars the St. Johns came prominently forward. The elder line, represented by the Earl of Bolingbroke, and by that great lawyer—over whose birth was the bar sinister, but who was destined to become a chief-justice of England and to adorn his high office—were in conspicuous opposition to the Crown. The younger line, represented by John St. John, who lost three sons in the field, were as conspicuously distinguished by their loyalty.

The days of trouble passed by, and the subsequent marriage of Sir Walter St. John, a member of the Royalist branch, with Joanna, a daughter of the chief-justice, probably composed political differences. The young couple settled at Battersea, to the manor of which Sir Walter had succeeded by the death of his nephew. The virtues of the Lady Joanna were long remembered in the neighborhood. Her husband's munificence is more imperishably recorded in the school which he founded nearly two centuries ago, and which has ever since been one of the ornaments of Battersea. His crest and motto may still be seen over the gate; his portrait still adorns the walls. He died at an advanced age in 1708. The issue of this marriage was a daughter Barbara and a son Henry, of whom we know little, and that little is not to his credit. The dissipated habits of the young man probably alarming his parents, they resorted to the expedient usual in such cases, and the lad became the husband of Mary, second daughter and joint-heiress of Robert Rich, Earl of Warwick.* The remedy, however, only aggravated the disease. Henry became worse than ever. At last he brought his reckless and dissolute career to a climax by the murder of St. William Escourt in a brawl. He was arrested. His friends were in despair. After much anxious deliberation, his counsel advised him to plead guilty, and to throw himself on the mercy of the King. For some time it was doubtful whether the united influence of the St. Johns and the Riches could prevent him from expiating his crime at Tyburn, or whether indeed the King could, even if he wished it, stretch his prerogative so far as to pardon a subject convicted of so grave an offence. At last the culprit was

---

* The youth appears to have added to his other vices that of hypocrisy, as we find him described in the "Autobiography of Mary, Countess of Warwick," as a "young gentleman very good-natured and viceless." See "Autobiography," edited by T. C. Croker for the Percy Society, p. 35.

permitted to retire to Battersea. A bribe was accepted. The case was dropped, and he dragged on a listless and good-for-nothing life for nearly half a century longer. Six years before this event his wife had borne him a child, who was destined to inherit all his vices, but with those vices to unite abilities which, if properly directed, and less unhappily tempered, might have given him a place in history beside Pericles and Chatham, and a place in letters beside Bacon and Burke. Henry St. John, afterwards Lord Viscount Bolingbroke, was born at Battersea in the October of 1678, and was baptized on the tenth of that month. The house in which he first saw the light has, with the exception of one wing, which is still preserved, been long since levelled with the ground.

For his early education he was indebted to his grandparents, who shared the family residence with their son and daughter-in-law. Sir Walter was a member of the Established Church, and appears to have been a kind and tolerant man. But his wife had been bred among the Puritans, and to the ascetic piety of her sect she added, we suspect, something of her father's moroseness. She ruled the house at Battersea. She superintended the education of her grandchild. It was conducted on principles of injudicious austerity, and Bolingbroke never recurred to this period of his life without disgust. The good lady delighted in perusing the gigantic tomes in which the Puritan Fathers discussed the doctrine of the Eucharist and the Atonement. Patrick's "Mensa Mystica" had been written under her roof, and she had shared with her husband the honor of the dedication; but Patrick held only the second place in her affections—her favorite was Dr. Manton. This stupendous theologian—five of his folios still slumber in our libraries—prided himself on having written a hundred and nineteen sermons on the hundred and nineteenth Psalm, and to the perusal of these hundred and nineteen sermons she compelled her grandson to betake himself.* There is reason for believing that the child was for some time under the tuition of Daniel Burgess, a learned and eccentric Nonconformist, who is now remembered chiefly as the butt of Swift, but who was in those days celebrated as one of the most popular of metropolitan preachers. His definition of a lawsuit and of thorough-paced doctrine are still treasured by collectors of good sayings.

In due time Henry was removed to Eton, where he remained for some years. About his career there tradition is silent. We know that Walpole was one of his contemporaries; and Coxe has added that the seeds of that long and bitter rivalry which ever afterwards existed between the two school-fellows were sown in the class-room and the play-ground. This, however, is highly improbable. Walpole acquitted himself creditably during his school career, and is not likely either by indolence or dulness to have permitted a lad two years his junior to assume the position of a rival. What became of him after leaving Eton it is now impossible to discover. His career is indeed at this point involved in more obscurity than his biographers seem to suspect. They assert, for example, that on leaving Eton he matriculated at Oxford, and became an undergraduate of Christ Church, and they have described with some circumstantiality his University career. But of this residence at Oxford there is no proof at all. There is no entry of his matriculation on the books of the University, and these books are not, we believe, in any way deficient dur-

* This is Bolingbroke's own account, but a reference to Dr. Manton's folio shows that the number was not a hundred and nineteen, but a hundred and ninety.

ing the period of his supposed connection with Oxford. There is no trace of his residence at Christ Church on the Buttery Lists, and the Buttery Lists have from the midsummer of 1695 been kept with scrupulous exactness. There is no trace of his residence to be found in the entry books of the Dean. We cannot find any allusion to his ever having been a resident member of the University in the correspondence of those accomplished men who must have been his contemporaries. But one circumstance seems to us conclusive. He was the patron of John Philips, and that pleasing poet has in two of his poems spoken of him in terms of exaggerated encomium. Philips was a student of Christ Church, and in his "Cyder" he takes occasion to celebrate the eminent men connected with that distinguished seminary; but though he mentions Harcourt and Bromley, he makes no allusion to St. John. The error, we suspect, arose from this. On the occasion of Queen Anne's visit to Oxford in 1702 St. John was made an honorary doctor and entered on the books of Christ Church. He was proud of the honor which the College of Atterbury and Harcourt had done him, and not only delighted to speak of himself as a Christ Church man, but ever afterwards considered that a member of that foundation had a special claim to his patronage. But Christ Church is not entitled to number him among her sons.

Wherever he pursued his studies, he probably pursued them with assiduity. He was all his life distinguished by attainments the groundwork of which is seldom or never laid in after-years. The specimen which he has left of his Latin composition, with the letters to Alari, prove that he had paid some attention to the niceties of verbal scholarship. Much of the recondite learning which he so ostentatiously paraded in his philosophical works was it is evident, the trophy of adroit plagiarism, but it is no less evident — as every page of his writings shows—that his classical acquirements, if not exact, were unusually extensive. He was conversant with the Roman prose writers, from Varro to Aulus Gellius, and the frequency with which he draws on them for purposes of analogy, comment, and illustration, the felicity with which he adapts their sentiments and opinions, the ready propriety with which their allusions and anecdotes respond to his call is a sufficient guarantee for the assimilative thoroughness with which he had perused them. Indeed his acquaintance with Cicero and Seneca appears to have been such as few scholars have possessed. He had studied them as Montaigne studied Plutarch, as Bacon studied Tacitus. To the poets he had not, we suspect, paid the same attention, though his quotations from Lucretius, Horace, and Virgil are often exquisitely happy. Whatever may have been his attainments in Greek, he had at least mastered the rudiments, could discuss the relative signification of words, and had read in some form or other the principal orators, Homer and Hesiod among the poets, and most of the historians.

It is the privilege of later years to mature and apply, rarely to initiate, such studies. We are therefore inclined to suspect that his biographers have plunged him into debauchery a little prematurely, and that these years of his life, wherever they may have been passed, were judiciously and profitably employed. But the scene soon changed. In 1697 we find him in London, where he abandoned himself to the dominion of the two passions which ever afterwards ruled him—inordinate ambition and inordinate love of pleasure. At thirty he was in the habit of observing that his heroes were Alcibiades and Petronius; at twenty his model, he said, was his cousin John Wilmot, Earl of

Rochester. That unhappy nobleman had, ten years before, terminated a career to which it would be difficult to find a parallel in the annals of human folly. Everything that can make the life of man splendid, prosperous, and happy, both Nature and Fortune had lavished on him. Nature had endowed him with abilities of a high order, with literary instincts, with refined tastes, with brilliant wit, with a lyrical genius which, if properly cultivated, might have placed him beside Béranger and Herrick, with a handsome and engaging person, with manners singularly winning and graceful. Fortune had added rank and opulence, and had thus opened out to him all sources of social and intellectual enjoyment; had enabled him to gratify every ambition, to cultivate every taste, and to enter that sphere where the qualities that distinguished him could be seen to the greatest advantage. Unhappily, however, a depraved and diseased mind counteracted these inestimable blessings. He was anxious only to be pre-eminent in infamy. A premature death had been the just penalty for his madness; but the tradition of his genius and of his brilliant parts had, in the eyes of young and giddy men, lent a romantic interest to his career. They learned his poems by heart. They retailed his witticisms. They listened with eagerness to stories about his bravery at Bergen, his wit-combats with Villiers, his amours, his convivial excesses, and they were anxious to follow in his footsteps. Indeed, the influence of Rochester on the youth of London in the latter quarter of the seventeenth century appears to have resembled, in some degree, the influence of Byron on the same class a hundred and twenty years later. But St. John was not content to be a mere zany, he aspired to rival his master as a wit, and to outstrip him as a libertine. He was now in his twentieth year, overflowing with animal spirits, drunk with vanity, and burning to indemnify himself for the restraints of Eton and Battersea. He allied himself with a band of reprobates who were striving to recall, under the purer rule of William, the wild license of the Restoration, and he became, while a mere boy, the worst member of that bad clique. His excesses moved astonishment even in those who had witnessed the orgies of his cousin. He passed whole weeks in unbroken rounds of riotous debauchery. He could drink down veteran drunkards. He ran naked through the Park.* He was a match for old Wycherley in ribald profanity and in all the arts of licentious intrigue. To the poetical genius of Rochester he had indeed no pretension, but he did his best to remedy the deficiency. He sought the acquaintance of Dryden, whom he visited on more than one occasion in Gerrard Street. The poet had just completed his version of Virgil, and St. John wrote a copy of verses which may still be read among the commendatory poems prefixed to that work. They are remarkable for nothing but the grossness of their imagery, and for the skill with which literary compliment is conveyed in the allusions of the bagnio.

He now set out on his travels, probably leaving England in the autumn of 1697. He was away nearly two years. Of his movements during that time nothing certain is known, but it may be gathered from an allusion in one of his letters that he visited Milan. Whatever portion of this period he may have spent in Italy, we are inclined to think with Mr. Macknight that much the greater part of it was spent at Paris. The Peace of Ryswick had

* The authority for this is Goldsmith. Pöllnitz was an eye-witness of a similarly disgusting freak in the same place.—*Memoirs*, vol. ii., p. 470.

just been concluded, and the attractions of the French capital were once more open to English visitors. In 1698 the Earl of Jersey had succeeded Portland as Ambassador. He was connected by family ties with St. John. He was on intimate terms with Sir Walter, and was in a position to be of great service to a lad beginning the world. It is indeed by no means improbable that young St. John, if not attached to his suite, at all events shared his protection, and was introduced by him to the salons of the Faubourg St. Germain and to the antechambers of Marly. It would be difficult on any other supposition to account for the delicate purity with which he ever afterwards both wrote and spoke the French language, and for his possession of an accent so perfect that even the fastidious ear of Voltaire was unable to detect a jarring chord. With this useful accomplishment he returned to England about the beginning of 1700. He at once devoted himself to his old pursuits, which appear to have been in a measure interrupted during his residence on the Continent. He composed a long Pindaric ode, in which he informs his readers that he had for some time been "wandering from the Muses' seat" and been visiting the "gloomy abodes of Wisdom and Philosophy," but that he had repented of his folly, and was returning to Poesy and Love. His return to the latter took the form of an intrigue with an orange girl who hung about the lobby of the Court of Requests; his return to the former, a poetical epistle addressed to his sordid paramour. These verses Lord Stanhope not only pronounces to be beautiful, but sees in them evidence of genius. They appear to us neither better nor worse than a dozen other poems of a similar character which might be selected from the miscellanies of that day, and the miscellanies of that day moved the derision of Pope. Many years later, indeed, he produced three stanzas, which are by no means contemptible.*

The ostentatious dissoluteness of his life was about this time aggravated by his taking a step which must have made Sir Walter tremble for the family estates. A woman whose beauty was a tradition in London circles, even as late as the days of Goldsmith, but whose extravagance had already completed the ruin of three lovers, was now under his protection. It became necessary to resort to extreme measures. Menaces were vain: exhortations were vain. The abilities of the young libertine were unquestionably great. His family was influential. He was now twenty-two, and his relatives wisely resolved to appeal to the only passion which rivalled in any degree his devotion to pleasure—the passion of ambition. They offered him

---

* As these verses have escaped the notice of all Bolingbroke's biographers, we will transcribe them. They were written for insertion in the masque of "Alfred," as part of "Rule Britannia," and are to be found in Davies's "Life of Garrick," vol. ii., p. 39.

> "Should war, should faction shake the isle,
>   And sink to poverty and shame;
> Heaven still shall o'er Britannia smile,
>   Restore her wealth and raise her name.
>   Rule Britannia, etc.

> "How blest the Prince reserved by fate
>   In adverse days to mount thy throne!
> Renew thy once triumphant state,
>   And on thy grandeur build his own.
>   Rule Britannia, etc.

> "His race shall long in times to come
>   (So Heaven ordains) thy sceptre wield;
> Rever'd abroad, beloved at home,
>   And be at once thy sword and shield.
>   Rule Britannia, etc."

a seat in Parliament. They suggested that he should take a wife, and they offered in the event of his marriage to settle on him the family estates in the counties of Wilts, Surrey, and Middlesex. To these proposals he acceded. At the close of 1700 he became the husband of Frances Winchescombe, daughter and one of the co-heiresses of Sir Henry Winchescombe, a descendant of the famous Jack of Newbury. The lady had a handsome fortune, and succeeded on the death of her father to a fine estate near Reading. She was, moreover, possessed of considerable personal attractions. John Philips has celebrated her charms, and in 1713 we find Swift writing to Stella: "Lady Bolingbroke came down while we were at dinner, and Parnell stared at her as if she were a goddess." The Dean delighted in her society, and humorously declared himself her lover. The married life of youthful libertines has been the same in all ages. St. John returned her affection, which was on more than one occasion in the course of his eventful life very touchingly evinced, at first with indifference, and subsequently with contempt. But Frances Winchescombe was a true woman. The conclusion of fifteen years of domestic misery, aggravated by his studied neglect and shameless infidelities, found her still clinging to him—"a little fury if they mention my dear lord without respect, which sometimes happens." On hearing, however, of his connection with the Marquise de Villette at Marcilly she became entirely estranged from him, altered her will, and left him nothing when she died in 1718. One or two angry paragraphs about the pecuniary loss he had sustained, and a bitter reflection on the suppleness of religion, to which he appears in some way to have attributed her conduct, was all the notice he took of her death. Shortly after the celebration of this inauspicious marriage he succeeded his father as member for Wootton Basset in Wiltshire, and he took his seat in the Parliament which assembled on February 6, 1701.

He entered public life at one of those conjunctures which veteran statesmen contemplate with dismay, but which have in all ages been hailed with delight by young and aspiring spirits. For fourteen years the country had been convulsed with the struggles of two great factions. These factions owed their origin not to superficial and accidental differences, which easily arising are easily reconciled, but to differences which admit of no compromises, and are in their very nature substantial and inveterate. Each was the representative of principles which can never under any circumstances meet in harmony, which should and may balance each other, but which were at that time in violent and terrible collision. Each was animated by those passions which are of all passions the most malignant and abiding. In the perplexity of an awful crisis they had for a moment suspended their animosities. Their leaders had come to terms. There had been a semblance of unity. Scarcely, however, had the Prince of Orange ascended the throne, than they had again broken out into tenfold vehemence and fury. For some time William scarcely seems to have been aware of the nature of the struggle which was raging round him, and had persisted in attempting to appease the belligerents; at last he saw, and he saw with the deepest regret, that all conciliatory measures were out of the question, and that he must attach himself to one of the two factions. He decided in favor of the party which had raised him to the throne, which would in all probability support his foreign policy, and which had since 1691 been gradually gaining ground. In September, 1697, the Peace of Ryswick was signed. It was indeed a mere armistice to enable William and Louis to discuss a complicated and momentous question. That mighty empire on which the sun never set was in all likelihood about to be left without an heir. It was necessary to settle the succession, for on the ultimate destination of those vast dominions hung the fate of Europe for many generations. William was anxious that they should not pass into the hands of the French claimant; Louis was equally anxious that they should not pass into the hands of Austria, or into the hands of the Electoral Prince. The two kings determined therefore to divide them between the three competitors, and the First Partition Treaty was arranged. Meanwhile William turned his attention to affairs in England, for all depended on the cordial support of the English Ministry and of the English people. In England, however, everything was going wrong; a Tory reaction was setting in. The first symptoms of that reaction were evident in the Parliament which assembled after the Peace of Ryswick; the reaction itself set in in full force when Parliament assembled in December, 1698. On that occasion there was a schism in the Whig ranks; on that occasion the first definite blow was aimed at William's foreign policy. The army was reduced. The navy was reduced. The Dutch guards were dismissed. Then followed the attack on Montague; next came the inquiry into Orford's administration, and, lastly, the question of the Crown grants. Suddenly arrived the intelligence that the Electoral Prince was no more. Again Louis and William resorted to diplomacy, and the Second Partition Treaty was arranged. At length the King of Spain died. It was known that he had made a will; it was known that in that will he had nominated a successor, and all Europe was anxious to know the terms of it. On the 3d of November,

1700, the Duke of Abrantes presented himself before the ambassadors and grandees who were thronging the antechambers of the Escurial, and announced that the whole Spanish monarchy had been bequeathed to the grandson of Louis. In the event of Louis refusing the succession for his grandson, it was to pass to Charles, Archduke of Austria. William at once saw what would happen; and when, a few weeks afterwards, his rival, in spite of all his solemn engagements, accepted the bequest, he could only watch with patience the course of events. There was, in truth, little to encourage him. The Tories were now completely in the ascendant. Their animosity against the King and against his Ministry had reached its climax. The power of the Whigs was everywhere declining. The session of April, 1700, had been abruptly closed without a speech from the throne, and William had been forced, with tears of humiliation in his eyes, to dismiss from his councils the wisest and the most faithful of his servants. In July the death of the Duke of Gloucester left the successor to the Crown without an heir. The state of the country was deplorable; from 1690 to 1699 there had been scarcely one year of average prosperity. A succession of wretched harvests had spread ruin among the farmers. In some districts trade was almost at a stand-still.* Bread riots had broken out in many of the provincial towns. The failure of the Land Bank had exasperated the country gentlemen who were watching with malignant jealousy the rise of the moneyed classes. Nine clergymen out of ten were Jacobites, and had been completely alienated from the throne by the Toleration Act. The King was not merely unpopular, but detested. His cold and repulsive manners, his systematic

* See Lecky's "History of England in the Eighteenth Century," and the authorities there quoted, vol. i., p. 17.

attempts to embroil England with foreign powers, his Dutch favorites, his exorbitant grants to those favorites, the protection he extended to needy aliens, his struggles to maintain a standing army, his suspensions of the Habeas Corpus Act, his abandonment of the Darien Colonists, his frequent retirements to the Continent, his secluded court—all tended to aggravate the public discontent. William now saw that the party on which he had relied for support was so broken and so powerless that there was nothing left for him to do but to throw himself into the arms of the Tories. He accordingly dissolved the Parliament in December, 1700, and summoned another for the following February. The Ministry was remodelled and the Tories came in. Godolphin was placed at the head of the Treasury; Tankerville was Privy Seal, while Hedges succeeded Jersey as one of the Secretaries of State. February arrived. The Houses met, and St. John took his seat in one of the most intemperate and turbulent assemblies which had since the days of the Plantagenets disgraced our parliamentary history.

The leader of the Lower House was Robert Harley, a man who was destined in a few years to reach the highest eminence which a British subject can attain, and to leave a name embalmed forever in the verse of Pope and Prior, and in the prose of Arbuthnot and Swift. On his entrance into public life he had played the part of an intolerant and vindictive Whig, but he had since, while retaining many of his original principles unimpaired, allied himself with the Tories. He had none of those gifts with which Nature endows her favorites. His features were gross and forbidding, his figure mean, his voice inharmonious, his gestures singularly uncouth.* To the art of engaging the passions,

* "The mischievous darkness of his soul"—the Duchess of Marl-

or of captivating the reason of the great assembly over which he presided, he made no pretension. As a speaker he was tedious, hesitating, confused, and not unfrequently unintelligible. Indeed, to the end of his life he remained incapable of framing ten sentences of lucid and coherent English. His intellect was both small and sluggish, his parts were scarcely above mediocrity. But he possessed qualities which seldom fail of being rated at many times their intrinsic value. He was cunning, decorous, reticent. His temper was not naturally good, but it was under strict control, and seldom betrayed him into an indiscreet or discourteous expression. His studies had been neither various nor profound, but they had been judiciously directed. In knowledge of the law of Parliament he was not excelled either by Seymour or Nottingham. His acquaintance with affairs was great, his memory tenacious, his judgment sound, his tact consummate. In all the arts of parliamentary diplomacy he was without a rival. Though in private life he sometimes made himself ridiculous by the frivolity of his amusements, he loved the society of men of genius and letters, and he was the first of English statesmen who had the sagacity to employ the press as an engine of political power. To these qualities he added others not so respectable. He was deeply tainted with those vices which ambition engenders in timid and pusillanimous natures. His meanness and treachery would have been conspicuously infamous even in that bad age in which his po-

---

borough is speaking—"was written in his countenance, and plainly legible in a very odd look disagreeable to everybody at first sight, which being joined with a constant awkward motion, or rather agitation of his head and body, betrayed a turbulent dishonesty within even in the midst of all those familiar airs, jocular bowing and smiling which he always affected."—*Conduct of the Duchess*, p. 261.

litical morality had been learned. Dilatory and irresolute, his aspirations were sordid and narrow. His indifference to truth shocked even the least scrupulous of his colleagues. His promises were like the promises of Granville, as ready and profuse as they were feigned or forgotten. At this moment, however, he stood well with all parties, for his real character was as yet unsuspected even by those who knew him best, as men are slower to detect than to practise dissimulation.

St. John probably saw that the star of Harley and the Tories was in the ascendant, and that even if a reaction set in there would be no room for him in the ranks of the Whig oligarchy. To Harley and the Tories he accordingly attached himself, and to Harley and the Tories he adhered, so long as it served his purpose, through all vicissitudes of fortune. Some of his biographers have labored to show that in taking this step he was acting in strict accordance with the principles he had inherited, and probably in accordance with his own independent convictions. Such a theory is partly false and partly ludicrous. His father and his grandfather, in the first place, were Whigs: most of his relatives were Whigs; and he had in early life been trained up in doctrines from which the Tories shrank in abhorrence. Nor had his subsequent career been more favorable to the formation of such convictions. The religious tenets of the Tories—and those religious tenets were of the essence of their politics—he systematically outraged in his life, and systematically ridiculed in his conversation. Of politics themselves, as he afterwards frankly confessed, he knew nothing. But with politics, in any legitimate sense of the term, the House was not at that instant engaged. There were, indeed, two questions of the last importance awaiting discussion—the question of maintaining the balance of power in Europe, and the question of providing for the Protestant succession in England. The first had been rendered pressing by an act of unparalleled audacity on the part of Louis, an act which would, under ordinary circumstances, and should under any circumstances have been passionately resented. Having obtained the consent of the Spanish Government, Louis had suddenly despatched an army into the Spanish Netherlands and seized the Barrier Fortresses. No such calamity had befallen Protestant Europe within the memory of man. There was now every probability that Holland would fall under the dominion of France, and the subjugation of Holland would not only fatally disarrange the balance of power but involve consequences to England such as all who had her interests at heart trembled to contemplate.

The Tories were, however, in no humor for anything but party vengeance. Their hour of triumph had come: their enemies were at their feet, and they resolved to trample on them. They proceeded to impeach the Ministers who were responsible for the Partition Treaties. Long and tedious controversies resulted. Every day there were unseemly collisions between the two Houses. The business of the Government stood still. Nothing had been arranged but the Act of Settlement, and the Act of Settlement had been arranged in such a way as to insult the King. Then the country was roused. The Kentish Petition was presented. The Legion memorial was drawn up. Fierce debates ensued. On the 14th of June William prorogued the Parliament. On the 7th of September the Grand Alliance was concluded. Ten days afterwards occurred an event which completely changed the face of affairs. James II. died at St. Germains, and Louis XIV. proclaimed the titular Prince of Wales King James III. of England. In a few hours a courier was at Loo with the intelligence. William saw that his time had come. He knew the English; he hurried to London; he remodelled the Ministry. The indignation of the English people at the insult they had received knew no bounds. The whole country was transported with fury. Both parties were unanimous for war. A bill was passed for attainting the Pretender, and so completely had the Whigs triumphed that the Abjuration Bill was also carried. On the 15th of May, 1702, war was proclaimed by concert in London, at Vienna, and at the Hague. But William was no more.

In the debates on the Partition Treaty Impeachments, on the Act of Settlement, and on the Kentish Petition, young St. John appears to have distinguished himself. A high compliment had indeed been paid him. He had been appointed by the House to assist Hedges in preparing and bringing in an important measure—the bill for the further Security of the Protestant Succession—and from this moment he rose rapidly to eminence.

On the accession of Anne the position of the two parties was a very peculiar one. The point on which all eyes were turned was the war, and the war had created a violent reaction in favor of the Whigs. It had been the triumph of the Whig policy. It had been the realization of the Whig hopes. It had, to a great extent, been the work of the great Whig ruler. But the new Queen was a Tory, indeed a bigoted and intolerant Tory; the great general on whom the conduct of the war depended was a Tory; the Ministry on which he thought it expedient to rely was a Tory Ministry; the Privy Council, to which he looked for support, was a Privy Council in which the names of Somers, Halifax, and Orford were not to be found. On the prosecution of the war the two factions had met

for a moment on common ground, and by one of the most
singular revolutions in history the Tories had been enabled
to supersede their rivals by adopting their policy. For a
few months all went well. Scarcely, however, had Marlborough's cannon begun to thunder on the Meuse, when
dissensions began. In the Parliament which assembled in
October three parties may be distinguished: the Whigs,
who predominated in the Upper House, but who were in
a minority in the Lower; the extreme Tories, who were
represented by Rochester, Nottingham, Jersey, and Nor-
manby in the Lords, and by Hedges and Seymour in the
Commons; the moderate Tories, in whose ranks were to
be found Harley, now for the third time elected Speaker,
Harcourt, the solicitor-general, and St. John. But the
two men on whom everything turned were Marlborough
and Godolphin. Godolphin was now far in the decline of
life. In official experience and in practical sagacity he had
no superior among contemporary politicians; as a financier he was eminently skilful. He had borne a prominent,
but by no means honorable part in the events of the last
fifteen years. He had been false to James, and he had
been false to William, but his character stood deservedly
high for virtues which were rarely in that age found conjoined with laxity of principle. He was incorruptible by
money. In his management of the Treasury he had shown
himself scrupulously honest; in his transactions with men
of business he was never known to break his word, and he
had therefore succeeded in inspiring confidence where confidence is slow to express itself. Though in debate he confined himself as a rule to the mere expression of his opinion, delivered in a few bluff sentences, and set off by no
play on his sullen and impassive features, he had more
weight with the House than the most accomplished ora-

tors of those times. At Court, indeed, and among men of letters he found no favor; for his manners were the manners of a carter, and his tastes not exactly those of a Mæcenas or a Leo. They were, in truth, such as little became either his age or his position. His awkward gallantries he had had the good sense to abandon; but his addiction to gambling, horse-racing, cock-fighting, and the card-table amounted to a passion. These frivolous pursuits detracted, however, nothing from the respect with which he was regarded by his colleagues, as there was no levity in his conversation, which was, as a rule, confined to monosyllables, or in his demeanor, which was remarkably grave and reserved. Between Marlborough and himself there existed the tie of a singularly close and affectionate friendship, and this tie had recently been drawn closer by a family alliance.

The main object of Godolphin's policy was to support his friend, to find the necessary funds for sustaining the war, and to silence those who wished either to control its operations or to change its character. Moderate, and cautious even to timidity, he tried at first to govern by a Ministry in which all parties were represented. Though a Tory himself, and dependent on the Tories for support, he was unwilling to place himself entirely in their hands, for he knew that he only could look for their co-operation up to a certain point, and that as soon as the war extended its area and assumed an aggressive character he would in all likelihood be obliged to fall back upon the Whigs. Such a step he could not, however, contemplate without apprehension, for the Queen regarded that party with peculiar aversion. His hope was that he might by skilful parliamentary diplomacy be enabled to form out of the moderate Tories a body of partisans who would support his war policy, while he could rely with some confidence on securing the Queen through the influence of the Countess of Marlborough.

The first point in which the two bodies came into violent collision was the Bill against Occasional Conformity. This was introduced by St. John and two other Tory members. He distinguished himself not only by the conspicuous part he took in the stormy debates which attended its progress through the House, but in the Conference held subsequently in the Painted Chamber. In the financial inquisition for incriminating Halifax we find him one of the Commissioners, and in the Disqualification Bill he was for the first time pitted against his future enemy Robert Walpole, who had taken his seat among the Whigs as member for Castle Rising.

Godolphin and Marlborough soon clearly saw the necessity of breaking with the High Tories. Though the conduct of the war had not as yet been openly assailed in either of the two Houses, symptoms of discontent had already declared themselves. The resignation of Rochester in 1703 had already relieved them of a troublesome colleague. Nottingham, however, still represented his views, and had on more than one occasion expressed his disapproval of the conduct of the Government. Indeed he made no secret of his intention to put himself at the head of an opposition, and if possible to supplant Godolphin without resigning office. He began by insisting on the removal of Somerset and Devonshire from the Privy Council. This was a test question: and this was refused. Upon that he resigned, and his resignation was eagerly accepted by Godolphin, who hastened to place the seals in the hands of Harley. Next went Jersey and Seymour, Wright, the Lord-keeper, followed. Blaithwayte, the Secretary of War, then vacated office, and on the 23d of April, 1704, St. John was appointed to succeed him.

As he had not completed his twenty-sixth year when he was raised to a post which involved a more than usual amount of responsibility, his biographers have concluded that he must have owed his advancement to the personal intercession of either Harley or Marlborough. He owed it, we suspect, to Marlborough. Marlborough was in England at the time, and it had been at his suggestion that the changes in the Ministry had been made. In a letter to Godolphin, not long afterwards, he speaks of St. John as a man would speak of one for whose conduct he had in a measure made himself responsible.* St. John did not disappoint the expectations of his friends. Though his private life continued to be marked by the excesses which characterized his earlier days, he discharged his public duties in a way which called forth the admiration even of his enemies. The position of a Secretary of War in the teeth of a powerful Opposition is a position of no ordinary difficulty. It is a position, indeed, to which the tact and experience of veteran statesmen have not always been found to be equal. Never were the labors of that onerous office more exigent and harassing than during the four years of St. John's tenure. A war beyond all precedent, complicated and momentous, was raging. That war had spread itself over the vast area of Europe. Our position in it was undefined. The amount of our contingents, both of men

---

* See Marlborough's Letter to Godolphin, Coxe, vol. i., p. 152, and the Stuart Papers, Macpherson, "Original Papers," vol. ii., p. 532, where it is said, "Lord Marlborough was always very fond of Harry St. John, and on the loss of his son, the Lord Blandford, said he had no comfort left but in Harry St. John, whom he loved and considered as his son."

and resources, was variously assessed and angrily disputed. Every step taken in it was submitted to the malignant scrutiny of party jealousy. Every manœuvre had to be accounted for to a captious and irritable Opposition. Whoever is acquainted with Marlborough's correspondence at this period will be at no loss to understand the difficulties with which the young Secretary had to contend. We find him constantly before the House — arguing, explaining, pleading, refuting. Indeed, his energy, decision, and zeal were of infinite service both to Godolphin and Marlborough in the troubled and anxious interval between the August of 1704 and the June of 1706.

At the beginning of 1707 it became more and more evident that if the war was to be continued, the Ministry must throw itself entirely on the Whigs; for the recent successes of Marlborough in Flanders, of Eugene in Italy, and of Peterborough in Spain, had, according to the Tories, satisfied the ends of the war, and the Tories were resolved to oppose its continuance. Godolphin had therefore acceded to the wishes of the Whigs in removing Hedges, and in placing the seals in the hands of Sunderland, the son-in-law of Marlborough and an uncompromising Whig. The chiefs of the Tory party were removed from the Privy Council, and from this moment the administration of Godolphin and Marlborough assumed a new character. It was no longer a Tory but a Whig Ministry; though for a time, at least, Harley still continued to hold the seals with Sunderland, and St. John retained the post of Secretary at War. Harley's conduct excited some surprise. The truth is he had seen all along that the Church and the Queen would ultimately triumph; that the only tie which connected Anne with Godolphin and his colleagues was her personal affection for the Duchess of Marlborough; and that her affection was, owing to the overbearing and imperious character of the favorite, daily declining. He saw the annoyance with which she regarded the recent changes in the Cabinet—her intense dislike of Sunderland—her increasing coolness to Godolphin. He saw that the predominance of the Whigs depended mainly on the successful prosecution of the war, on its continuance, on its popularity. He saw that a financial crisis was at hand. He saw that the High-church Party were gaining ground, and he perceived how completely the Queen's sympathies were with them. He proceeded, therefore, to open a secret communication with her by means of his cousin Abigail Hill, and while he pretended to be cordially co-operating with the Treasurer, he did all in his power to inflame the Queen against the foreign and domestic policy of the Cabinet. To throw Godolphin off his guard, he redoubled his protestations of fidelity; and with Marlborough he practised the same elaborate duplicity in a series of letters, which have scarcely a parallel in the annals of political treachery. At what precise period St. John became a party to these ignoble intrigues it is by no means easy to decide. It is clear from the correspondence of Marlborough and from the "Conduct of the Duchess," that they both looked upon him as the ally of Harley, and that they regarded him with suspicion, though without being able to satisfy themselves of his guilt. We are, on the whole, inclined to suspect that it was not till the autumn of 1707 that he had any share in these scandalous tactics. For upward of a year Harley managed with consummate hypocrisy to conceal his machinations. At last all was discovered, and the Whigs, whose difficulties had been increased by the inactivity of the campaign in the Netherlands, by the disastrous defeat at Almanza, and by the failure of the enterprise against Toulon, resolved to get rid of Harley. Anne fought hard for her favorite Minister. She refused to give any credence to the Greg scandal; she refused to see anything which incriminated him in the affair of Vallière and Bara.* She dilated at mortifying length on his eminent services, on his great experience, on his sound judgment. Godolphin and Marlborough then plainly told her that if Harley remained in office they would at once give in their resignation, and that she must choose between sacrificing Harley and throwing the affairs of Europe into hopeless perplexity. Then, and then only, she yielded. On the 11th of February Harley laid down the seals; and St. John not only followed him out of office, but, on the dissolution in April, resigned his seat.

His premature departure from a scene in which he had so conspicuously distinguished himself, not unnaturally excited a good deal of surprise. It is not, we think, difficult to account for. Had he continued in Parliament he must have taken one of two courses. He must have apostatized and joined the Whigs, or he must have adhered to his party and taken his place in the ranks of the Opposition. Both courses were fraught with embarrassment. The triumph of the Whigs was certainly complete, but it had been won at the price of the Queen's favor, in the teeth of the Church, and in the teeth of the party opposed to the war. A reaction was obviously merely a matter of time, and that reaction would in all probability involve the downfall of the dominant faction. If, on the other hand, he joined the Opposition, he would be compelled to assail a policy which he had for some time zealously supported; he would be compelled to ally himself with men whom he regarded as enemies against men whom he regarded as friends; and

* See Burnet's "History of his Own Times," pp. 821, 822.

he would, moreover, be forced to the indelicate necessity of going all lengths against his patrons Marlborough and Godolphin. From his country-house he could watch in security the course of events, and take a definite step when a definite step was prudent. These were, we believe, his real motives in withdrawing at this conjuncture to Bucklersbury.

He abandoned himself with characteristic impetuosity to his new whim. He had now, he said, done with politics. He was weary of the world. He would devote himself henceforth to Philosophy and Literature. He would leave affairs of State to meaner men. These remarks—for with these remarks he now began to regale his friends—were received with roars of laughter, and Swift quotes an epigram which was proposed by one of them as an appropriate inscription for the summer-house of the young Recluse. It is, we regret to say, quite unfit for repetition here. That he applied himself, however, with assiduity to literary pursuits may well be credited. He had arrived at that period in life when curiosity is keenest, when sensibility is quickest, when the acquisitive faculties are in their greatest perfection. Indeed, he always spoke of these two years as the most profitable he had ever spent.

In the autumn of 1710 fell that great administration which is in some respects the most glorious in our annals —the administration of Godolphin and Marlborough—an administration which had distinguished itself by no ordinary moderation in the midst of no ordinary trial; which had in the intoxication of success been conspicuous for that calm wisdom which it is the lot of most governments to learn only in reverses; which, founded on faction, had endeavored with rare magnanimity to adopt a policy of concession and reconciliation which could look back on the victories of Blenheim, Ramillies, Oudenarde, Malplaquet, and Saragossa—on the expulsion of the French from Flanders and from Germany—on the capture of Gibraltar and Minorca—as the trophies of its foreign policy; and which could, among many other liberal and salutary measures, point to the union of England and Scotland as one of the glories of its policy at home. The immediate cause of a revolution which altered the course of European history was, as every one knows, the impeachment of Sacheverel—perhaps the only act of imprudence of which Godolphin had ever been guilty. It has been asserted that he took this impolitic step from motives of personal resentment. He took it, we know, in direct opposition to the advice of Somers* and of the solicitor-general; he took it, there is reason to believe, in opposition to the advice of Marlborough and Walpole; but he took it, we suspect, with a deliberate object. The truth is that the party of which Sacheverel was the mouth-piece was beginning to assume a mischievous activity in political circles. Half the nation learned, as Godolphin well knew, their politics from the pulpit, and the pulpits were filled with Tories who were advancing from philippics against the Whig doctrines to philippics against the Whig government. He perceived with anxiety the growing power of the Opposition; and he perceived with alarm that a great crisis in public opinion was approaching. He resolved, therefore, to strike a decisive blow while the strength of the Government was as yet unimpaired, and there was some chance of its being able to grapple successfully with its formidable adversaries. The blow was struck, and the Whigs were ruined. It

* Indeed Somers prophesied that if the prosecution was undertaken it would be the ruin of the Whigs.—SWIFT, *History of the Four Last Years* (Scott's Swift), v. p. 172.

would, however, be an error to suppose—as many historians do suppose—that the prosecution of Sacheverel was the real cause of the sudden collapse of the Whig Ministry. The train had long been laid. The prosecution was merely the match which fired it. Had Godolphin taken the advice of his coadjutors, the catastrophe might have been postponed—it could scarcely have been postponed for long; it was unavoidable, it was inevitable. The Queen had never looked upon the Whigs with favor, and at such a time, when the two parties were so nicely balanced, no Ministry could subsist for long apart from that favor. She suspected their political principles; she detested their religious toleration; she looked upon many of them as little better than infidels: she considered that they had imperilled the Church; that she had been personally aggrieved by them; that they had insulted her husband; that they had forced Ministers on her whom she hated, and had compelled her to dismiss Ministers whom she respected. They were, she said, constantly outraging her feelings. In July, 1708, for example, they had driven her almost frantic by threatening to propose in Parliament that the Electoral Prince should be invited to settle in England. On the occasion of her husband's illness in 1707, and of his death in 1708, their conduct had been marked not merely by disrespect, but by gross indelicacy. Nor was the domestic tyranny to which she was subjected by the Duchess of Marlborough less galling. All these passions and prejudices had moreover been sedulously inflamed by Harley and Mrs. Masham.

But everywhere the current was running in the same direction. A reaction was setting in against the Dissenters. The Naturalization Act had crowded London with a rabble of needy and turbulent aliens who had—such was the language of Tory demagogues—diverted charity from its proper channel, and been invited over by the Whigs to assist in the subversion of the Church. Marlborough's recent application for the captain-generalship for life had seriously impaired his popularity. He already possessed, it was said, more power than it became a subject to enjoy, and men were beginning to mutter about Cromwell, standing armies, and military despotism. The unsatisfactory conclusion of the Conferences at the Hague in the spring of 1709, and the recent failure of the Conference at Gertrudenberg, had irritated the middle classes, who were complaining heavily of the war—the unnecessary protraction of which they attributed to the ambition of Marlborough and to the party necessities of the Ministry. The resources of Godolphin had been taxed to the uttermost to avert a financial crisis which was now to all appearance at hand. For some time Godolphin clung to power with indecent pertinacity; but on the 8th of August he received a brief note from the Queen, in which she curtly intimated that she had no further occasion for his services, desiring at the same time that instead of bringing the White Staff to her he would break it. The note was delivered by a lackey in the royal livery, not to the Lord-treasurer himself but to his hall-porter. Godolphin, irritated at this mean and gratuitous insult, broke the staff, and flung, in a fit of petulance, the fragments into the fireplace. Such was the ignominious conclusion of a long and brilliant ministerial career, and such is the gratitude of princes.

The Treasury was placed in Commission, but Harley became Chancellor of the Exchequer. He at once proceeded to form a Ministry, and he attempted with characteristic caution to trim between the two parties. He was by no means inclined to throw himself entirely on the Tories. He was anxious for a coalition. He had interviews with

Cowper, Halifax, and Walpole. He importuned them to retain their places. "There was," he said, "a Whig game intended at bottom;" but when asked to explain himself, he became unintelligible. Cowper and Halifax gathered, however, that if they would consent to remain in the Government, St. John and Harcourt should be admitted only to subordinate offices. They declined the proposal. "If any man was ever born under the necessity of being a knave, he was"—was the quiet comment which Cowper entered in his diary when recording a former interview with Harley.* It was indeed soon evident that a mixed Ministry was out of the question, that the days of coalition were over. A faction had triumphed, and a faction must rule. Rochester succeeded Somers as President of the Council, and St. John received the Seals as Secretary of State for the Northern Department: Boyle having the good sense to prevent disgrace by a voluntary resignation. So entered on its stormy and disastrous career the last Ministry of Queen Anne.

When St. John received the Seals he was in his thirty-third year. It has been said, and it is by no means improbable, that he owed this splendid elevation principally to his knowledge of the French language, an accomplishment which neither Harley nor any member of the Cabinet possessed in an adequate degree, but an accomplishment which the negotiations contemplated about this time with Versailles rendered indispensable in one at least of the two secretaries. At the end of September Parliament was dissolved. The nation was now on fire with faction. The panic excited by Sacheverel had not yet subsided. The elections were almost universally in favor of the Tories, and were marked by such excesses of party feeling that life

* "Diary of William, Earl Cowper," p. 33.

was in jeopardy. By day the bells clanged joyously from the Tory strongholds, by night the bonfires roared in the squares. Mobs wild with excitement paraded the streets; conventicles and meeting-houses were gutted. An appalling riot convulsed Westminster, and some of the provincial towns presented the appearance of places which had been exposed to the ravages of war. Meanwhile addresses from all quarters of England came pouring in. The doctrines most dear to the Stuarts were everywhere proclaimed. The Court was thronged with Jacobites and High Tories, who publicly congratulated the Queen on what they termed her emancipation from captivity. "Your Majesty," said the Duke of Beaufort, "is now Queen indeed." In November Parliament met, and St. John took his seat as member for Berkshire.

In the vicissitudes of political history there are certain conjunctures in which power is more easily acquired than maintained, and it was at one of these conjunctures that the new Ministry assumed the reins of government. Its position was in the highest degree perilous and embarrassing. "It rested," wrote Swift, "on a narrow bottom, and was like an isthmus between the Whigs on one side and the extreme Tories on the other." Harley saw from the very first the precariousness of the tenure by which he held. He saw that the Tories could not stand alone. He estimated at its real value the popular panic to which he had been immediately indebted for his elevation. In the Commons he beheld with alarm an Opposition conspicuous by their abilities and steady co-operation, and he beheld with perplexity a ministerial majority conspicuous mainly by their insolence, their numbers, and their tumultuous fanaticism. In the Lords he beheld against him the most formidable combination of enemies that ever sought the destruction of a rival faction. The finances were in deplorable confusion. Immense supplies were needed, and without the confidence of the moneyed class nothing could be raised; but the moneyed class had little confidence in the Ministry. Among his colleagues there was no one, with the exception of Dartmouth, on whom he could depend. St. John and Harcourt were for extreme measures, and had been in a manner forced on him. Rochester was already in open mutiny. Buckinghamshire, whom he regarded with suspicion and dislike, was impracticable; Paulet was a mere cipher. He was compelled, therefore, to grapple single-handed with the difficulties of his position; to satisfy, on the one hand, the party which had befriended him, and to conciliate, so far as he could, the party which were opposing him. His ultimate object was a coalition, his immediate object was to prepare the way to it. He saw that the health of the Queen was failing, and the question of the succession imminent. He shrank, therefore, from compromising himself either at Hanover or at St. Germains. He wrote to the Elector, assuring him of his good intentions. He put himself as soon as possible into communication with the Pretender. At home he fenced, he trimmed, he equivocated. The necessity of a peace with France was obvious; without it he was at the mercy of his opponents; but to conclude a peace on anything but on the most advantageous terms to England would in all probability cost the Cabinet their heads. With consummate tact he declared, therefore, his resolution of supporting the Allies, while he took measures to undermine them in popular estimation. He provided for the vigorous prosecution of the war, while he enlarged on the expediency of peace. He did everything in his power to conciliate Marlborough, while he connived at attacks on him. He upheld him in the field, while he annihilated his influence in the closet. He prepared also, in addition to these devices, to call in the assistance of a more formidable power.

In the preceding August the Tories had, at the suggestion of St. John, started the *Examiner*. Several numbers had already appeared. They had not been distinguished by conspicuous ability, but during the course of the elections a pamphlet, entitled a "Letter to the *Examiner*," had attracted so much attention that it had elicited a reply from the pen of Earl Cowper. The paper in question was an attack on the Duke and Duchess of Marlborough, on the protraction of the war, and on the ruinous selfishness of the Allies. It pointed out in angry and declamatory terms that England was the dupe of Austria and the tool of Holland, "a farm to the Bank and a jest to the whole world;" that she had engaged in the war as a confederate, that she was now proceeding in it as a principal; that the objects of the Grand Alliance had long since been attained, and that ruin and bankruptcy were now staring her—the prey of a wicked faction—in the face. The pamphlet was, as every one knew, the work of St. John. It was a sufficient indication of the policy he meant to pursue as a Minister; it was an indication, indeed, of the policy Harley intended to pursue. But Harley was by no means inclined to trust to his impetuous colleague either the development of his schemes or the interpretation of his policy. He proceeded, therefore, to put the press under his own control. He had an interview with De Foe, whose *Review* was at that time the most influential paper in the kingdom, and De Foe was instructed to dilate on the First Minister's well-known inclination towards the Whigs. He sought the assistance of Charles Davenant, whose name is scarcely remembered now, but who was in 1710 one of the ablest writers on politics and finance that British journalism could boast. He won over Prior, Rowe, and Parnell. He made overtures to Steele; and though Steele preferred to remain in the Whig ranks, a more illustrious apostate was preparing to quit them. Swift had recently arrived in London. He had been received with coldness by Godolphin. He had been treated with duplicity, he said, by Somers. He had been grossly insulted by Wharton. He had done great services for the Whigs. These services had been ignored, and his sensitive pride was wounded. He called on Harley, and Harley, by a few courteous words, succeeded in securing the aid of the greatest master of political controversy which this country had ever seen.

At the beginning of November Swift undertook the editorship of the *Examiner*, and for upward of three years he fought the battles of the Ministry as no one had ever yet fought the battles of any Ministry in the world. With a versatility unparalleled in the history of party warfare, he assailed his opponents in almost every form which satire can assume; in Essays which are still read as models of terse and luminous disquisition; in philippics compared with which the masterpieces of Cicero will, in point of vituperative skill, bear no comparison; in pamphlets which were half a century afterwards the delight of Burke and Fox: in ribald songs, in street ballads, in Grub Street epigrams, in ludicrous parodies. He had applied his rare powers of observation to studying the peculiarities of every class in the great family of mankind, their humors, their prejudices, their passions; and to all these he knew how to appeal with exquisite propriety. He was a master of the rhetoric which casts a spell over senates and tribunals, and of the rhetoric which sends mobs yelling to the tar-barrel or the club-stick. With every weapon in the whole armory of scorn he was equally familiar. In boisterous scurrility he was more than a match for Oldmixon. In delicate and subtle humor he was more than a match for Addison. In an age when the bad arts of anonymous polemics had been brought to perfection, his lampoons achieved a scandalous pre-eminence. His sarcasm and invective were terrific. His irony made even the Duchess of Marlborough quail; his pasquinades drove Eugene in ignominy from our shores; his broadsides made it perilous for the Opposition to show their faces in the streets. But however remarkable were his abilities as an unscrupulous assailant, his abilities as an unscrupulous advocate were not less consummate. Where his object was persuasion, he was indifferent to everything but effect. He hesitated at nothing. When the testimony of facts was against him, he distorted them beyond recognition. When testimony was wanting, he invented it. When the statements of his opponents admitted of no confutation, he assumed the air of an honest and stout-hearted Englishman who refused to be duped. His diction — plain, masculine, incisive — came home to every one; and the monstrous effrontery of his assumptions was seldom suspected by readers whose reason was enthralled by the circumstantial conclusiveness with which he drew his deductions. In truth, of all writers who have ever entered the arena of party politics, Swift had, in a larger measure than any, the most invaluable of all qualifications—the art of making truth assume the appearance of elaborate sophistry, and the art of making elaborate sophistry assume the appearance of self-evident truth. With these formidable powers he entered the camp of Harley.

For a few weeks all went well. The cautious policy of

Harley was steadily pursued. The supplies were voted and raised. The war was vigorously prosecuted. The language of the Tory press was the language of moderate Whigs. In December Marlborough arrived in England. He had a long interview with St. John. St. John candidly explained to him the intentions of the Ministry. They would support him in the war so long as the Queen continued him in command. They had no ill-feeling towards him. They should be sorry to lose him. He must, however, consent to two things—he must insist upon the removal of his wife from Court, and he must "draw a line between all that had passed and all that is to come:" in other words, he must quit the Whigs, who were his enemies, and he must join the Tories, who were his friends. He then proceeded to give him a long lecture on the difference between the two parties. To all this Marlborough listened with patient urbanity. He was, he said, worn out with age, fatigue, and misfortune; he had done wrong in joining the Whigs, he would return to his old friends. He did nothing of the sort, and he never meant to do so. He struggled hard to prevent the degradation of his wife, but all was in vain, and the high offices she had held were divided between the Duchess of Somerset and Mrs. Masham. The failure of this negotiation with Marlborough was a severe blow to Harley, who found himself more and more thrown into the power of the extreme Tories. Party-spirit was now running high in both Houses. The conduct of the war in Spain was the point at issue. The Whigs took their side by Galway, and the Tories by Peterborough. St. John, at the head of the Tories, harangued against Galway. The war, he said, had been grossly neglected in Spain to give effect to the triumphs of Marlborough in Flanders, and he had, he continued, no doubt that to the scandalous

—to the criminal—neglect of the war in Spain was to be attributed not only the disaster at Almanza, but the failure of the expedition to Toulon. At last a vote of censure was passed on Galway, and a vote of thanks to Peterborough. The Tories were mad with joy, and the Whigs with chagrin.

Meanwhile a schism was forming in the Tory ranks. The extreme members of that faction—and the extreme members formed the majority—began to clamor against Harley. They would have no half measures. They would have no dallying with the Whigs. Why was the *Examiner* speaking civilly about Marlborough? How long were they going to be a farm to the Bank? When were they going to have a peace? Why were not the Whig dogs impeached? At the head of these malcontents was Rochester. Every day their complaints became more intemperate and more insolent. The October Club was formed. Nightly meetings were held. The crisis was alarming, and Harley fell ill. "The nearer I look upon things," wrote Swift to Stella, "the worse I like them. The Ministry are able seamen, but the tempest is too great, the ship too rotten, and the crew all against them." It was rumored that the Duchess of Somerset was superseding Mrs. Masham in the Queen's affections, and that Somers had been twice admitted to a private audience. Suddenly an event occurred which completely changed the face of affairs.

In the course of his licentious pleasures St. John had made the acquaintance of a dissolute French adventurer. His name was Antoine de Guiscard. Originally an abbé, he had become successively a political demagogue, a soldier, and a parasite. His life had been stained by almost every vice to which human depravity can stoop. His abbey resembled, it was said, the groves of Paphos. Even the vestals of his religion had not been safe from his sacrilegious libertinism. One of his mistresses he had poisoned. A steward whom he suspected of peculation he had put with his own hand to the rack. In Rouergue, where he had excited a rebellion and left his colleagues to be broken on the wheel, he had been hung in effigy by the magistrates. Entering subsequently into the service of the English, he had proposed several wild schemes for the invasion of his own country which had not been regarded with much favor, and since the battle of Almanza he had resided on a pension in London. There St. John, at that time Secretary of War, fell in with him. Their acquaintance soon ripened into intimacy. They gambled and drank together. They paid court to the same mistress and lived for some time in sordid community of pleasures. The woman gave birth to a child. A dispute about its paternity arose, and the two friends parted in anger. At the beginning of 1711 Guiscard attempted to open a secret correspondence with France. His letters were intercepted. He was arrested on a warrant signed by St. John, and carried by the Queen's messengers to the Cockpit. The scene which ensued is well known. In the course of his examination he rushed forward, and with a penknife which he had managed to secrete stabbed Harley in the breast. For about six weeks the First Minister was the most popular man in England. His house was besieged by crowds of anxious inquirers. He had fallen a victim, it was said, to his patriotism. Guiscard had no doubt selected him because of his hostility to France and to Popery. Guiscard had meant—such was the audacious assertion of Swift—to make his way to Windsor and to assassinate the Queen, but, failing that, had aimed his blow at the most faithful of her servants. The truth really was that Guiscard's dastardly act had been prompted merely by personal resentment, as Harley had struck off a hundred pounds from his pension, and had at the same time declined to put it on the permanent list. Indeed there is reason to believe that the wretch had originally intended to attack St. John, with whom he twice attempted, in the course of his examination, to have a private interview. But Harley had been stabbed—and Harley was the martyr. At the end of May he was Earl of Oxford. A few days afterwards he was presented with the White Staff. Nor was this all. Shortly before the fortunate accident to which he owed so much, he had with the assistance of St. John organized a committee to inquire into the expenditure of the last Ministry. This scrutiny, undertaken with the object of casting a slur on Godolphin and his colleagues, was conducted with scandalous unfairness. The Report was issued, and the Report announced that upward of thirty-five millions sterling had been unaccounted for. The effect produced was the effect intended. The Whig leaders became more unpopular than ever, and the confidence which had once been placed in Godolphin was immediately transferred to Harley. His position was now to all appearance impregnable. His credit was high. The Queen, and the two favorites who ruled the Queen, were his friends. The death of Rochester had relieved him of his most troublesome colleague. Even the October Club had relented. From this moment, however, his power began gradually to decline. "It soon appeared," says Burnet, "that his strength lay in managing parties, and in engaging weak people by rewards and promises to depend upon him, and that he neither thoroughly understood the business of the Treasury nor the conduct of foreign affairs."

The star of St. John now rose rapidly into the ascendant. The struggle between the two Ministers had indeed already begun. While Harley was confined to his chamber by the knife of Guiscard, the subordinate had passed into the rival. The truth is, recent events had convinced St. John of three things—the real strength of the Tory party if judiciously consolidated; the impossibility of a coalition with the Whigs; the ruinous folly of trimming and equivocating. But he saw also that the Ministry could not stand without a peace, and without securing the unprovided debts, and that these measures could be carried only by Oxford, who had the ear of the Queen, the confidence of the moderate Tories, and the supreme direction of affairs. To break with the Treasurer before he could step into his place would be destruction. He would therefore co-operate with him so far as the common interests of their party went, but he would have no share in his dealings with the Whigs. He would put himself at the head of the extreme Tories, arm and inflame them against the Whigs, and force on through every obstacle the peace with France. He now plunged headlong into those dark and tortuous intrigues which finally drove him in shame from his country, and have made his name ever since synonymous with all that is most odious in a reckless and unprincipled public servant, and all that is most contemptible in a treacherous and self-seeking diplomatist.

In the preceding January secret communications had been opened with France. In the middle of August it was suspected that a peace was in contemplation. In the middle of October it became known that preliminary articles had been signed. In a moment the whole kingdom was in a blaze. The Allies were beside themselves with anger and chagrin. Marlborough remonstrated with the Queen. Buys had already been sent over from Holland to protest.

Bothmar followed with a memorial from the Elector. De Gallas, the Austrian Ambassador, behaved with such insolence that he was forbidden the Court. The fury of the Whigs knew no bounds, and they prepared for a desperate effort to defeat the Government. Deputations were formed, protests signed, meetings summoned. The public mind, which had for many months been kept in a state of the most exquisite irritability by party pamphleteers, was now goaded almost to the verge of madness. Every press was hard at work. On the side of the Whigs were enlisted the boisterous scurrility of Steele, the mature polemical skill of Burnet and Maynwaring; Oldmixon and Ridpath, with their rancorous myrmidons; and Dunton, with half Grub Street at his heels. On the side of the Tories appeared—with Swift towering in their van—Atterbury and Mrs. Manley, King and Oldesworth, Freind and Arbuthnot. On the 17th of November a terrible riot was expected, and the trained bands were called out.

In the midst of this ferment Marlborough arrived from the Hague, and at once took counsel with the chiefs of the Opposition. It was resolved to open overtures with Nottingham, who, having been passed over in all the recent nominations, made no secret of his enmity to Oxford. A bargain was soon struck. Nottingham consented to move a resolution against the peace. The Whigs, in return, agreed to support the Bill against Occasional Conformity. They then proceeded to secure Somerset, whose wife was generally understood to divide with Lady Masham the affection of the Queen. The sympathies of Anne were altogether with the Tories. "I hope," she said to Burnet, "the Bishops will not be against the peace." "If," replied Burnet, with characteristic bluntness, "the present treaty with France is concluded, we shall all be ruined;" in three years your Majesty will be murdered and the fires will be raised again in Smithfield." The Houses were to assemble on the 7th of December. "On Friday next," wrote St. John to a friend at the Hague, "the peace will be attacked in Parliament. We must receive their fire, and rout them once for all." The anxious day arrived. The Queen informed the Houses in her Speech from the Throne that the time and place had been appointed for opening the treaty of a general peace, "notwithstanding," she added, "the arts of those that delight in war." Having concluded her address she retired, laid aside the royal robes, and returned to the House *incognita*. Then Nottingham rose, with more than usual emotion on his harsh and gloomy features. He inveighed against the articles signed by Mesnager, declared that hostilities ought to be carried on with the utmost vigor till the objects of the Grand Alliance had been fully attained, and concluded a long and intemperate harangue by moving that no peace could be safe or honorable to Great Britain or Europe if Spain or the West Indies were allotted to any branch of the House of Bourbon. He was supported by the whole strength of the Whig party, by Wharton and Sunderland, by Cowper and Burnet. As the debate grew more acrimonious the remarks became more personal. At last a taunt of one of the Tory Speakers called up Marlborough. He had been accused, he said, of wishing to protract the war for his own interests. Nothing could be falser. He desired—he had long desired peace, and he called that God, before whom he would have, in the ordinary course of nature, so shortly to appear, to witness the truth of what he was saying. But he could not, compatibly with his duty to his sovereign, to his country, to Europe, acquiesce in any peace which was not honorable and not likely to be lasting. He alluded with great pathos and dignity to his advanced years, to the hardships he had undergone, and to the cruel aspersions which had been cast on his character and on his motives. It was impossible even for the Tories to listen unmoved to such words coming from such a man. The House was deeply affected, and the flush of shame was on more than one face when the hero of Blenheim and Ramillies resumed his seat. In the division which ensued the Whigs obtained a complete victory. It was evident, too, that the feelings of the Queen were changing. Oxford and St. John, whose secret negotiations with France had now fatally committed them, were in terrible perplexity. The crisis was, indeed, appalling. Swift gave up all for lost. "I," he said to Oxford, half seriously, "shall have the advantage of you, for you will lose your head; I shall only be hanged, and carry my body entire to the grave." For some days it was believed that the Ministry would be turned out; that the Queen had settled that Somers was to have the White Staff; that the Parliament would be dissolved, and that the Whigs would carry the elections.

The storm blew over. But it became every week more evident that the languid and indecisive policy of Oxford, to which the late defeat was almost universally attributed, was not the policy which the exigencies of the time required. The Whigs must be crushed. Their coadjutors, the Allies, must be silenced. The peace with France must at all cost be consummated. A Tory despotism must be established. Such had long been the course prescribed by St. John. Recent events had proved his wisdom, and he now virtually directed affairs. He rushed at once into every extreme, and into every extreme he hurried the Treasurer and the Cabinet. A series of measures which were without precedent in parliamentary history now followed in rapid succession. The Tory minority in the Upper House was corrected by the simultaneous creation of twelve peers, and, added St. John in insolent triumph, "if those twelve had not been enough, we would have given them another dozen." Then came the astounding intelligence that Marlborough had been removed from all his employments. On the 18th of January Walpole was in the Tower. On the 19th Somerset had been dismissed. By the middle of February the Barrier Treaty had been condemned, and Townshend, who had negotiated it, voted an enemy to his country. Meanwhile all opposition was quelled with summary violence. The Tory press, with Swift at its head, was encouraged to proceed to every length of libellous vituperation against the victims of ministerial vengeance; but whenever a Whig journalist presumed to retaliate, he was at once confronted with a warrant from the Secretary. At the end of the session the Stamp Act was passed. In the Lower House the same system of tyranny and intimidation was practised. Supported by a vast majority, and without a rival in eloquence and energy, St. John carried everything before him. "You know," he wrote some years afterwards to Wyndham, "the nature of that assembly; they grow like hounds fond of the man who shows them game, and by whose halloo they are wont to be encouraged," and he gave them that halloo as none but Jack Howe had given it them before. Indeed, the audacity and insolence which characterized his conduct at this period were long a tradition in parliamentary memory. The "Journals" of the Commons still testify how in the course of one of the debates he threatened a recalcitrant Whig with the Tower.

The Whigs had now, in Oxford's phrase, been managed. The Allies remained, and the Allies were busier than ever against the peace. Swift's pamphlets had already done them considerable damage in popular estimation. St. John resolved to deal them such a blow as would effectually paralyze their efforts. That blow was dealt by the Representation, and that blow they never recovered. The Representation was drawn up by Hanmer under the direction of St. John. It was an elaborate exposure of the selfishness and ruinous folly of the Whigs and the Allies in continuing to prosecute the war when the objects for which the war had been undertaken had been long attained. It pointed out that the whole burden of the contest fell on England, the only Power which had nothing to gain by it; that the Emperor and the Dutch, who reaped all the benefit, had never contributed what they had stipulated to contribute; and that while in 1702 the cost of the war had amounted to £3,706,494, in 1711 it had, in consequence of this shameful breach of contract on the part of the Allies, risen to £8,000,000. "We are persuaded"—so ran the concluding paragraph—"that your Majesty will think it pardonable in us to complain of the little regard which some of those whom your Majesty of late years trusted, have shown to the interests of their country in giving way at least to such unreasonable impositions upon it, if not in some measure contriving them." This was sensible, this was temperate, this was to the point; and it was observed that after the Representation appeared many even of the advanced Whigs quitted the ranks of the War party.

But whatever were the difficulties with which St. John had to contend in the House and in the Cabinet, the difficulties with which he had to contend in the closet were formidable indeed. He had to unravel every thread in the whole of that vast and perplexed labyrinth of interests which were involved in the Treaty of Utrecht. He had to grapple—and to grapple virtually alone—with the most accomplished diplomatists in Europe, with an exacting and imperious enemy, and with a factious and malignant Opposition. His colleagues in France and Holland were dogged and dilatory, his colleagues at home were timid and helpless. At every step he was traversed, and at every step new and unexpected complications arose. The clandestine negotiations which had by means of Gautier and Mesnager been opened with France, were every day sinking the Ministry deeper and deeper in ignominy and embarrassment. They had already violated the most sacred ties which can bind one nation to another. They had already, for the most ignoble of all objects, stooped to the most ignoble of all expedients. St. John now resolved to abandon the Allies to the vengeance of Louis. We cannot linger over those shameful transactions which preceded the Treaty of Utrecht. They may be read at length in Bolingbroke's "Political Correspondence"—an everlasting monument of his genius and of his infamy.

In the midst of these labors Parliament was prorogued. St. John was anxious for a seat in the Upper House. The Earldom of Bolingbroke, which had for some time been in the possession of his family, had recently become extinct, and he aspired to revive it. In the interests of his party he had already waived his claim to a peerage. His services had been greater than those of any other Minister in the Cabinet. He had borne the whole burden of the last session. He had all but conducted to a prosperous issue the negotiations with France. An earldom, however, the Queen would not hear of. She had promised, she said, a viscounty, and a viscounty was all she would concede. In the middle of July, therefore, he accepted, with feelings of rage and mortification which he took no pains to conccal, the title of Viscount Bolingbroke and Baron St. John of Ledyard Tregoze. To employ his own phrase, he was dragged into the Upper House in a manner which made his promotion a punishment, not a reward. This conduct on the part of the Queen he always attributed to Oxford, whom he had long regarded with jealousy, and whom he now began to regard with hatred. The truth seems to be that Anne had conceived an aversion to him on account of the profligacy of his private life,* a profligacy which his official duties had by no means suspended, and which had indeed given great scandal to the more decorous of his colleagues.

Meanwhile several minor details had to be settled in the treaty with France. Bolingbroke was irritable and moody. To soothe his wounded pride and to put him in a good-humor, it was resolved to send him on a diplomatic mission to Paris. The incidents of that visit were long remembered by him. He had no sooner left Calais than it became known, in spite of his precautions, that he had arrived on French soil. The intelligence spread like wildfire. Crowds poured forth to meet him. Joyful acclamations rent the air. He was the friend of a war-worn nation. He was their savior; he was the Herald of Peace. He could scarcely make his way through crowds so ecstatic with enthusiasm that they covered his very horses with kisses. In the capital his visit was one continued ovation. When he appeared in the streets he was overwhelmed with tumultuous expressions of popular gratitude. When he presented himself at Court the noblesse vied with one an-

---

* This is Swift's view. See his "Enquiry into the Behaviour of the Queen's Last Ministry;" and see particularly the "Wentworth Papers," p. 395, where details are given of Bolingbroke's reckless debauchery at this period.

other in pressing on him their splendid hospitality. When he entered the theatre the whole audience rose up to receive him. He had a satisfactory conference with Louis at Fontainebleau. In a few days everything had been arranged with De Torcy. The rest of his time he devoted to social enjoyment. It has been asserted that he had, during the course of this visit, two interviews with the Pretender. Such a thing is, however, in spite of the assurance of Azzurini, very improbable. His intrigues, at this time at least, were, we suspect, of another kind. His gallantries betrayed him indeed into a serious official indiscretion. In truth De Torcy was not a man to observe such a weakness without turning it to account. He threw the susceptible diplomatist in the way of an accomplished but profligate adventuress, who robbed him of some important documents, which were at once communicated to the Minister. The effects of Bolingbroke's folly soon became apparent. He arrived in England with a damaged reputation. It was whispered by some that he had established a private understanding with the French Court; by others, that he had turned traitor and divulged the secrets of the English Cabinet; while others, again, asserted that he had come to terms with the Pretender. These reports, equally improbable and equally unfounded, were, however, eagerly caught at by Oxford, whose jealousy had been roused by his rival's reception in Paris. On this occasion he scarcely acted with his usual prudence. He removed the Foreign Correspondence out of Bolingbroke's hands, and placed it in the hands of Dartmouth. The consequences were easy to foresee. Affairs became more and more complicated. Dartmouth was as helpless as the Treasurer. France became more exacting, Holland more insolent. A wretched squabble between the suite of Rechtheren, one of the Dutch deputies, and the suite of Mesnager, the French plenipotentiary, had suspended the conferences at Utrecht. Prior wrote from Paris complaining that he had "neither powers, commission, title, instructions, appointments, money, nor secretary." The Whigs were in league with the Allies, and the peace threatened to come to a stand-still. At last the rivals began to understand their folly. Bolingbroke swallowed his chagrin, hurried up from Bucklersbury and resumed his duties at Whitehall. On the 31st of March, 1713, the Treaty of Utrecht was signed.

The verdict which history has passed on the masterpiece of Bolingbroke's statesmanship is well known. It is a verdict which no judicious biographer would, we think, attempt to question, which no sophistry can reverse, and which no future grubbing among State papers and family documents is ever likely to modify. That peace was expedient and even necessary to the welfare of England;*

---

* Bolingbroke's letter to Lord Raby, dated March 6, 1711, so admirably summarizes the reasons for peace that we will transcribe the principal paragraphs:

"We are now in the tenth campaign of a war the great load of which has fallen on Britain as the great advantage of it is proposed to redound to the House of Austria and to the States-General. They are in interest more immediately, we more remotely concerned. However, what by our forwardness to engage in every article of expense, what by our private assurances, and what by our public parliamentary declarations that no peace should be made without the entire restitution of the Spanish monarchy, we are become principals in the contest; the war is looked upon as our war, and it is treated accordingly by the confederates, even by the Imperialists, and by the Dutch.... From hence it is that our commerce has been neglected, while the French have engrossed the South Sea trade to themselves, and the Dutch encroach daily upon us both in the East Indies and on the coast of Africa. From hence it is that we have every year that the Allies, who had everything to gain by the protraction of the war, were throwing the whole burden of it on England, who had nothing to gain; that the actual union of Austria and Spain under the same sceptre would have been more prejudicial than the chance of such a union between France and Spain; and that the difficulties in the way of attaining peace were almost insuperable, may, we think, be fairly conceded. But how did Bolingbroke solve the problem? Even thus: he knew that we were bound by the most solemn obligations not to enter into any separate treaty with France. He lied, equivocated,* and entered into a separate treaty. He knew that we were bound to defend the interests of our Allies. He leagued with the common enemy to defeat them. He knew that we were bound by every consideration of good faith and humanity to protect the Catalans, whose liberties we had promised to secure, and who in return for that promise had rendered us eminent services. In defiance of all his engagements

added to our burden which was long ago greater than we could bear, while the Dutch have yearly lessened their proportions in every part of the war, even in Flanders. Whilst the Emperor has never employed twenty of his ninety thousand men against France. . . . From hence it is that our fleet is diminished and rotten, that our funds are mortgaged for thirty-two and ninety-nine years, that our specie is exhausted and that we have nothing in possession and hardly anything in expectation. . . . From hence, in one word, it is that our government is in a consumption, and that our vitals are consuming, and we must inevitably sink at once. Add to this that if we were able to bear the same proportion of charge some years longer, yet from the fatal consequences, should certainly miss of the great end of the war, the entire recovery of the Spanish monarchy from the House of Bourbon."—*Letters and Correspondence*, vol. i., pp. 117-119.

* His political correspondence reveals such a mass of duplicity and falsehood as will not be easily paralleled in the records of diplomacy.

he abandoned them to the vengeance of Philip; and in defiance of ordinary humanity he despatched a squadron to assist Philip in butchering them. He knew that the renunciations, which he palmed off on the English people as valid, were worth no more than the paper on which they were inscribed. The honor of England was, as he was well aware, pledged to provide for the Dutch a substantial barrier against France. The barrier provided for them by the treaty was a mere mockery. By ceding Lille he ceded to Louis the key of Flanders. He compelled Holland to restore Aire, Bethune, and St. Venant. He allowed France to retain Quesnoy, and he was, as his correspondence with De Torcy proves, only deterred from sacrificing Tournay by his fear of public opinion. Austria fared even worse. For the loss of Spain, the Indies, and Sicily, she was condemned to satisfy herself with the kingdom of Naples, the Duchy of Milan, and the Spanish Netherlands; her tenure of the Netherlands being indeed of such a kind as to render it little more than nominal. With regard to the concessions exacted on behalf of England, we are not inclined to take so unfavorable a view as most historians do take. It is true that France had been reduced to the lowest ebb. It is true that the concessions which she made in 1713 were by no means the concessions she had offered to make either in 1706 or in 1709. But it is no less true that in spite of our successes in Germany, Italy, and Flanders, our chances of success in Spain, which was the main object of the struggle, were all but hopeless. The possession of Gibraltar, Minorca, Hudson's Bay, Nova Scotia, Newfoundland, and the French portion of St. Christopher — the Assiento Treaty, the demolition of Dunkirk, and Louis's recognition of the Act of Settlement, were assuredly no contemptible trophies.

The triumph of Bolingbroke was, however, very short-lived; and when, on the 16th of July, Parliament was prorogued, it was evident that the current was running strongly against the Ministry. The Bill to make good the Commercial Treaty had been defeated; and the Commercial Treaty was the point on which Bolingbroke had especially prided himself. The Cabinet had been charged, absurdly charged, with attempting to ruin the mercantile interests of England in favor of the mercantile interests of France, and had lost ground in consequence. The Malt Tax had thrown the Scotch members into the ranks of the Opposition. A scandalous attempt had been made to dissolve the Union. Argyle was at open war with Oxford. Another schism had broken out among the Tories themselves. The Cabinet was divided. There was no money in the Treasury. Oxford and Bolingbroke were scarcely on speaking terms, and everything was going wrong. All through the autumn this state of things continued. It was plain that the health of the Queen was breaking. It was plain that if at this conjuncture the throne became vacant, one of two things must happen: either the Act of Settlement would be carried out by the Whigs, and the Tories be trampled under the feet of their victorious foes, or the Act of Settlement would be set aside by the Tories and a civil war convulse the country. The proper course for the Ministry to take was obvious. If they were strong enough to set aside the Act of Settlement—and, provided the Pretender would have made the necessary concessions, or even have affected to make them, there is no reason to suppose the Ministry would not have been strong enough —they should have cordially co-operated; should have rallied their partisans; should have remodelled the army; should have gained the confidence of their party; should have made with firmness and prudence the requisite arrangements. If, on the other hand, the Pretender persisted in his bigotry, and thus rendered it impossible to set aside the Act without ruin to Liberty and to the Church, they should at once have declared war against him; should have cleared their policy of all ambiguity: should have vied with the Whigs in ostentatious zeal for the Protestant Succession, and have cultivated in every way the good-will of the Elector. But the more pressing became the emergency, the more dilatory and irresolute became the Treasurer. He was apparently anxious about nothing but the establishment of his family. He could rarely be induced to open his lips about affairs; and when he did so it was impossible to understand what he meant. He was frequently intoxicated. He was always out of the way—sometimes on the plea of ill-health, sometimes on the plea of domestic concerns, and sometimes on no plea at all. Bolingbroke was furious. He attributed to him the recent ministerial defeat, and all the perplexities which had arisen since. He saw that everything was going to pieces. He saw that the Ministry were on the brink of ruin. He saw that an awful crisis was at hand; but he could not induce his infatuated colleague to take one step, and without him he could take no decided step himself. He could only ingratiate himself with Lady Masham and the Duchess of Somerset, and that he did.

The new year found things worse than ever. The Queen was apparently on the point of death, and the question of the succession was now agitating every mind even to madness. The Whigs were in paroxysms of delight, and the Tories in a panic of perplexity. In February, however, she recovered, and on the 16th opened Parliament with an address which bore unmistakable traces of Bolingbroke's hand. The Tories were at this moment decidedly in the majority both within the Houses and without; indeed Bolingbroke assured D'Iberville that seven-eighths of the people in Great Britain might be reckoned as belonging to that faction, and the Tories were, on the whole, averse to Hanover. But there was no harmony among them. Some were willing to accept the Pretender without exacting any securities from him. Others, again, insisted on such securities as the condition of their co-operation. In some of them an attachment to the principles of the Revolution struggled with an attachment to High-church doctrines, and with an antipathy to Dissenting doctrines. Many of them belonged to that large, selfish, and fluctuating class, who, with an eye merely to their own interests, are always ready to declare with the majority on any question. The Whigs, on the other hand, though numerically inferior, were weakened by no such divisions.. Their policy was simple, their opinions never wavered, their feelings were unanimous. Their leaders were of all public men of that age the most resolute, the most united, and the most capable.

It may assist our knowledge of the character of this conjuncture, and of the political profligacy of those at the head of affairs, to observe that Oxford, Buckingham, Leeds, Shrewsbury, and Bolingbroke were publicly proclaiming their devotion to the Elector, and at the same time secretly assuring the Pretender of their allegiance. Nor can Anne herself be altogether acquitted of similar duplicity. She never, it is true, gave her brother any encouragement in writing; but her aversion to the Elector was well known, and she led both Buckingham and Oxford to infer that, provided James would consent to change his religion, she should not scruple to follow "the bent of her own inclinations."*

The Houses soon showed that they were in no mood for trifling, and Bolingbroke saw that the time had come for him to take, at any hazard, decisive measures. He determined to hesitate no longer, but to seize the reins of government by assuming, in opposition to Oxford, the leadership of the extreme Tories, and by undermining him not merely at Kensington, but at Bar le Duc and at Herrenhausen. He could thus, he thought, make himself master of the position without at present definitely compromising himself either with James or the Elector. He could heal the schisms which were paralyzing a triumphant majority. He could supplant the Treasurer without alienating the Treasurer's adherents, and remodel the Ministry without weakening its constituent parts. He could thus, at the head of a great Tory Confederation—such was his splendid dream—dictate the terms on which the Elector should be received, or set aside the Act of Settlement, and escort the Pretender to the throne. Nor were these designs altogether without plausibility. He stood well with the Queen, whose prejudices had probably not been proof against his singularly fascinating manners, with Lady Masham and with the Duchess of Somerset. He could reckon certainly on the assistance of Ormond, Buckingham, Strafford, Atterbury, who had recently been raised to the see of Rochester, Harcourt, Bromley, Trevor, Wyndham, and the Earl of Mar. He had hopes of Anglesea and Abingdon; he

* It is, we think, quite clear that the sole obstacle in the way of Anne's espousing the cause of her brother lay in his refusing to change his religion. See particularly Macpherson's "Original Papers," vol. ii., pp. 504, 603; Berwick's "Memoirs," vol. ii., pp. 192; Lockhart's "Comment," p. 317.

had hopes of Shrewsbury, and he proceeded at once to make overtures to others. He continued to assure the Elector of his fidelity, and he kept up simultaneously a regular correspondence with the Jacobite agents D'Iberville and Gaultier. When, in the House, he found it necessary to proclaim hostile measures against James, he at once privately wrote to suggest the means of evading them, or to insist that they were not to be received as indications of his own feelings. Meanwhile he did everything in his power to ruin Oxford. In the motion for the further security of the Protestant succession he affected to misunderstand his meaning. When the Queen was insulted by the demand made by Schutz, he informed her that the demand had been suggested by the Treasurer. When Oxford had nominated Paget as envoy to Hanover, Bolingbroke sent Clarendon. In May he drew up that Bill which is one of the most infamous that has ever polluted our Legislature — the Schism Bill, with the double object of conciliating the extreme Tories, and of reducing his rival to a dilemma—the dilemma of breaking with the Moderate Party and the Dissenters by supporting it, or of breaking with the extreme Tories by opposing it. Oxford saw through the stratagem. Angry recriminations followed. Violent scenes occurred every day in the House, and in the Cabinet. Bolingbroke taunted Oxford with incapacity and faithlessness, and Oxford retorted by declaring that he had in his hands proofs of Bolingbroke's treachery to Herrenhausen. Swift, who had on other occasions interposed as mediator between his two friends, saw with concern the progress of these fatal dissensions. He hurried up to London, and had several interviews with the rivals. He implored them, in their own interests, in the interests of their party and in the interests of the whole Tory cause, to lay aside these internecine hostilities. He pointed out that everything depended on their mutual co-operation; that their partisans, every day becoming more scattered and perplexed, must be united; that they could only be united in the union of their leaders; that too much precious time had already been wasted; that if the death of the Queen, which might be expected at any hour, surprised them, they would be buried under the ruins of their party. All, however, was in vain, and a final interview at Lord Masham's convinced him that reconciliation was out of the question. As a parting word, he advised Oxford to resign, and then with a heavy heart hurried off to bury himself at Letcombe. Oxford and Bolingbroke now lost all control over themselves. Their unseemly altercations grew every day more violent, and became not only the jest and scandal of coffee-house politicians and ribald wits, but outraged in a manner gross beyond precedent the decorum of the Presence Chamber. Meanwhile everything was hurrying from anarchy into dissolution. "Our situation," wrote Swift to Peterborough, "is so bad that our enemies could not without abundance of invention and ability have placed us so ill, if we had left it entirely to their management." At last these lamentable scenes drew to a close. On the 27th of July Oxford was removed, but the Queen was in a dying state.

Bolingbroke was now virtually at the head of affairs. He proceeded at once with characteristic energy to grapple with the difficulties of his position. His immediate object was, we make no doubt, to amuse the Whigs and the Hanoverians while he rallied the Tories and the Jacobites. With this view he entertained at dinner, on the night succeeding Oxford's dismissal, a party of the leading Whigs, solemnly assuring them of his intention to promote the

Protestant Succession in the House of Hanover. He instructed his friend Drummond also to send Albemarle with assurances of a similar effect to the Elector himself. On the same day he had by appointment an interview with Gaultier, informing him that his sentiments towards James had undergone no change, but observing at the same time that James should immediately take such steps as would recommend him to the favor " of all good people." It may help to throw some light on his ultimate designs, to observe that almost every member of his projected Ministry was to be chosen from the ranks of the most advanced Jacobites. Bromley was to retain the Seals as Secretary of State; Harcourt was to be Chancellor; Buckingham, President of the Council; Ormond, Commander-in-chief; Mar was to be Secretary of State for Scotland; and the Privy Seal was to be transferred to Atterbury. For himself he merely proposed to hold the Seals of Secretary of State, with the sole management of the foreign correspondence. He would willingly have possessed himself of the White Staff, but he feared Shrewsbury, and he had the mortification of perceiving that even his own colleagues doubted his fitness for such a post. "His character is too bad," wrote Lewis to Swift, "to carry the great ensigns." He thought it prudent, therefore, to keep the Treasury in commission, with his creature Sir William Wyndham at the head of it.

In the midst of these preparations alarming intelligence arrived from Kensington. The Queen had been stricken down by apoplexy. A Council was summoned to the palace. Bolingbroke was in an agony of apprehension. He feared that the crash had come. He knew that Marlborough was on his way to England, and that in a few hours the army would be awaiting his orders. He knew that Stanhope had, in the van of a powerful confederation of Whigs, made arrangements for seizing the Tower, for obtaining possession of the outposts, and for proclaiming the Elector. He knew that Argyle and Somerset had been busy, that Somers had shaken off his lethargy, and that the Whigs were mustering their forces in terrible strength. He saw that the Tories—torn with internal dissensions, divided in their aims, scattered, helpless, and without leaders—must go down before the storm. But he clung desperately to one hope. If Shrewsbury would declare in favor of them, all might yet be well. Shrewsbury had been his ally in the great crisis of 1710. Shrewsbury had recently stood by him in an important debate. He had not, it was true, committed himself to any definite expression of his opinions, but his bias towards the House of Stuart was well known.* That treacherous, fickle, and pusillanimous statesman had, however, already made up his mind. With every desire to serve the Tories, he had satisfied himself of the impossibility of rallying them in time, and had decided therefore to abandon them. With all his sentiments in unison with those of Bolingbroke and Ormond, he saw that Bolingbroke and Ormond were on the losing side, and he had therefore concerted measures with Argyle and Somerset. The Council met on Friday morning, July 30th. On Friday afternoon it became known that Shrewsbury had coalesced with the Whigs, and had received the White Staff from the hands of his dying mistress. On Saturday afternoon almost every arrangement had been

---

* That Bolingbroke had good reason for believing that Shrewsbury would support him is shown by the fact that Shrewsbury was not long afterwards in league with the Jacobites—"frankly engaged and very sanguine." For this remarkable fact see the "Stuart Papers," under date August 20, 1715.

completed for carrying out the Act of Settlement. On Sunday morning Anne was no more, and Bolingbroke was a cipher. "The Queen died on Sunday. What a world is this, and how does Fortune banter us!" were the words in which the baffled statesman communicated the intelligence to Swift. Fortune was, however, bent on something more serious than banter.

But here for the present we pause. Up to this point the biography of Bolingbroke has been the parliamentary history of England during fourteen stirring and eventful years. He was now about to figure on a widely different stage, in a widely different character.

LORD BOLINGBROKE IN EXILE.

SUMMARY.

Importance of this period, p. 79-81—Retrospect at the close of Bolingbroke's political career—What next? p. 81—Bolingbroke's schemes, p. 82, 83—His advances not encouraged by the Elector: arrival of the King in England, p. 84—The Whigs come into power: their feelings against the late Government, p. 84-86—Bolingbroke's attempt at self-justification unsuccessful, p. 85, 86—Threatening prospects, p. 86, 87—Bolingbroke, scared, takes to flight, p. 87, 88—Imprudence of this step, p. 89-91—His arrival in Paris: intrigues with both Parties, p. 90—His arraignment in Parliament by Walpole: considerations thereon, p. 90-92—His indictment and condemnation as an outlaw, p. 93—Character of the Pretender: reasons which guided Bolingbroke in espousing his cause, p. 93-98—Bolingbroke organizes the Jacobite movement in Paris: disappointments and trials, p. 97-99—Circumstances favorable to the cause, p. 99-101—Bolingbroke as a negotiator, p. 100-102—Inauspicious events: death of Louis XIV., flight of Ormond, p. 102-104—Declining prospects of the Jacobite cause: its collapse, p. 104, 105—Bolingbroke's self-devotion thanklessly rewarded: his dismissal by the Chevalier, p. 106-108—Satisfaction at the Court of St. James, p. 108—Bolingbroke kept in expectancy, p. 109—His retirement and private studies, p. 109-114—Connection with the Marquise de Villette and subsequent marriage, p. 113, 114—Literary pursuits, p. 114-117—Friendship with Voltaire, p. 117-121—His desire to return to England repeatedly thwarted: at last acceded to, p. 121—Bolingbroke's overtures to Walpole and Carteret, p. 121-124—His offer of intercession at the French Court declined by Walpole, p. 125, 126—Walpole averse to restore him to his civil rights: at last forced to do so by the King, p. 125-127—Bolingbroke's double life, p. 128.

LORD BOLINGBROKE IN EXILE.

WE now propose to trace the fortunes of Bolingbroke from an event which speedily, indeed, reduced him to insignificance as a statesman, but which marked the commencement of what is, beyond question, the most interesting and instructive portion of his personal history. From 1690 to 1704 his career differs little from that of other clever and dissolute youths with indulgent relatives and with good expectations. From 1704 to 1714 it is, if we except the short interval of his retirement, that of a thriving and busy politician, whose life is too essentially bound up with contemporary history to present those features of individual interest which are the charm of biography. But from 1714 to 1752 it assumes an entirely new character. During this period he passed, in rapid succession, through a series of vicissitudes which it would be difficult to parallel even in fiction. During this period he played innumerable parts. He became identified with almost every movement of the public mind in Europe, with political opinion, with polite letters, with the speculations of science, with the progress of free-thought, with historical and metaphysical discussion. He became the teacher of men whose genius has shed lustre on the literature of two nations, and with whose names his own is imperishably associated. He produced writings which are, it is true, too unsound, too immature, and too fragmentary to hold a high place in didactic philosophy, but which were of great service in stimulating inquiry, and which are, regarded as compositions, second to none in our language. From 1726 to 1742 the influence he exercised on English politics was such as it is scarcely possible to overestimate. He was the soul of the most powerful Coalition which ever gathered on the Opposition benches. He kept the country in a constant ferment. He inaugurated a new era in the annals of Party. He made Jacobitism contemptible. He reconstructed the Tory creed. Of the Patriots he was at once the founder and dictator. To his energy and skill is, in a large measure, to be attributed that tremendous revolution which drove Walpole from office, and changed the face of political history. And yet this is the period of his life of which his biographers have least to say. With them he ceases to be important when he ceases to be conspicuous. They do not perceive that the part he played was exactly the part which Thucydides tells us was played by Antiphon in the great drama of B.C. 411—the part of one who, unseen himself, directs everything. Of his literary achievements their account is, if possible, still more vague and meagre. Indeed, Mr. Cooke and Mr. Macknight appear to have no conception of the nature and extent of his influence on the intellectual activity of his age. They have not even discussed his relations with Pope and Voltaire. They have not even furnished us with a critical analysis of his principal works; and what they have omitted to do no one has done since. We shall therefore make no apology for entering with some minuteness into the particulars of this portion of his life. It divides itself naturally into three periods. The first extends from his fall, in 1714, to his reappearance in England in 1723; the second extends from 1723 to his departure for the Continent in 1735; and the third is terminated by his death in 1752.

On the death of Anne it became at once apparent that any attempt to set aside the Act of Settlement would be vain. Atterbury, indeed, importuned Bolingbroke to appeal to the nation, and to declare open war with Hanover. He offered, himself, to lead the forlorn hope. He was willing, he said, to head a procession to Charing Cross, and to proclaim, in full canonicals, the accession of James III. But his proposal found little favor. Bolingbroke saw that all was over, and that for the present, at least, things must take their natural course. It must, in truth, have been obvious to a man of far less discernment than he that the position of the Hanoverians was impregnable. Their leaders were united, their arrangements had been judicious. They were in possession of all the means which command dominion—of the fleet, of the army, of the garrisoned towns, of the Tower. The recent divisions in the Cabinet, the unpopularity of the Commercial Treaty, and the sudden death of the Queen, had confounded the Tories. Their only chance was to outbid the Whigs in loyal zeal for Hanover, to purify themselves from all taint of Jacobitism, and to leave the few desperate fanatics who still held out for James to their fate. Such was clearly their policy, and such was the course that Bolingbroke now prepared to take. That it was his original intention to set aside the Act of Settlement it would, in spite of his repeated assurances to the contrary, be absurd to doubt. It would be equally absurd to suppose that he had, so far as conscience or feeling was concerned, any bias in favor either of Hanover or St. Germains. He was as destitute of sentiment as he was destitute of principle. From the moment he entered public life his interests had centred and ended in himself. To crush Marlborough and to supplant Oxford he had found it expedient to ally himself with the extreme Tories. In allying himself with that faction it had become necessary to identify himself with the Jacobites. But he knew his danger. He had tried hard to stand well with George as well as with James. He had regularly corresponded with both of them. He had sworn allegiance to both of them. The exigencies of his struggle with Oxford had, however, necessitated a decided course, and at the beginning of 1714 he was fatally compromised. He saw that the Whigs had then succeeded in making the succession a party question. He saw that if the Elector ascended the throne, he would ascend it as the head of the Whig faction; and that if the Tories were to maintain the supremacy, they must maintain it under a Tory king. He saw that the Elector regarded him with suspicion and dislike. He saw that the return of the Whigs to power would in all likelihood consign him at once to impotence and ignominy. He was therefore bound by all considerations of self-interest to attach himself to James, and of his intrigues in favor of James we have ample proofs. Circumstances had, however, gone against him, and it was now necessary to retrace his steps. Though his prospects were far from promising, they were not hopeless.

If he could not transform himself into a Whig, he could at least abandon the Jacobites and figure as a zealous Hanoverian. It was just possible that the new king might adopt the policy of William, and consent to a coalition. The Tories were, after all, a formidable body, and there was little likelihood of repose in any government in which the land interest and the Church were not powerfully represented. Of these representatives he was the acknowledged leader. The Elector was notoriously a man of peace, and averse to extreme measures. He had undoubtedly flung himself upon the Whigs, but it had been from motives of policy. Such, if we may judge from his correspondence, were Bolingbroke's reflections as he watched from his window in Golden Square the flare of the bonfires in which his effigy was crackling.

He lost no time in expressing in abject terms his devotion to his new master. "Quoique je crains d'être importun"—so ran his letter—"je ne saurois me dispenser plus long-tems et de suivre mon inclination et de m'acquitter de mon devoir." He enlarged on the fidelity with which he had served Anne, congratulated himself on being the servant of so great a prince as her successor, and concluded by observing that in whatever station he might be employed he could at least promise integrity, diligence, and loyalty. During the next three weeks there was much to encourage him. The Council of Regency had, it is true, submitted him to the indignity of being superseded by their secretary. But Clarendon's despatches from Hanover were favorable. Goertz, one of the Elector's confidential advisers, was openly enlisted in the Tory cause. There were already signs of disunion in the Ministry, and Halifax had even suggested that Bromley should be Chancellor of the Exchequer, and Hanmer one of the Tellers. It was confidently rumored that the King, so far from having decided to crush the Tories, was even hesitating as to which of the two factions should be preferred to honor. This report emanated, we suspect, from Bothmar. That wily diplomatist had seen all along the expediency of amusing the Tories till the arrival of George should settle the kingdom. The general tranquillity of affairs had by no means thrown him off his guard. He was too well acquainted with the history of revolutions not to know that the first thing generated by them is ambition, and that the last things changed by them are principles.

It was now late in August, and Bolingbroke was awaiting with some anxiety a reply to his letter. The answer arrived on the twenty-eighth, in the form of an express, addressed not to himself but to the Council of Regency. He was summarily dismissed from his post of Secretary of State; his office was to be put under lock and key; his papers were to be seized and sealed up. This disagreeable intelligence he affected to receive with indifference. It shocked him, he says—for at least two minutes; "but," he added, "the grief of my soul is this—I see plainly that the Tory party is gone."*

On the evening of the 18th of September, the King landed at Greenwich, and Bolingbroke hurried up from Bucklersbury to offer his congratulations. His worst fears were soon verified. The Tories had learned, indeed, some days before that they were to be excluded from all share in the Government, but they had not yet learned that they were to be excluded from all share in the royal favor. They were at once undeceived. Their leaders were treated with contempt. Ormond and Harcourt failed to extort even a glance of recognition; Oxford was openly insulted; Bolingbroke was not permitted to present himself. This was the signal which had been long expected. For some weeks the struggle between the two great factions had been suspended. A great victory had been won, but the ultimate issue of that victory depended upon the attitude of the new sovereign. The prostrate Tories trusted to his moderation, for protection; the Whigs to his gratitude, for revenge. Till he declared himself, the combatants could only stand glaring at one another. Between the death of Anne and his reception at Greenwich, George's policy

* Letter to Atterbury, Macpherson's "Original Papers," vol. ii., p. 651.

had been studiously concealed; his Ministers had been feeding both parties with hopes, and the majority of men had been deceived. Now, however, all was clear. His pretended neutrality had been a mere trick to effect a peaceable entrance. He had come, not as a mediator but as a partisan; not as the guardian of the common interests of his people, but as the leader of an insolent and vindictive faction. In less than a month the three kingdoms were again on fire with civil fury. The Whigs, eager to indemnify themselves for long oppression, were bent on nothing less than the utter destruction of their rivals. The Tories, fighting against fearful odds, were driven in despair to take a course which, for forty-five years, reduced them to impotence in the Senate, and which brought many of them to the scaffold.

On the 17th of March the Houses met, and Bolingbroke appeared as leader of the Opposition. The King's Speech, which was read by Cowper, was judicious and temperate. With the Addresses in answer the war began. The Opposition took their stand on a clause in which the House had expressed their hope that his Majesty would recover the reputation of the kingdom. This the Tories very properly interpreted as a reflection on the conduct of their chiefs. A warm debate ensued, and Bolingbroke rose for the last time to address that assembly which had so often listened to him with mingled aversion and pleasure. His speech was an elaborate defence of his foreign and domestic policy. He paid a pathetic tribute to the memory of the late Queen, and he addressed a still more pathetic appeal to the wisdom, equity, and moderation of the reigning sovereign. He was willing to be punished if he had done amiss, but he thought it hard to be condemned unheard. He then proceeded to deal in detail with the transactions in which he was so deeply concerned, and he concluded a long and masterly harangue by moving that the word "maintain" should be substituted for the word "recover." He was supported by the Earl of Strafford and the Duke of Shrewsbury. But all his efforts were vain. The motion was rejected by an overwhelming majority. In the Lower House the late Government fared even worse. There Walpole openly charged them with being in league with James, and stated that it was his intention and the intention of his colleagues to bring them to justice. What Walpole announced was repeated with still more emphasis and acrimony by Stanhope. Endeavors had, he said, been made to prevent a discovery of the late mismanagement, by conveying away several papers from the Secretaries' offices; but there still remained ample evidence against them, evidence which would not only prove their corruption, but place it beyond doubt that far more serious charges could be established.

Bolingbroke now saw that the storm was gathering fast. His private secretary had indeed succeeded in defeating the vigilance of the Government, by concealing such papers as might be prejudicial. Almost all those witnesses who could conclusively prove his treason were either out of reach or above temptation to treachery. Azzurini was in the Bastile, Gautier had retired to France, D'Iberville was protected by his diplomatic character, De Torcy was the soul of honor. But there was one man whom Bolingbroke had for many years loved and trusted as a brother, who had been his companion in business and pleasure, who had shared all his secrets. That man was Prior. Prior had recently arrived from France. The emissaries of Stanhope and Walpole had been busy with him, and Bolingbroke heard with terror and astonishment that his old friend had promised to reveal everything. This report, for which, as it afterwards turned out, there was not the slightest foundation, had the more weight because it appeared to confirm what had reached him from another quarter. He had been informed that the Whigs had engaged to bring him to the scaffold, that they had entered into an alliance of which his blood was to be the cement, and that all attempts to defend himself would be vain, for sentence had virtually been passed. There is reason to believe that this alarming intelligence was, under the guise of friendship, conveyed to him by Marlborough, and that it was part of an ingenious manœuvre suggested by Walpole and Stanhope to induce him to leave the country—a step which would enable them to proceed against him by Act of Attainder, and to accomplish without difficulty his destruction. The stratagem succeeded.

On Saturday, the 26th of March, it was reported in London that Bolingbroke had fled. The report was at first received with contemptuous incredulity. He had been seen by hundreds the night before in his usual high spirits at Drury Lane, where he had, from his box, complimented the actors and bespoken a play for the next evening. He had repeatedly assured his friends—and his friends were to be found in every coffee-house in the town—that he was under no apprehensions of what his enemies might do. He was only anxious for an opportunity to clear himself, and that opportunity would, he said, be provided by the Parliamentary inquiry then pending. In a few days all was known. The greatest excitement prevailed in political circles, and this excitement was shortly afterwards increased by the intelligence that a man who had assisted in effecting the escape of the fallen Minister was in custody. The man's name was Morgan, and he held a commission in the Marines. In the course of his examination before the Privy Council he stated that he had met Bolingbroke, disguised as a French courier, and travelling as the servant of a king's messenger, named La Vigne, at Dover; that he had at one time been under obligation to him, and that when Bolingbroke revealed himself and begged for a passage to Calais, he had not had the heart to refuse him. This statement had been already supplemented by communications from Bolingbroke himself. He had written to Lord Lansdowne and he had written to his father. The letter to Lansdowne was published. It was dated from Dover. He had left England, he said, not because he was conscious of any guilt, not because he shrank from any investigation, but because his foes had resolved to shed his blood. And he challenged the most inveterate of those foes to produce a single instance of criminal correspondence on his part, or a single proof of corruption. Had there been the least hope of obtaining a fair trial he should have stood his ground; but he had been prejudged. His comfort in misfortune would be the memory of the great services he had done his country, and the reflection that his only crime consisted in being too patriotic to sacrifice her interests to foreign allies. This letter was not considered even by his friends as a very satisfactory explanation of the step he had taken. Several harsh comments were made on it, and his conduct was generally regarded as reflecting little credit either on his judgment or his courage.

His flight was, in truth, the greatest blunder of his life —a blunder which it is scarcely credible that any one possessing a particle of his sagacity and experience could ever have committed. A moment's calm reflection might have shown him that any attempt on the part of his enemies to

bring him to the block would be futile. Whatever may
have been the measure of his moral guilt in the negotiations with France, there had been nothing to support a
capital charge. Whatever had been most reprehensible
in his conduct had been sanctioned by the Queen, had
been sanctioned by two Parliaments. In the intrigues with
James several of the leading Whigs had been as deeply
involved as himself, and of his own intrigues it would, even
if Prior had turned traitor, have been very difficult to obtain corroborative evidence. The temper of the nation
was such as to make extreme measures eminently impolitic. There was not an observant statesman in England
who did not perceive that affairs were on the razor's edge.
The King had already made many enemies. The Government was becoming every day more unpopular, the Opposition more powerful. The Tories were beginning to rally.
The schisms which had at the end of the last reign divided
them showed symptoms of healing. A reaction was to all
appearance merely a matter of time. That reaction could
scarcely fail to be hastened by the impeachment of a Minister so representative and so popular as himself. By
awaiting his trial he would, therefore, have run comparatively little risk. By his flight he ruined everything.
Bolingbroke has, however, seldom the magnanimity to acknowledge himself in error; and to the end of his life he
continued, both in his writings and in his conversation, to
defend this suicidal step. The account which he afterwards gave of it is a curious instance of his disingenuousness. He left England, as his letter to Lord Lansdowne
proves, in panic terror, to save himself from the scaffold.
He left England, according to his subsequent statement,
after mature deliberation, not to save himself from the
scaffold, not because he was afraid of his enemies, but to

avoid the humiliation of being beholden to the Whimsicals for protection, and to embarrass Oxford.

On his arrival at Paris he immediately put himself into communication with Lord Stair, the English Ambassador. He solemnly promised to have no dealings with the Jacobites, and these promises he reiterated in a letter to Stanhope. Within a few hours he was closeted with Berwick, assuring him of his sympathy, assuring him that all was going well for James in England, but adding that, for the present at least, he must refrain from any public co-operation with the Jacobites.* Having thus, by a piece of double duplicity, established relations with both parties, and provided for either alternative, he proceeded to Dauphiné to watch the course of events.

Meanwhile his enemies in England had not been idle. Prior had been arrested. The papers relating to the negotiations with France had been called for and produced. A secret committee had been appointed to collect and arrange evidence. The most unscrupulous means had been resorted to to make that evidence complete. Private correspondence had been seized and scrutinized. The escritoires of the late Queen had been ransacked, and such was the malignant industry of this inquisition that in six weeks the evidence accumulated by them amounted to no less than twelve stout volumes. An abstract of this evidence was drawn up by Walpole with great ability in the form of a Report. On the 2d of June he informed the House that the Committee were in a position to communicate the result of their inquiries, and the day fixed for the communication was that day week. The news of these proceedings had for several weeks kept the two factions in a state bordering on frenzy. The Whigs were eager to enhance

* "Memoirs of the Duke of Berwick," vol ii., p. 198.

the glory of their recent triumph by the meaner satisfaction of being able to trample on a fallen foe. The treachery of Bolingbroke and Oxford would now, they said, be incontrovertibly established. They would be punished as they deserved. The Tories, on the other hand—though Bolingbroke's flight had been a great shock to them—professed to anticipate very different results. They had no fear at all, they answered, of any such investigation, provided only it were properly conducted; they would never believe that their leaders had been guilty either of treason or misdemeanor. The Whigs, therefore, took their stand by Walpole and Stanhope; the Tories, with the exception of the Whimsicals, identified themselves with the cause of Bolingbroke and Oxford.

The important day arrived. The House was densely crowded. Walpole announced, amid a breathless silence, that before producing his Report he had a motion to propose. He must request the Speaker to issue warrants for the apprehension of several persons. Upon that the lobby was cleared, the doors were locked, and the keys laid upon the table. The persons named by him were at once arrested, and among them were Thomas Harley and Matthew Prior. With these alarming preliminaries he proceeded to deliver his Report. The ceremony occupied many hours; when the House adjourned it was not concluded, and it was late in the afternoon of the following day before the last folio was read. The Whigs had triumphed. The Tories saw that defence was hopeless. The charge of Jacobitism had not, indeed, been satisfactorily established, and it was open to doubt whether anything had been brought forward which was technically sufficient to support a charge of high-treason. But of the moral guilt of the two Ministers there could be no doubt. They had sullied the national honor, they had set at naught the most sacred ties which can bind nations together, they had sacrificed to party considerations the common interests of their country, they had had recourse to the most dishonorable subterfuges. The desertion of the Dutch, for example in the negotiations with France, and the suspension of arms in the spring of 1712, are two of the most scandalous incidents in the annals of diplomacy. A skilful advocate might undoubtedly have shown that these misdemeanors, grave though they were, had been accompanied with extenuating circumstances. He could have been at no loss to prove that the termination of hostilities with France was not only expedient but necessary, and he might have reasoned that if the means employed had been reprehensible, if the terms accepted had been inadequate, the blame lay with the vexatious opposition of the Whigs and the Allies. He would not, we think, have had much difficulty in refuting such evidence as the prosecution had then been able to obtain touching the intrigues with James. He could have protested, and have protested with justice, against the sophistry to which Walpole had resorted in his endeavors to heighten the minor charge of high crimes and misdemeanors into the most serious charge which the law knows. On this point the Whigs undoubtedly went too far. The moral delinquency of Oxford and Bolingbroke can scarcely be exaggerated, but there had been nothing in their conduct to warrant a charge of high-treason. The evidence on which the Whigs succeeded in establishing their case is well known. It was proved that in the negotiations with De Torcy, Bolingbroke had endeavored to procure for France the city of Tournay. The possession of Tournay was for the advantage of the French, with whom we were at that time in open hostility. The attempt was, therefore, interpreted as an adherence to the Queen's enemies, and adherence to the enemies of the Crown had, by a Statute of Edward III., been pronounced high-treason. The answer to this was obvious. Tournay, as a matter of fact, had not been surrendered. Had the place been actually abandoned the sacrifice would have done no injury to England, for Tournay did not belong to her. The proposal, moreover, had been made not with a view to benefit the French, but with a view to benefit the English. The Queen herself had been a party to the proposal, and when there seemed probability of disapprobation the project had been abandoned. But the temper of the House was such that none of the partisans of the late Ministers had the courage to undertake their defence. Hanmer, indeed, rose to move that further consideration of the Report should be deferred till the members had been served with copies. To this Walpole and Stanhope declined to accede. Walpole then rose and impeached Bolingbroke of high-treason. On the 6th of the following month Walpole presented himself at the bar of the Upper House. On the 14th of September Bolingbroke was an attainted outlaw. We have little doubt that had he remained in England this terrible sentence would never have been passed. Many of the Whigs had, we now know, serious misgivings about its justice. Some had even refused to sanction it. The wise and moderate Somers had expressed his dissent in the most emphatic terms, and had even gone so far as to compare the vindictive proceedings of Walpole and Stanhope to the proscriptions of Marius and Sulla. But the minds of the most scrupulous were soon to be set at rest. Before the measure had passed into law it had unhappily received its justification.

We have now arrived at a period in Bolingbroke's life

of which he has himself left us an elaborate account. In the Letter to Sir William Wyndham he narrates the circumstances under which he attached himself to the interests of the Pretender, and he professes to lay bare without reserve the motives which induced him to take this unfortunate step. That his narrative of the events of 1715 is substantially correct we have not the smallest doubt. His principal object in penning it was to cover James and his projects with ridicule, and to show the Tories that an alliance with the Jacobites meant nothing less than alliance with disgrace and ruin. This object was, as he well knew, best attained by stating simple truth. There was no necessity for fiction; there was no necessity for over-coloring. Everything that the art of the satirist could do to render the character of James contemptible Nature had actually done. To exaggerate his incapacity was superfluous, for his conduct had been in itself the quintessence of folly. To make his Cabinet the laughing-stock of Europe, all that was needed was to preserve with exact fidelity its distinctive features, for those features presented in themselves everything that the most malignant caricaturist could desire. The whole drama of 1715 was in truth such a ludicrous exhibition of recklessness and mismanagement as to be almost without parallel in history. There is, however, one portion of this narrative in which we are not inclined to place much confidence. Bolingbroke informs us that he allied himself with the Jacobites, not from motives of self-interest, but from the loftiest and purest motives which can animate a man of honor. Till his departure from England he was the acknowledged leader of the Tory party. To that party he was, he said, bound by every tie, both of sentiment and principle. Since his exile those ties had been drawn closer. The Tories had been submitted to a grinding despotism. They had been excluded from all share in the favor of the new king. In Parliament they had been reduced to political impotence. Principles for which they would gladly have shed their blood were trampled under the feet of savage and vindictive foes. Their very lives were at the mercy of sycophants and informers. The very existence of Toryism was at stake. At last, partly owing to the conviction that the only remedy for their misfortunes lay in a change of dynasty, partly owing to continued persecution, and partly moved by resentment at the measures which had doomed their chiefs to the fate of traitors, they had thrown themselves into the arms of the Pretender. In this extremity they appealed to their banished leader, and he responded to their call. He anticipated failure, but he had, he said, no choice. As the servant of the Tories he was therefore forced to cast in his lot with the Jacobites, and as the servant of the Tories he accepted the seals from James.

Now nothing is more certain than that Bolingbroke had made overtures to Berwick several weeks before any appeal had been made to him from England at Commercy. Nay, nothing is more certain than that from the October of 1712 he had, in his communications with D'Iberville and Gautier, repeatedly declared himself in favor of the Pretender. He had accepted the seals at least six weeks before the Bill of Attainder had been passed — a fact which he always denied, but which is now placed beyond doubt by the date of his first letter to James, preserved in the Stuart Papers. That many of the Tories who, previous to the coronation of George, held no communication with the Jacobites, had, by the violence of the Whigs, been driven to open communications with them is unquestionably true; but that Bolingbroke should have believed for one instant that the majority of the Tories would have consented to set a Papist on the throne is ludicrous. And that there was little likelihood of the Pretender changing, or even affecting to change his religion, he has himself admitted.

The appeal made to him emanated, as he well knew, from a small knot of men as desperate as himself. And the simple truth is, that in taking this step he was guided, as he always was guided, by purely personal considerations. In England the game had been played out. The Tories were too feeble to become his tools, and the Whigs too wise to become his dupes. His only hope lay in mischievous activity and in the chances of fortune. He clung to the cause of James, not as an honest zealot clings to a principle, but as desperate adventurers clutch at opportunity.

His first interview with his new master was not encouraging. "He talked," says Bolingbroke, "like a man who expected every moment to set out for England or Scotland, but who did not very well know which." Of the state of his affairs the Chevalier gave, indeed, a very glowing account; though it appeared on investigation that he had arrived at his satisfactory conclusions by a somewhat unsatisfactory process. In other words, he had invented much, assumed more, and colored everything. For the furtherance of his designs it was soon obvious that, in spite of all his blustering, he had done nothing. He assured Bolingbroke, however, that everything was in readiness, and he was, he said, convinced that in a few weeks he should be on the throne of his ancestors. Bolingbroke consented to accept the seals, which at the conclusion of the interview were pressed on him, but he left his new master with no very exalted ideas either of his character or of his capacity. Indeed, he afterwards assured Wyndham that he had already begun to repent of the step he had taken, almost as soon as he had taken it. His penetrating eye had probably discerned in the young prince the germs of those odious qualities which had, in the person of the Second James, made the name of Stuart a synonyme for folly, and in the person of the Second Charles a synonyme for ingratitude. In a few hours he received his instructions. He was to proceed to Paris, which was to be the basis of operations. He was to put himself at the head of the Jacobite party. He was to open communications with the United Kingdom, and to lose no time in soliciting the assistance of Louis.

Bolingbroke arrived in Paris at the end of July. He was anxious to meet his coadjutors, and orders were at once issued for the Jacobite Ministry to meet. His interview with James had been a shock, but when his eyes rested on the spectacle which now presented itself, his heart sank within him. He saw before him a sordid rabble of both sexes. They appeared to have no bond of union, but had gathered in knots, and in a few minutes he was enabled to discover that they represented the scum of four nations. Their hopes were high, their voices were loud; their air and gestures indicated boundless self-importance. Those who could read and write had papers in their hands, and those who could neither read nor write were contenting themselves with looking mysterious. On analyzing this assembly into its constituent parts, he perceived that it consisted of hot-headed Irish vagrants, largely recruited from the least reputable sections of Parisian society; of a few Englishmen who had been glad to put the Channel between themselves and their infuriated creditors; and of several women whose characters were more obvious than respectable. To these had been added a small body of Scotch adventurers, desperate from poverty and mad with fanaticism. As each of these politicians recognized no leader but James, each, in the absence of James, had proceeded on the principle of doing what was right in his own eyes. Each regarded his neighbor, not in the light of an ally, but in the light of a rival; and as nobody had looked beyond himself, nobody had advanced one step towards the attainment of what could only be attained by mutual co-operation. The temper of such assemblies has been the same in all ages. The only counsellors in whom they have any confidence are those who flatter their hopes; the only counsellors to whom they refuse to listen are those who would teach them how those hopes may be realized. Everything is seen by them through a false medium. Their imagination is the dupe of their vanity. Their reason is perverted by their passions. As their distinguishing features are ignorance and credulity, they are, of all bodies of men, the most impracticable; for the first renders them incapable of discerning their true interests, and the second keeps them in a state of perpetual agitation. Never were these peculiarities more strikingly illustrated than by the crowd which now surrounded Bolingbroke. The public discontent in England was multiplied a thousand-fold. Every riot was a rebellion. Every street brawl portended revolution. Scotland and Ireland were on the point of rising. The Whig Cabinet had collapsed. The army had mutinied. Nothing was more certain than that in a few weeks James would be at Whitehall, and George in exile. Letters and despatches, which had in truth emanated from men of the same character as those with whom they corresponded, were produced to prove the truth of this rhodomontade. It was useless to reason with these fanatics. It was useless to point out to them that the battle had yet to be fought, and that, if victory came, it would not come spontaneously, but as the prize of valor and prudence.

Bolingbroke now clearly saw that to have any chance of success he must stand alone. He could rely on no assistance from his master, he could expect nothing but embarrassment from his colleagues in Paris. He proceeded at once to grapple with the difficulties of his position, and he grappled with them as few men have ever grappled with difficulties so arduous and complicated. At this moment the prospects of the Jacobites were not unpromising. Among the States of Europe there was scarcely one which regarded the accession of the House of Hanover with favor. Louis XIV. took no pains to conceal the fact that nothing but national exhaustion, occasioned by recent disaster, prevented him from openly re-espousing the cause of James. The sympathies of Spain were entirely on the side of Jacobitism. The policy of Portugal was to stand well with France. The Emperor, incensed at the provisions of the Peace of Utrecht, kept sullenly aloof from both parties, but it was generally understood that he viewed the elevation of the Elector with feelings of suspicion and jealousy. Indeed, the only Powers which could be described as in any way attached to George were Holland and Prussia. Of these Holland was too deeply involved in financial embarrassment to be of much service, and Prussia was not in a condition to do more than contribute a few troops for the preservation of Hanover. In Scotland the discontent was deep-seated and general. In Ireland the prospect of James's accession was hailed with joy. In England, though affairs had by no means advanced so far as the Jacobite agents represented, there was ample ground for hope. Berwick indeed asserts that of the body of the people five out of six were for James; not, he adds, because of his incontestable right, but from hatred to the House of Hanover, and to prevent the total ruin of the Church and of popular liberty.*

These advantages were, however, of a negative character; the task before Bolingbroke was to discover in what way they might be turned to the best account. The ground was cleared; the material lay ready; but the edifice had yet to be raised. His proper course was easy to discern. He must unite the scattered forces of his party by establishing a regular communication between them. He must make the Jacobites, who lay dispersed through France, through England, through Scotland, through Ireland, act in unison. When they rose they must rise not in detachments and at intervals, but simultaneously, under the command of competent officers. He must obtain assistance from France, for without that assistance no manœuvre could be effectual. He must endeavor by dint of skilful diplomacy to secure the co-operation of Spain and Sweden.

To these difficult duties he devoted himself with admirable skill and temper. Never, indeed, were his eminent abilities seen to greater advantage. In a few weeks he had not only induced Louis to provide the Jacobites with ammunition, but he had kindled in the breast of the aged King the same ardor which glowed within his own, and he had brought him almost to the point of declaring war with England. He had obtained pecuniary assistance from Spain. He had opened negotiations with Charles XII. He had put himself into communication with the leading Jacobites in the three kingdoms, and had exactly informed them both of what it was necessary for them to do, and of what it behooved them to guard against. He had twice

* "Memoirs," vol. ii., p. 202.

saved James from taking steps which must inevitably have ruined him. Affairs which were, before he left Dauphiné, in the utmost possible perplexity, now began to assume an aspect so promising that some of the leading members of George's Government were meditating treachery, and the Chevalier could number among his adherents the great names of Marlborough and Shrewsbury. Measures had, moreover, been concerted for seizing Bristol, Exeter, and Plymouth. It would not, we think, be going too far to say that, had Bolingbroke been suffered to continue as he commenced, had he been properly supported by the Jacobite leaders, had his warnings been regarded, had his instructions been carried out, had his supremacy in the Council been seconded by Berwick's supremacy in the field, the whole course of European history might have been changed. The more closely we examine the Rebellion of 1715, the more apparent will this appear. It began as a desperate enterprise on the part of a few hot-headed adventurers. It promised, under the direction of Bolingbroke, to become the first act of a tremendous drama. The scheme of operations as designed by him was without a flaw. He had provided for all contingencies except those contingencies which no human foresight can meet. In the United Kingdom he had laid the foundation of a coalition which would in all probability be irresistible; on the Continent he was sure of the neutrality of those Powers which could oppose his designs, and he had ample reasons for supposing that those Powers would, on the first appearance of success, declare in his favor. But the levity and faithlessness of James, and the insane folly of the Jacobites, were unhappily in exact proportion to his own wisdom and foresight. At the end of August he was astounded to hear that Ormond, on whom everything depended in England, and who had in a recent despatch promised to hold out, had deserted his post and was in Paris. The flight of Ormond was shortly afterwards succeeded by the death of Louis XIV. "He was," said Bolingbroke, "the best friend the Chevalier ever had, and when I engaged in this business my principal dependence was on his personal character, my hopes sunk when he declined, and died when he expired."

These events were, indeed, a severe blow. For the flight of Ormond augured ill for the prospects of the Jacobites in England, and the death of Louis augured ill for their prospects in France. Still he did not despair. The next three weeks were spent in receiving and in answering despatches from England and Scotland, and in sounding the new French Government. The Regent was courteous and sympathetic, but Bolingbroke was not long in discerning that the interests of that wily prince were by no means compatible with running any risks for the Jacobites. The state of France was indeed such as to preclude all hopes of assistance. Louis had left his kingdom in a deplorable condition. Her provinces were desolated by famine. Her finances were hopelessly involved; her capital was torn by faction. The only thing which could enable her to recover herself was peace, and the maintenance of peace was therefore the Regent's first consideration. There was also another question which entered largely into his calculations. The rickety and sickly child whose place he filled was scarcely likely to survive infancy. Philip of Spain, who was, in order of succession, next heir to the throne of France, had by the Treaty of Utrecht solemnly renounced all claims to it. The Regent, therefore, was heir-presumptive. But Philip had recently announced that he had no intention of abiding by his former decision, and that the renunciations he made at Utrecht were, as the lawyers had at the time justly asserted, invalid. His claim was good, and it was his intention, should occasion offer, to assert it. This claim Orleans very naturally determined to resist, and was anxious to form such alliances as might enable him to make this resistance effectual. He shrank, therefore, from compromising himself with the English Government by assisting the Jacobites, and from compromising himself with the Jacobites by assisting the English Government, for either party might serve his turn. His policy was to leave the two parties to settle the question of supremacy between them, and to maintain a position of strict neutrality until that question should be decided. It was a matter of little importance to him whether George or James sat on the throne of England, but it was a matter of great importance to him that the king who filled that throne should, in the event of young Louis's death, consent to guarantee the succession of the House of Orleans. Such was, we believe, the real policy of the Regent at this conjuncture. He was certainly in communication with Ormond and Bolingbroke; he was certainly in communication with Stair and Stanhope.

And now everything began to go wrong. The Jacobites were apparently bent on nothing but self-destruction. The chief objects of their leaders appeared to be to outbid each other in folly, and to defeat the efforts of the two men who might have saved them. The only coadjutors in whom James had any confidence were those who were betraying him to Stair. The only counsellors who had any weight with Ormond were two harlots and a hare-brained priest. Bolingbroke and Berwick had scarcely a voice in the conduct of affairs. If they were consulted, they were consulted only to be laughed at; if they issued instructions, their instructions were either countermanded or set at naught.

This was bad, but this was not all. To men situated as the Jacobites then were, nothing was more indispensable than secrecy; but their secrets were, as Bolingbroke bitterly observed, the property of everybody who kept his ears open. "For no sex," he adds, "was excluded from our ministry. Fanny Oglethorpe kept her corner in it, and Olive Trant was the great wheel of our machine." In consequence of this indiscreet loquacity, it was soon known that a small armament, assembled at Havre, had been assembled for the purpose of assisting the Chevalier. Stair demanded, therefore, that it should be surrendered to the English Government. To this request, however, the Regent refused to accede, but a compromise was accepted, and the flotilla was disarmed and broken up. Having thus succeeded in ruining themselves by sea, the Jacobites lost no time in ruining themselves by land. In the middle of September, Bolingbroke addressed a despatch to Mar, who had undertaken the management of affairs in Scotland, pointing out to him that it would be worse than useless to raise the Highlands without support from France, and without providing for a simultaneous movement on the part of the Jacobites in England. But Mar had already assembled the clans before Bolingbroke's despatch arrived. It appears, indeed, that James had had the inconceivable folly to issue, on his own responsibility, and without consulting either Bolingbroke or Berwick, previous instructions ordering Mar to take this insane step. All that ensued was of a piece with all that preceded. Blunder followed on blunder, disaster on disaster, in rapid succession. Ormond sailed for Devonshire to find, instead of loyal multitudes rallying round his standard, a solitary coast, a churlish fellow who refused him a night's lodging, most of the leading Jacobites in custody, and warrants out for the arrest of Jersey and Wyndham. The Chevalier, not to be outdone in folly, dallied at St. Malo, debating about what was the best thing to do till it was too late to do anything but despair, and then hurried off to head a forlorn hope in Scotland.

In a few months all was over. A tragedy, the particulars of which it is difficult, even at this distance of time, to peruse without tears, had been enacted. A large multitude of brave and generous enthusiasts had, in obedience to a noble impulse, and after making heroic self-sacrifices, rushed to destruction. Everything that could be effected by a spirit which rose superior to privation and reverses, by fidelity strong even to martyrdom, and by a fortitude which death could subdue only by extinguishing, these gallant men had done. For a cause which was in their eyes the cause of Justice, they had sacrificed their fortunes; for one who was to them merely the representative of a righteous claim, they had poured out their blood. Whatever may have been the motives which guided their leaders in France, the motives of these unhappy men had at least been pure and honorable. But terrible, indeed, had been their fate. Many who had not had the good-fortune to find a grave in the field, had been condemned to die the death of felons. Two chiefs, distinguished by rank and opulence, and still more honorably distinguished by the virtues of heroism, had been led to the scaffold, their blood attainted, their property confiscated. The hopes of the Jacobites had been blighted; their power had been destroyed; their very names had become a byword.

One thing, and one thing only, was now wanting to make James and his counsellors completely contemptible. If their party contained a man whose sagacity and good sense had, during the general frenzy, been above imputation, and whose services had entitled him to the respect and gratitude of the Jacobites, that man was Bolingbroke. Of all James's servants, he had been the most able and the most zealous. He had furnished the Jacobites with a plan of operations which nothing but their own temerity and wrongheadedness could have defeated. He had amply forewarned them of their errors; and when they had set his warnings at defiance, he had toiled with almost superhuman energy to extricate them from the consequences of those errors. When the prospects of Jacobitism were blackest, when everything was lost in England, and when everything was on the point of being lost in Scotland, he had not despaired. He had renewed his applications to Spain and Sweden; he had been at great pains to procure and ship off ammunition and soldiers. He had submitted to every indignity to gain access to the Regent, and, in Berwick's emphatic phrase, "he had moved heaven and earth" to obtain assistance from the French Court.* His official duties he had performed with punctilious exactness, and from the day on which he took up the Seals at Commercy to the day on which he was ordered to resign them, he had done nothing inconsistent with the character of a wise and honest Minister. All this weighed, however, very little with men who saw that they might, with a little management, make him the scape-goat of their own follies. With the Jacobite clique in the Bois de Boulogne he had never been popular. From the Jacobite rabble he had always stood contemptuously aloof. Scandalous stories were

---

* Berwick gives eloquent and indignant testimony to the services of Bolingbroke and to the folly and ingratitude of James.—*Memoirs*, vol. ii., pp. 253-257.

therefore without difficulty vamped up against him and industriously circulated. He was charged, among other things, with having at a supper-party spoken disrespectfully of James, which was possibly true; with having lavished on his mistress money which had been intrusted to him for State purposes, which was certainly false; with having neglected his duties, which carried with it its own refutation. Mar and Ormond, with scandalous indifference to truth, attributed to his incapacity and negligence the misfortunes in Scotland, and the fact that no assistance had been obtained from France. The Chevalier, glad to find an opportunity of imputing to his Minister the calamities for which he had himself been mainly responsible, caught eagerly at these calumnies. At the end of January, therefore, Bolingbroke suddenly received his dismissal, the dismissal being accompanied with gross insult, and succeeded by a storm of obloquy. So terminated his unfortunate connection with the Jacobites.

We have thought it desirable to enter at some length into this episode in his career, first because of the influence it subsequently exercised both on his conduct and on his opinions, and secondly because it has, we think, been very generally misunderstood. Few parts of his public life have been so malignantly assailed, and no part of his public life was, we are convinced, more creditable to him. He served James as he had never before served Anne, and as he never afterwards served any master. At no period was his political genius seen to greater advantage, at no period were his characteristic defects under better control. During these few months he exhibited, indeed, some of the highest qualities of an administrator and a diplomatist, and if he failed, he failed under circumstances which would have rendered Richelieu powerless, and have baffled the skill of

Theramenes or Talleyrand. The motives which originally induced him to join the Jacobites were, as we have already shown, anything but laudable, but an estimate of the motives which induced him to join the Chevalier, and an estimate of his conduct as the Chevalier's Minister, ought by no means to be confounded. What he did he did well, though it should never have been done at all.

The news of his disgrace was received with much satisfaction by the English Cabinet. The character of Bolingbroke was too well known to admit of any doubt as to the course he would take. All who knew him knew that his recent allies had transformed the most formidable of their coadjutors into the most formidable of their enemies; and he would, it was expected, run into all lengths that revenge and interest might hurry him. The Jacobites had, indeed, suffered too severely in the recent struggle to make it probable that they were in a position to renew hostilities, but their real strength was still unknown, their numbers were still uncertain, their movements were full of mystery. If Bolingbroke would consent to throw light on these points —and no man was more competent to do so—he would relieve the Ministry from much embarrassment. If he could be induced to open the minds of the Tories to the real character of James, he would do much to restore public tranquillity. It was resolved, therefore, to see what could be done with him, and instructions were forwarded to Stair to solicit an interview. The two statesmen met at the Embassy. Bolingbroke behaved exactly as Stair anticipated. He longed, he said, to get back to England. His sole anxiety was to be enabled to serve his country and his sovereign with zeal and affection. He would do everything that was required of him. He would show the Tories what manner of man the Pretender was, and how grossly they had been deceived in him. He could not, as a man of honor, either betray individuals or divulge private secrets, but he would throw all the light he could on the movements and on the designs of the Jacobites. "Time and my uniform conduct will," he added in conclusion, "convince the world of the uprightness of my intentions, and it is better to wait for this result, however long, than to arrive hastily at one's goal by leaving the highway of honor and honesty." To all this Stair listened with sympathy and respect. His instructions had, however, gone no further than to hold out "suitable hopes and encouragement," and suitable hopes and encouragement were all that Bolingbroke could obtain from him. Bolingbroke left the Embassy, little thinking that seven years were to elapse before those hopes were even partially to be realized.

Those seven years were perhaps the happiest years of his life. He was, it is true, pursued by the unrelenting malevolence of the Jacobites, and he was kept in a state of uneasy expectation by Stanhope and Sunderland, who would neither definitely refuse nor definitely promise a pardon. But, for the rest, his life was without a shadow, and he had in truth little occasion for the exercise of that stoicism which he now began with so much ostentation to profess. He was in the prime of manhood. His excesses had not as yet begun to tell upon his fine constitution. A fortunate speculation had secured him a competence. A fortunate connection was soon to win him from grosser indulgences to more refined enjoyments. He was the centre of a society which numbered among its members some of the most accomplished men and women of those times. In the salons of the Faubourg Saint-Germain he was a welcome guest. In the Société d'Entresol he had a distinguished place. He was enabled to gratify to the full, first at Marcilly and subsequently at La Source, the two passions which were, he said, the dominant passions of his life —the love of study and the love of rural pursuits. Ambition had still its old fascination for him, but the nature of that ambition had undergone a complete change. Up to this time he had been the leader of a party; he now aspired to be a leader of mankind. Up to this time the prize for which he had been contending had been popularity; the arena on which he had fought, an arena crowded with ignoble competitors. He now aspired to enter that greater arena where, in a spirit of more honorable rivalry, nobler candidates contend for nobler prizes.

At the beginning of this period he produced, within a few months of each other, a work of which the best that can be said of it is that it would not disgrace a University prizeman, and a work which has by many of his critics been pronounced to be his masterpiece—the "Reflections on Exile," and the "Letter to Sir William Wyndham." The "Reflections on Exile" is in truth little more than a loose paraphrase of Seneca's "Consolatio ad Helviam," garnished with illustrative matter from Cicero and Plutarch, and enlivened with a few anecdotes derived principally from the Roman historians and from Diogenes Laertius. It reproduces in a diffuse and grandiloquent style those silly paradoxes by which the followers of Zeno affected to rob misfortune of its terrors. As exile has been the lot of some of the most exalted characters of antiquity, exile involves no dishonor, and dishonor is all that a good man has to fear. To a philosopher exile is impossible, for a philosopher is a citizen of the world, and how can a man be banished from his country when his country is the universe? If exile is a misfortune, exile is a blessing, for without misfortune there can be no virtue, and without virtue there can be no enjoyment. These sentiments, which would have been ridiculous in the mouth of Cato or Brutus, become doubly ridiculous when proceeding from a man like Bolingbroke, and their inconsistency is the more grotesque when we remember that at the time this Essay was written the profligacy of his private life, though on the eve of reformation, had reached its climax, and that he was, in his letters and conversation, expressing the greatest impatience to return to England.

In striking contrast to this absurd and puerile declamation stands the Letter to Wyndham, which must not be confounded—and we are surprised to see that so well-informed a writer as M. Charles de Rémusat does confound it—with the shorter "Letter to Wyndham," dated September 13, 1716, and preserved among the "Townshend Papers." The immediate cause of the composition of this celebrated work was the appearance of a pamphlet, entitled "A Letter from Avignon," a publication in which the Jacobites had at great length enumerated the crimes and blunders of which they accused Bolingbroke. Incensed at this libel, which he afterwards described as a medley of false fact, false argument, false English, and false eloquence, he determined not only to refute once and forever the calumnies of his contemptible assailants, but to do everything in his power to sow dissensions between the Tories and the Jacobites, and to furnish posterity with an elaborate vindication of his conduct and policy, from his accession to office in 1710 to his dismissal from the Pretender's service in 1716. Of the historical value of this work we have already spoken. Of its literary value it would be impossible to speak too highly. As a composition it is almost faultless. It exhibits in perfection that style of which Bolingbroke is our greatest master—a style in which the graces of colloquy and the graces of rhetoric harmoniously blend—a style which approaches more nearly to that of the finest disquisitions of Cicero than any other style in the world. Walpole never produced a more amusing sketch than the picture of the Pretender's Court at Paris and of the Privy Council in the Bois de Boulogne. Burke never produced anything nobler than the passage which commences with the words—" The ocean which surrounds us is an emblem of our government." The account of the state of affairs during the last years of Anne, at the accession of George I., and during the course of the Rebellion, are models of graceful and luminous narrative, and we shall have to go to Clarendon or Tacitus to find anything superior to the portraits of Oxford and of James.

Its serious reflections, its strokes of humor, its sarcasm, its invective are equally admirable. It is singular that though this Letter was, as we have seen, written with the immediate object of crushing the Jacobites, it was never published, perhaps never even printed, until after Bolingbroke's death. Of this curious circumstance no satisfactory explanation has been given. Mr. Macknight's theory is that Bolingbroke withheld its publication in consequence of the suspension of his pardon, and afterwards forgot it. This is not, we think, very probable. Our own opinion is that when busy with the work he altered his mind, and, attaching more importance to it as a vindication of his conduct in the eyes of posterity than as a contribution to ephemeral polemics, resolved to keep it by him until death had removed those who might challenge his assertions and shake his credit. The Letter abounds in statements which rest on no authority but that of the writer—statements which may be false or which may be true, but which, true or false, would not have passed unquestioned by contemporaries. It bears, moreover, all the marks of careful revision. No work of Bolingbroke is more highly finished.

Bolingbroke was now in his thirty-ninth year. Since his residence in France his relations with the other sex had either been those of a libertine or a trifler. Sensual pleasures were beginning to pall upon him. Platonic gallantries were becoming wearisome. His wife was in England, and his wife he regarded with contempt. But in the spring of 1717 he met a woman who inspired him with a passion very different from anything which he had experienced before. Marie-Claire Deschamps de Marcilly was the widow of the Marquis de Villette, and the niece of Madame de Maintenon. As a school-girl at Saint-Cyr, she had attracted the attention of Louis XIV., by the skill with which she had supported the character of Zarès, when, under the auspices of Madame de Maintenon, Racine's "Esther" was acted by the scholars of that famous seminary. She was now upward of forty, and her beauty had lost its bloom. But her grace, her vivacity, her accomplishments, made her the delight of the polished circles in which she moved. Her wit has been celebrated by Walpole, and her conversation was, even among the coteries of Versailles, noted for its brilliancy. In the majority of women such qualities are perhaps more calculated to strike than to charm, to impress the mind than to touch the heart; but in the Marquise de Villette they were tempered with the feminine charms of amiability and good taste. Bolingbroke was soon at her feet. His mistress was not obdurate, and the two lovers appear to have divided their time between the Rue Saint-Dominique, Faubourg Saint-Germain, where the marquise had a town residence, and Marcilly in Champagne, where she possessed a fine chateau. The death of Lady Bolingbroke in November, 1718, removed the only impediment to their marriage, but the ceremony was deferred till 1720, when they were in all probability married at Aix-la-Chapelle. A little before this event occurred, Bolingbroke was relieved by a great piece of good-luck from the disagreeable necessity of being dependent on his wife's fortune. He had been induced to take some shares in Law's Mississippi stocks when the shares were low, and those shares he had sold out in time to realize large profits. He afterwards observed that if he could have condescended to flatter Law for half an hour a week, or to have troubled himself for two minutes a day about money markets, he might have gained an immense fortune; but such transactions were, in his opinion, little worthy either of a philosopher or of a gentleman.

At the beginning of 1720 he removed with his wife to that romantic and picturesque spot which is still associated with his name, La Source, near Orleans. Here he amused himself with laying out his grounds, with scribbling Latin inscriptions for his summer-houses, and with trying to persuade his friends and himself that the world and the world's affairs were beneath his notice. In his Letters to Swift he affects the character of an elegant trifler, indulges with absurd affectation in the cant of the Porch and the Garden, and writes in a style in which the best vein of Horace and the worst vein of Seneca are curiously intermingled. Such was Bolingbroke as he chose to describe himself to his acquaintances in England, but such was not the Bolingbroke of La Source. His habits were, in truth, those of a severe student. He rose early, he read hard. His intimate companions were men of science and letters, and the time that was not spent in study was spent for the most part in literary and philosophical discussion. Since his retirement from Paris he had been engaged on works which could have left him little leisure for idling. We find him busy with antiquities, with patristic and classical literature, with researches into the credibility of ancient annals, and with a comparative criticism of the various systems of chronology. We learn, moreover, from his correspondence, that he had, in addition to all this, struck out some new theory about history, and that he was meditating an account of Rome and England to be written in accordance with that theory. Since his residence at La Source his undertakings had been still more ambitious. By the end of 1722 he had probably produced — for it is extremely difficult to settle the exact date of his earlier works—the Letters to Pouilly, of which he subsequently published an interesting abstract; a "Treatise on the Limits of Human Knowledge," of which he speaks in a letter to Alari, and which is perhaps substantially identical with the first of the Four Essays addressed to Pope; the "Letter occasioned by one of Archbishop Tillotson's Sermons;" and the "Reflections on Innate Moral Principles." In a word, he had, before he quitted La Source, formulated the most important of those historical and philosophical theories which were afterwards developed in works given to the world. He had forged the weapons which, variously tempered, were in a few years to be wielded with such tremendous effect by his disciples. This is a circumstance which, in estimating his influence on contemporaries, and pre-eminently on Voltaire, it is very necessary to bear in mind. But it is a circumstance which has, we believe, escaped the notice of all his biographers and critics. The consequence has been that they have fallen into error of a fourfold kind. They have represented Bolingbroke as following, where in reality he was leading. They have attributed to his disciples what undoubtedly belongs to him; they have confounded his theories with the theories of the English Freethinkers, and they have supposed that the movement of which he was the central figure in France was identical with the movement of which Toland and Tyndal were the central figures in England. Nothing is, it is true, more natural than to estimate the influence of an author upon his age by the influence of his published writings, and yet in Bolingbroke's case nothing would be more misguiding. The era inaugurated by him in the history of political opinion dates, indeed, from the appearance of his papers in the *Craftsman;* but the era he inaugurated in a far more important revolution dates from a period long antecedent to the publication of a single treatise by him. This era was marked, not by what he printed, but by what he spoke; not by what he dictated to an amanuensis, but what he dictated in familiar intercourse to his friends. Many years before his appearance as an author, his work as an initiator had been done. Many years before he appealed himself to the public mind, he had appealed to those by whom the public mind is moved. While the circulation of his writings was confined to private cliques, the substance of his writings had been interpreted to Europe in prose as matchless as his own, and in verse more brilliant than that in which Lucretius clothed the doctrines of Epicurus; for his first disciple was Voltaire, and his second disciple was Pope.

We believe, then, that when young François Arouet arrived, in the winter of 1721, as a visitor at La Source, Bolingbroke had made considerable progress in the First Philosophy, had formulated his creed, and was perhaps not unwilling to provide the new creed with neophytes. Voltaire—to call him by the name he afterwards assumed—

was in raptures with his host. He found him almost omniscient: "J'ai trouvé dans cet illustre Anglais," he is writing to his friend Theriot, "toute l'erudition de son pays et toute la politesse du nôtre. Cet homme, qui a passé toute sa vie dans les plaisirs et dans les affaires, a trouvé pourtant le moyen de tout apprendre et de tout retenir. Il sait l'histoire des anciens Égyptiens comme celle d'Angleterre; il possède Virgile comme Milton; il aime la poésie Anglaise, la Française et l'Italienne." The young poet was at that time busy with his epic poem, which Bolingbroke pronounced to be superior to anything which had yet appeared in French poetry. Their conversation soon turned, however, on more serious topics than the virtues of Henri Quatre; and Voltaire, who entered La Source meditating the "Henriade," quitted it meditating "Le Pour et le Contre." How long he remained under Bolingbroke's roof it is now impossible to say, but he evidently remained long enough to become impregnated with his ideas. The intimacy thus commenced in France was afterwards renewed in England, where for upwards of two years the friends lived within a few miles of each other.

The nature and extent of Bolingbroke's influence on Voltaire is one of the most interesting questions in the literary history of the eighteenth century, and it is a question which has never, in our opinion, received half the attention it deserves. English biographers have, as a rule, ignored it; French critics have contented themselves with making a few general observations, in which a very laudable desire to do justice to Bolingbroke struggles with a very natural desire to do honor to Voltaire. Now Voltaire himself never made any secret of his obligations to Bolingbroke. When the two friends first met at La Source, Bolingbroke discussed, he listened. To the end of his life he regarded him as his master. To the end of his life he continued to speak of him with mingled feelings of reverence and affection. When the two friends first met, Bolingbroke was just at that age when the individuality of men is most pronounced; Voltaire was just at that age when the mind is most susceptible and most tenacious of new impressions. The one was aspiring to open out fresh worlds of thought, to initiate a fresh era in the history of inquiry; the other had, up to that time, aspired to nothing higher than to polish verses and to point epigrams. Bolingbroke assumed, therefore, naturally enough, the authority of a teacher; Voltaire accepted, naturally enough, the position of a disciple. When they met in England they met on a similar footing: the one eager to impart, the other eager to acquire; the one covering reams of manuscript with his thoughts, the other storing his memory with recollections. In conversation Bolingbroke delighted in long monologues, the diction of which was, we are told, as perfect as that of his printed dissertations. "He possessed," says Chesterfield, "such a flowing happiness of expression that even his most familiar conversations, if taken down in writing, would have borne the press without the least correction either as to method or style." In these monologues he dealt at length with the topics which form the substance of his philosophical works. Indeed, it was notorious among those who knew him well, that there was scarcely a theory, an opinion, or even an idea, in his posthumous writings which had not been repeatedly anticipated by him in conversation. To these conversations Voltaire sat for two years a delighted listener. It would not, of course, be true to say that what he learned in the drawing-room at Dawley was the sum of what he gathered during his residence among us. For he studied our literature and our history, our institutions and our character, as none of his countrymen have ever done before or since. But there is, we think, a distinction to be drawn between what he derived from observation and study, and what he derived immediately from his intercourse from Bolingbroke. What he saw and read, sent him from our shores a master in the niceties of our tongue, a scholar familiar with almost everything which English genius had produced in poetry, in criticism, in satire, in metaphysical speculation; the champion of civil and intellectual liberty, the disciple and exponent of Locke and Newton. From Bolingbroke he learned the application of those studies. He emerged from the school of Locke and Newton a logician and a philosopher. He emerged from the school of Bolingbroke the Prince of Iconoclasts and the Apostle of Scepticism. It was Bolingbroke who taught him to pervert the "Essay on the Human Understanding" into a vindication of materialism, and the "Novum Organon" into a satire on metaphysics. Nor was this all. The writings and the conversation of his friend furnished him not only with the hint and framework of those doctrines which the world has for many generations recognized as most characteristic of Voltaire, but with an inexhaustible store of illustrative matter; with references, with illustrations, with arguments. This will be at once evident if we compare what Voltaire has written on metaphysics, on early Christianity, on theological dogma, on the nature of the Deity, on the relation of man to the Deity, on inspiration, on religious sectarianism, on the authenticity of the Hebrew Scriptures, on the authenticity of the Gospels, on the credibility of profane historians, on the origin of civil society, on the origin of evil, on the study and true use of history, with what Bolingbroke has written on the same subjects. Should any one be inclined to question the correctness of what we have advanced, we would exhort him to compare the "Traité de Métaphysique," the "Dieu et les Hommes," and the "Homélie sur l'Athéisme," with the Abstract of the "Letters to Pouilly," and the "Essays" addressed to Pope; the "Examen Important de milord Bolingbroke," and the remarks on Jewish History in the "Essai sur les Mœurs," with the "Letter occasioned by one of Archbishop Tillotson's Sermons," and the dissertation on Sacred Annals in the "Third Letter on the Study of History;" the "Lettres de Memmius à Cicéron" with the "Minutes of Essays;" the tenth, eleventh, twelfth, and thirteenth articles in the "Fragmens sur l'Histoire" with the theories and principles inculcated in the "Letters on the Study of History." It would not, perhaps, be going too far to say that the historical dissertations of Bolingbroke suggested and inspired both the "Essai sur les Mœurs" and the "Essai sur le Pyrrhonisme de l'Histoire," as they certainly furnished models for the opening chapters of the "Siècle de Louis XIV."

To return, however, from our digression. Though Bolingbroke continued to assure his friends that his life at La Source left him nothing to desire, that his philosophy grew confirmed by habit, and that he was—we are quoting his own words—under no apprehension that a glut of study and retirement would ever cast him back into the world, his whole soul was ulcerated by discontent and impatience. He implored Lord Polwarth, whom he met in the spring of 1722, to remind the English Ministry of their promise. He applied to the Duke of Orleans and to Du Bois to exercise their influence with Walpole and Townshend. He expressed himself willing to submit to any conditions if he could only procure a pardon. It appears to have been attained chiefly through the influence of Carteret and Townshend, who had been induced, primarily by Stair and more recently by Polwarth, to remind the King of what had, seven years before, been promised in the interview at the Embassy.* At last, in May, 1723, the grant which enabled him to become once more a denizen of his native country passed the Great Seal. An Act of Parliament was still necessary for the restoration of his right of inheritance, and for the recovery of his seat in the Upper House. He was now, however, enabled to plead for himself. At the beginning of June he set out for England. As the ship was waiting for a favorable wind a curious incident occurred. A few weeks before, his old coadjutor Atterbury had been convicted of treasonable correspondence with the Jacobites, and had in consequence been ordered to quit the kingdom. The two men, formerly allied so nearly, and now so widely estranged, passed each other, without speaking, at Calais—the one the proselyte, the other the martyr, of a common cause. "I am exchanged," was the Bishop's very significant comment.

On his arrival in London, Bolingbroke found that the King had departed for Hanover, and that the two secretaries, Carteret and Townshend, were with him. Many months would in all probability elapse before the Houses reassembled. During the interval he hoped by dexterous diplomacy to form such alliances and to mature such schemes as would, in the following session, suffice to make the reversal of his attainder a matter of certainty. In the tactics of political intrigue he had few rivals, and he soon discovered that he was in a position eminently favorable for their application. The schisms which had from the

---

* See "Marchmont Papers," vol. ii., p. 184.

formation of George's first Ministry divided the Cabinet had now resolved themselves into one great struggle. The events of 1717 had left Sunderland and Stanhope masters of the field. The events of 1721 had ruined Sunderland and Stanhope, and had established the supremacy of Walpole and Townshend. That supremacy had been confirmed by the death of Stanhope in 1721, and by the death of Sunderland in 1722. There still remained, however, one formidable rival, a rival who had inherited all those principles of foreign and domestic policy which Sunderland had labored to uphold, who with those principles possessed abilities such as neither Stanhope nor Sunderland had any pretension to, and who, though he had not completed his thirty-third year, had more influence in the councils of Europe than either of the two Ministers. That rival was Carteret. As long as Carteret remained, Walpole and his brother-in-law saw that they would have no peace. But to get rid of Carteret was no easy matter. At this moment, indeed, it seemed probable that the struggle would terminate in favor of their refractory colleague. He stood well with the King; he stood well with those by whom the King was governed, with Berndorf and Bothmar, with the Countess of Darlington and with the Countess of Platen. At the Court of France his influence was paramount, for the English ambassador, Sir Luke Schaub, was his creature, and the late Regent's confidential adviser, Du Bois, was his friend. While the issue of this contest still hung doubtful, Bolingbroke prudently abstained from assuming the character of a partisan. Both of the rivals could, as he well knew, serve his turn; the opposition of either might be fatal to his interests. By estranging Carteret he would estrange the Court; by estranging Walpole and Townshend he would estrange the most influential members of the Upper and the Lower House. In a few weeks, however, it became more and more evident that the power of Carteret was declining, and at the end of July Bolingbroke attempted, by a skilful and well-timed manœuvre, to establish such relations with Walpole as must have imposed on that Minister the necessity of becoming his advocate. He was, he said, in a position to make a proposal, which would not, he hoped, in the present condition of affairs, be unacceptable. His friends, the leaders of the Tory party, Sir William Wyndham, Lord Bathurst, and Lord Gower, were prepared to form a coalition with the brother Ministers. They had already been invited to coalesce with Carteret, but they had no faith either in Carteret's policy or in Carteret's promises, and they were now willing to take their stand by Walpole as they had been a few months back ready to take their stand by his rival. Walpole at once discovered with what object these overtures had been made. He had little confidence in the Tories, he had still less confidence in their ambassador; and he not only peremptorily declined to enter into such a negotiation, but he boldly told Bolingbroke that he had been guilty of great indiscretion in entangling himself in Tory intrigues, when his political salvation depended on the favor of a Whig Parliament. This was not encouraging, but Bolingbroke had too much sagacity to display either resentment or chagrin; he gracefully acknowledged the justice of what Walpole had said, expressed himself perfectly satisfied with the result of their interview, and withdrew to try his fortune with Townshend and Carteret. In September he started for Aix-la-Chapelle, nominally on the plea of ill-health, really, no doubt, to see if he could succeed in obtaining an interview with the King, and to consider in what way he could turn to account the despicable intrigues which soon afterwards terminated in the fall of Carteret. During his visit at Aix-la-Chapelle he received, however, no encouragement to go on to Herrenhausen, and in a few weeks he proceeded to Paris. He found the Court of Versailles the centre of that struggle which was agitating Whitehall and Herrenhausen. It had now reached its climax. The English ambassador, Sir Luke Schaub, the nominee of Carteret, had been virtually superseded by Horace Walpole, the nominee of Walpole and Townshend. Paris was distracted with the quarrels of the rival Ministers. The partisans of Carteret united with Schaub in taunting Walpole; the partisans of Walpole united with his brother in insulting Schaub; and all was confusion.

In the midst of these ignominious squabbles the Duke of Orleans died, and the Duke of Bourbon succeeded him. It was a critical moment. Our relations with Foreign Powers were at that instant of such a kind that a change in the policy of the French Cabinet could not be contemplated without alarm. With Orleans and Du Bois our intercourse had been frank and cordial, with the Duke of Bourbon we were in a manner dealing with one who was almost a stranger. It became very necessary, therefore, not only to cultivate his good-will, but to ascertain, if possible, his views. The course of these events had been watched by Bolingbroke with anxious interest. He had now made up his mind that all was over with Carteret, he had accordingly determined to have nothing more to do with Schaub, and to come to an understanding with Schaub's antagonist. The accession of the Duke of Bourbon afforded him just the opportunity he wanted. He could now, he thought, repeat with a better chance of success the same stratagem which he had before attempted in England —

could, that is to say, force his services on the Cabinet in such a manner as to oblige them in common justice to assist him. With this object he waited on Horace Walpole. He had come, he said, to offer himself as a mediator between the Embassy and the Court, and for this post he was, he ventured to think, peculiarly well qualified. He had the good-fortune to be on intimate terms with the Duke, and with the only person who had influence with the Duke, with Madame de Prie. "And he seemed to appear," Walpole dryly remarks, "rather indifferent than over-fond of such a commission, taking it for granted, at the same time, as if this had been an application to him."* He wrote off in a similar strain to London, volunteering in lengthy despatches not only information but counsel. In a word, he managed with consummate dexterity to assume such importance in the conduct of affairs as must, in a few weeks, says Coxe, have thrown the principal management of the whole business into his hands, and have necessitated his complete restoration, both as an act of justice and as an act of expediency. This, however, Horace Walpole, whose official distrust of his artful coadjutor appears to have been sharpened by feelings of intense personal dislike, determined to prevent. By taking the bold step of directly communicating with the Duke, he rendered the interposition of Bolingbroke unnecessary; and though he continued to avail himself, in some degree, of his assistance, he took care to keep him in a position strictly subordinate. "I have," he writes to his brother Robert, "made good use of Lord Bolingbroke's information, without having given him any handle to be the negotiator of his Majesty's affairs." Before leaving Paris, Bolingbroke made another desperate attempt to force himself into prom-

* Coxe's "Memoirs of Horatio Lord Walpole," vol. i., p. 110.

inence, by undertaking the management of an intrigue, the details of which can have no interest for readers of the present day, and into which, therefore, we shall not pause to enter.* But all was in vain, and in the summer of the following year, weary, angry, and dejected, he hurried off to bury himself in his library at La Source.

Meanwhile the treachery of an English banker, who had been intrusted to invest a large sum of money belonging to the Marquise de Villette, but who now refused to refund it, on the plea that, as she was the wife of an attainted citizen, the money had been forfeited, necessitated the appearance of Lady Bolingbroke in London. She arrived in May. She pleaded her own cause with success, and her husband's cause with assiduity and skill. Her voluble eloquence appears, indeed, rather to have embarrassed than to have charmed the King, but the judicious present of eleven thousand pounds to the Duchess of Kendal purchased the services of the most persuasive of all advocates. The King promised to consult Walpole. Walpole, who had no desire to find himself confronted on the Opposition benches, or side by side on the Treasury benches, with a rival so able and so unscrupulous as Bolingbroke, expressed himself in the strongest terms against the measure. Several months passed by. The Duchess continued to importune her royal lover; Walpole persisted in entreating the King to let the affair stand over. Every day, however, the position of the Minister became more embarrassing. Strong though he was, he was not strong enough to brave the displeasure of the Duchess, who had already been instrumental in driving Carteret and Cadogan from the helm. He

* For the particulars of this intrigue, which related to the grant of a dukedom to De la Vrilliere, see Coxe's "Memoirs of Horatio Lord Walpole," vol. i., pp. 115–124.

was anxious, also, to oblige Harcourt, with whom he was then on very intimate terms; and of all Bolingbroke's advocates, Harcourt was the most indefatigable. Still the Minister held out. At last the King became so angry that Walpole was actually threatened with dismissal if he delayed the measure longer. Then he consented to a compromise.* The Bill for Bolingbroke's restoration should be introduced, if the restoration proposed should extend only to a restoration of property and of the right of inheritance. With this Bolingbroke, who had come over from France in the spring, and who saw that for the present at least nothing further was to be obtained, professed himself satisfied. Accordingly, in April, the Bill, presented by Lord Finch and seconded by Walpole, was brought in. Modified as it was, a large section of the Whigs, who had not forgotten the Treaty of Utrecht, and a large section of the Tories, who had not forgotten the events of 1717, united in opposing it. Finally, however, it became law, by a majority of 231 against 113, and Bolingbroke could now enjoy all the privileges of a private, though not of a public man.

From this moment he led two lives. In his villa at Dawley he played with still more ostentation the part which he had played at Marcilly and La Source, surrounded himself with poets and wits, discoursed, we are told, as no mortal had ever discoursed since Plotinus unfolded himself to Porphyry, and became so ethereal that Pope, with tears in his eyes, prophesied for him the fate of Elijah. But in his house in Pall Mall he underwent a very singular transformation. There the exponent of the Harmony of the Universe degenerated into a factious and mischievous incendiary; there the opponent of Plato and the Academy

---

* Coxe's "Memoirs of Horatio Lord Walpole," vol. i., p. 125.

sank into the opponent of Hoadley and Grub Street; and there the patriot, who had in the morning been cursing faction because it was ruining his country, and expressing contempt for civil ambition as unworthy of even the momentary consideration of a philosopher, was, in the evening, plotting with the chiefs of the Opposition the downfall of the Government, and ready to sell his very soul for a place.

LITERARY LIFE OF LORD BOLINGBROKE.

SUMMARY.

Bolingbroke chiefly noticeable as a polemic writer: his position and influence in the political contest, p. 131, 132 — Attitude of the Parties: the leaders of the Opposition, p. 133-137—Organization of the strife: launching of the Opposition paper, the *Craftsman*, p. 137, 138—Bolingbroke one of its chief contributors, p. 138—His interview with the King fruitless, p. 139, 140—Death of the King, p. 141—Critical aspect of affairs, *ibid*—Walpole restored to power, p. 142—Disgraceful party strife in Parliament: venality of office-holders, p. 142-144—The Opposition party playing on the popular feeling in order to discredit the Walpole Ministry, p. 144-147—Nearly successful, p. 147—The Excise bill, p. 147-149—Review of Bolingbroke's literary activity in the *Craftsman* from 1727 until 1734, p. 150—His "Remarks on the History of England," p. 151-153—His "Dissertation upon Parties," p. 154, 155—Bolingbroke as a writer on philosophical and metaphysical subjects: his rural pursuits at his country-house at Dawley, p. 155, 156—His open-handedness to friends, p. 157, 158—His friendship with Pope, p. 159—His influence on Pope's mind and studies, p. 159-163—His departure from England: reasons for same, p. 163-165—His residence in France: exclusive devotion to philosophic inquiries, p. 165, 166—His "Letters on the Study of History," p. 166, 167—His "Letter on the Spirit of Patriotism," p. 168—Character of the Prince of Wales, p. 169-171—Unscrupulous adulation of same in Bolingbroke's writings, p. 171, 172—His "Patriot King:" considerations thereon, p. 172-175—Walpole's influence declining: his resignation, p. 175, 176—Bolingbroke arrives too late from France: the Premiership has already been snatched from him, p. 176—Retrospect of Bolingbroke's literary career, p. 177—His unworthy conduct towards Pope, p. 177-179—His last days, p. 180—Afflictions of age: his death, p. 181—Review of his philosophical works, p. 181-186—Summary of his philosophy, p. 185, 186—Epilogue, p. 187.

LITERARY LIFE OF LORD BOLINGBROKE.

In our last article we left Bolingbroke on the eve of that tremendous struggle which continued for fifteen years to agitate the public mind in England, which was to end in the downfall of Whig tyranny, which was to revolutionize the creed of the Two Factions, and which was to establish new dynasties with new principles in party politics. To that great revolution no one contributed more powerfully than he. The more closely we follow its history in his essays and correspondence—and nowhere is its history written so fully and so legibly—the more obvious will this appear. Almost every manœuvre on the part of the Opposition we find traceable, in the first instance, to his suggestion. From him emanated the theories and sentiments which, promulgated at one time by the Whig and at another time by the Tory section of the minority, matured into the gospel of the Patriots. It was he who had the sagacity to discover where Walpole and his colleagues were most vulnerable. It was he who shook England with the tempest of 1733. It was he who barbed and aimed the deadliest of the bolts which Pulteney and Wyndham winged from the Opposition benches. Of all this we have ample evidence in such of his writings as have been given to the world. But his influence on political history during these years would, we suspect, be found to be even more considerable than we know it to have been, if his unpublished correspondence, now mouldering in the archives of Petworth, Hagley, and Hemel Hemsted, were properly examined. His biographers appear to have made no effort to obtain access to these collections. They have contented themselves with such extracts as have been given by Coxe, Phillimore, and the editor of the "Marchmont Papers."

But the period of Bolingbroke's literary activity has another side. Between 1726 and 1752 he was not merely the leader of the Patriots and the most indefatigable of political controversialists, he was the centre of other and calmer spheres. It will be our pleasant task to follow him thither, and our readers will doubtless be as glad as ourselves to exchange Pall Mall for Dawley, to quit Walpole and Townshend for Pope and Voltaire, and to escape from Excise Bills and Secessions to discuss the First Philosophy, and the "Essay on Man."

At the beginning of 1726 the position of Walpole and Townshend appeared impregnable. They stood high in the favor of the King and in the favor of the people. The removal of Carteret had relieved them of their only formidable rival in the Cabinet. The disgrace of Atterbury, four years before, had completed the paralysis of the Jacobites. The Opposition was too divided in its views, and too heterogeneous in its composition, to afford any grounds for apprehension. The clouds which had for many months obscured the horizon of foreign politics had been dispersed. The Treaty of Hanover had defeated the hostile designs of Spain and Austria. Comparative tranquillity at last reigned in Scotland and Ireland. But a great change was at hand. A new era in Parliamentary history had already begun.

Of all the enemies of Walpole the most active and the

most malignant was Daniel Pulteney. During the reign of Anne he had been envoy at Copenhagen. As a Commissioner of Trade and as a Lord of the Admiralty—for between 1717 and 1721 he filled both these appointments—he had proved himself a useful and industrious public servant. He had been the friend and confidant of Sunderland during the whole period when the feud between Walpole and Sunderland was deadliest. When Sunderland fell in 1721, Pulteney had borne a principal share in those cabals by which his patron sought to recover office. As the price of this co-operation he had, in the event of success, been promised the Seals, and he had therefore distinguished himself by his hostility to Walpole, for on the ruin of Walpole depended his own advancement. But the death of Sunderland dashed all these hopes to the ground. From this moment he became a soured and gloomy misanthrope. The prejudices which he had inherited from Sunderland, aggravated by his own bad passions, inflamed his animosity against Walpole to such a pitch that it resembled monomania. But he was a monomaniac of a very dangerous character. For with solid parts and methodical habits he united no small skill in the tactics of intrigue. Though he was no hypocrite, manners naturally graceful and pleasing, and a temper kindly and generous when unprovoked, served to conceal the implacable malignity of his disposition when anything occurred to ruffle him. His energy was indefatigable. As a speaker he was clear and weighty. His acquaintance with affairs was extensive; his Parliamentary connection considerable. He was now toiling night and day to form out of the scattered elements of the Opposition a coalition against Walpole. He lacked, however, the qualities necessary for organization; and though he was eminently fitted for the duties of a subordinate, he was by no means competent to lead.* What Daniel Pulteney lacked, that his kinsman William possessed. No politician of those times filled a larger space in the public eye than William Pulteney. He had entered office while still a very young man; his family was influential; no stain rested on his character; his private fortune was immense. His parts were so brilliant, his genius so versatile, that in whatever walk of life his lot had been cast, he would in all probability have achieved eminence. His political pamphlets and his papers in the *Craftsman* remain to testify his abilities as a writer.† One of his songs was for many years among the most popular in our language; and Pope has in a celebrated verse expressed his opinion that, had Pulteney chosen to cultivate light literature, he would have rivalled Martial. As a wit and a sayer of good things he was considered not inferior to Chesterfield, and many of his *bon-mots* still hold a distinguished place in literary *anas*. The extent and variety of his attainments were the wonder of all who knew him. With the masterpieces of ancient and modern literature he was equally conversant. His familiarity, indeed, with the Greek classics was such as was in that age very unusual, even with professed scholars. But no rust of pedantry dimmed the keen and brilliant intellect of William Pulteney. In practical sagacity and in official experience he was scarcely inferior, perhaps, to Walpole, and he needed only Walpole's equanimity and self-control to become as autocratic and successful. As an orator he had, since the retirement of

---

* For the character of Daniel Pulteney, see Speaker Onslow's "Remarks," Coxe's "Memoirs of Sir Robert Walpole," vol. ii., p. 559.

† The papers written by him are marked C., and those marked CA. were written conjointly with Amhurst. See Bishop Newton's "Autobiography," p. 123.

Bolingbroke and till the appearance of Pitt, no equal among contemporary statesmen. He shone alike in exposition and in debate, in set orations and in extempore speeches. At this moment, indeed, he had not yet arrived at that degree of excellence which, at the head of the Opposition, he shortly afterwards attained. Ever since his entrance into public life, he had distinguished himself as a firm and consistent Whig. When the schism took place in 1717, he had attached himself to Walpole, had resigned a valuable place, and had followed the fortunes of his friend. When Walpole returned to power, Pulteney was not invited to fill a seat in the Cabinet. An angry discussion between the two friends ensued. Walpole proposed an indemnity in the shape of a peerage. This Pulteney regarded as an aggravation of the slight. For some time he continued to remain a vexatious and irritable member of the Government. At last, in April, 1725, he was dismissed from a post which he held in the Household, and openly went over to the minority. Walpole, fully aware both of the influence and of the abilities of the man who had now declared war against him, made a desperate attempt to bribe him back. But affairs had gone too far. Nothing would satisfy Pulteney but the ruin of his old colleague. He had, he said, been grievously wronged, and he would have his revenge.

While the two Pulteneys were thus brooding over their grievances, and waiting for an opportunity of vengeance, another malcontent, not less rancorous and even more formidable, was similarly engaged. For two years Bolingbroke had submitted to every indignity that he might regain his seat. He had lackeyed and flattered Walpole, whom he hated. He had lackeyed and flattered Walpole's brother, whom he despised. He had been lavish of his money, of his energy, and of his time; and he had, after a long and weary struggle, been forced to accept a compromise, which rendered him capable of possessing fortune and incapable of enjoying it. For this restriction on his happiness he had been indebted to Walpole; and he now resolved not merely to obtain the removal of this restriction, but to make the Minister who had imposed it feel the full effect of his resentment. The Pulteneys and himself soon came to an understanding. The plan of operation was simple. It was obvious that the security of Walpole could never be shaken as long as his opponents remained disunited. At this moment the minority consisted of three distinct bodies of men: a large section of discontented Whigs, a large section of Tories who had abandoned Jacobitism, and a small section of Tories who still adhered to it. Could these factions be induced to coalesce? Could they be induced to bury minor differences in common hostility against a common foe? The co-operation of the Jacobite contingent was not, indeed, a matter of much moment; but the co-operation of the Hanoverian Tories was of the last importance. Now, the leader of this faction was Sir William Wyndham, and with Wyndham Bolingbroke lived not merely on terms of intimacy, but on terms of affection. Sir William was at once taken into the confidence of the conspirators, and in a very short time the party at the head of which were the Pulteneys, and the party at the head of which was Wyndham, had, by the mediation of Bolingbroke, consented to act together. Such was the origin of that famous Coalition, which continued for so many years to keep this country in a state of perpetual agitation, which inspired politics with new principles, and literature with a new spirit; which brought into being a new school of politicians, which destroyed Walpole and created Pitt, which numbered among its ranks in Parliament the most accomplished public men, and in its ranks out of Parliament some of the most distinguished men of letters then living; for among the first, in addition to the Pulteneys, were Wyndham, Carteret, Chesterfield, Argyle, Pitt, Polworth, Dodington, Lyttelton, and Barnard; and among the second, in addition to Bolingbroke, were Pope, Swift, Arbuthnot, Gay, Fielding, Akenside, Brooke, Thomson, Paul Whitehead, Glover, and Johnson.

Having concluded their arrangements for embarrassing the Government within the walls of St. Stephen's, Bolingbroke and Pulteney now proceeded to consider in what way they could rouse and engage the passions of the country. A few years before these events occurred, an undergraduate at Oxford, named Amhurst, had been expelled from his college on a charge of libertinism and insubordination. Since that time he had been engaged in libelling the University. He was now pushing his fortunes in London. Though his habits were squalid and profligate, he was, as his writings showed, a man of parts and wit; and as he possessed, in addition to these qualifications, an empty purse, loose principles, and a facile pen, he had already risen to distinction among journalists. Pulteney proposed, therefore, that negotiations should be opened with Amhurst, and that he should be invited to undertake the management of a periodical. This periodical was to be the mouthpiece of the Opposition. It was to demonstrate to the whole nation the tyranny, the insolence, and the rapacity of Walpole. It was to assail his foreign and domestic policy, and to point out that the one was a tissue of blunders, and the other a tissue of corruption. It was to charge him with making the King his dupe, that he might make him his tool, and the Cabinet his parasites, that he might make the people his slaves. There was little difficulty in inducing Amhurst to occupy a post for which he was so well fitted; and on the 5th of December, 1726, appeared the first number of the *Craftsman*. It is not now, we believe, possible to recover the names of all the contributors to this famous publication, which continued for upward of ten years to exercise an influence on public opinion without precedent in journalism. By far the largest, and beyond question the most valuable portion, is to be ascribed to Bolingbroke. Many papers were contributed by Pulteney, many by Amhurst, and many by Amhurst and Pulteney in conjunction. The circulation was, for those times, enormous. Indeed, it is said at one time to have exceeded ten thousand copies a week.

Bolingbroke was now all fire and hope. In the spring of 1727, in addition to his Essays in the *Craftsman*, he produced, under the title of the "Occasional Writer," three papers so acrimonious and personal as to ruffle even the imperturbable temper of Walpole. Into the particulars of these altercations we cannot enter; but as a specimen of the decency with which political controversy was, in the days of our fathers, occasionally conducted, we will transcribe a few sentences of the First Minister's rejoinder:

"Though you have not signed your name, I know you: you are an infamous fellow, a perjured, ungrateful, unfaithful rascal . . . of so profligate a character that in your prosperity nobody envied you, and in your disgrace nobody pities. You were in the interests of France and of the Pope, as hath appeared by your writings, and you went out of the way to save yourself from the gallows. You have no abilities; you are an emancipated slave, a proscribed criminal, and an insolvent debtor. You went out of the way to save yourself from the gallows, and Herostratus and Nero were not greater villains than you. You have been a traitor and should be used like one. And I love my master so well that I will never advise him to use you, lest you should jostle me out of my employment. I know you to be so hot-headed that when you read this you will vent all your malice against me. But I do not value it, for I would rather have you my enemy than my friend. Change your name and be as abusive and scurrilous as you please, I shall find you out. You may change to a flame, a lion, a bull, or a bear, I shall know you, baffle you, conquer you, and contemn you. All your opposition will redound to my honor and glory."

This was not exactly the style of Bolingbroke, and Walpole never afterwards ventured, we believe, to confront his adversary on paper. While the press was thus hard at work, Bolingbroke was busy also in another quarter. It was well known that the Duchess of Kendal and her niece, Lady Walsingham, were by no means favorably disposed towards Walpole. It was notorious, also, that the King and the Prince of Wales were at open war, and that the affections of the Prince were divided between his wife and Mrs. Howard. By assiduously cultivating the Duchess and her niece, Bolingbroke sought, therefore, to gain the ear of the King; and by assiduously cultivating Mrs. Howard, to secure the favor of the heir-apparent. This double intrigue was, however, a matter of considerable difficulty; for by paying court to the King he ran the risk of estranging the Prince, and by paying court to the Prince he was almost certain to estrange the King. He conducted it at first with consummate tact. In the first part of it, indeed, he was successful. The Duchess became his advocate. She even risked a large pension to serve him. He drew up an elaborate statement enumerating the blunders of Walpole, enlarging on his unpopularity, incapacity, and corruption, and offering, if the King would grant an interview, to demonstrate at length the truth of what he had asserted. This document the Duchess placed in the King's hands. He perused it and sent it on to Walpole. Walpole advised the King to grant the interview, and the interview was granted. On this critical occasion Bolingbroke acquitted himself with far less dexterity than might have been expected from so accomplished a diplomatist. He began with a florid eulogy of his own merits and abilities. He then went on to assail in general terms the character and the conduct of his opponent; and when the King, interrupting, asked for proofs and particular illustrations of what he was advancing, he merely proceeded to recapitulate in other words the same general charges. Walpole was notoriously unfit for his post: he was despised abroad, he was hated at home; he was involving affairs in inextricable confusion; he would, if he continued in power, make his royal master as unpopular as himself. "Is this," said the King, becoming impatient, "all you have to say?" And with these words he turned on his heel, and Bolingbroke was curtly dismissed.

It seems, indeed, quite clear that nothing that Bolingbroke had said had made any serious impression on his majesty, as the King afterwards spoke of him as a knave, and of the statements he had made as bagatelles. But it is equally clear that Walpole was, in spite of the King's assurance, greatly alarmed. The favor of princes was, as he well knew, a perishable commodity. He was surrounded by enemies; almost all those enemies were the coadjutors of his rival: his influence with the King was great, but the influence of the Duchess was greater; and with the Duchess the cause of Bolingbroke had now become in a manner her own. Indeed, Walpole is said to have been so convinced that his rival would ultimately supplant him, that he was on the point of resigning the Seals and of accepting a seat in the Upper House. The chances of Bolingbroke at this singular crisis have doubtless been exaggerated, but there is, we think, ample reason for supposing that had the King lived a few months longer, a revolution, of which it would have been difficult to foretell the consequences, might have ensued. Whether Bolingbroke would have succeeded in replacing Walpole, as he confidently anticipated, is, we think, very problematical, though Pelham assured Onslow—and Pelham in all likelihood was simply repeating what he had heard from Walpole—that, had the King lived to come back from Hanover, "it was very probable that he would have made Lord Bolingbroke his Chief Minister." That Bolingbroke would have succeeded in regaining his seat in the Upper House is more than probable. "As he had the Duchess entirely on his side," said Walpole to Etough ten years afterwards, "I need not add what must or might have been the consequence." At the beginning of June the King set out for Hanover. On the fourteenth a despatch arrived announcing his death.

In an instant everything was in confusion. Nothing seemed certain but the fall of Walpole. The new king ordered the First Minister to receive his instructions from Sir Spencer Compton. Two of his creatures were dismissed from their employment; his parasites abandoned him; his antechamber was a desert. The Opposition confidently anticipated that their time had come. Ten days afterwards all was changed. The ludicrous incompetence of Compton, Walpole's own tact, and the favor of the Queen, saved the Ministry. Bolingbroke and Pulteney, who had placed all their hopes on Mrs. Howard, soon found that Mrs. Howard was as helpless as themselves. Judging as men of the world would be likely to judge, they had concluded that the mistress would have more authority than the wife, and that the King, as a lover, would be more amenable to persuasion than the King as a husband. But they were as yet imperfectly acquainted both with the strange character of the new sovereign and with the still stranger character of the woman who shared his throne. In truth, the relation between a husband habitually uxorious and habitually unfaithful, and a wife who, to maintain her supremacy, condescends to superintend the amours of her consort, might well be misinterpreted even by the most penetrating observer. Before her accession the Queen had been the friend of Walpole, and had in strong terms expressed her aversion to Bolingbroke. After her accession she entered into the closest alliance with her favorite Minister, and became even more emphatic in her hostility to his opponent. Against such a coalition—for the secret of the Queen's power was soon known—Bolingbroke saw that it would be idle to contend. He abandoned, therefore, all hopes of making his peace with the King. Fortune had again played him false. His defeat had been complete and ignominious.

But he was not the man to despair. If victory had been lost on one field, it might be gained on another. If he could not appeal to the King, he could appeal to the country, and to make that appeal he now bent all his energies.

The Parliamentary history of the next twelve years is one of the most scandalous chapters in our national annals. At the head of the Government stood a Minister, experienced indeed, moderate, skilful, and sagacious, but selfish beyond all example of political selfishness, and ready at any moment to sacrifice his convictions to his interests, and his country to his place. At the head of the Opposition stood a body of malcontents, whose conduct was on all occasions dictated by motives of mere personal animosity, and whose policy, if policy it could be called, consisted simply in opposing whatever their rivals advocated, and in advocating whatever their rivals opposed. In neither party can we discern any of those qualities which entitle public men to veneration. The vices of Walpole were gross and flagrant. The virtues so ostentatiously professed by his opponents consisted of nothing more than a pompous jargon of words. By both parties the welfare of the country was, in the exigencies of their ignoble struggle, regarded as a matter of purely secondary consideration. To embarrass Walpole, the Opposition united to defeat measures the soundness and utility of which must have been obvious to a politician of the meanest capacity. To maintain himself against the Opposition, Walpole was often compelled to resort to expedients by which, as he well knew, temporary advantages were obtained at high prices and at great risk. The sole object of Walpole was at all costs to maintain his place. The sole object of the Opposition was to dislodge him. This they endeavored to effect, not so much by grappling with their enemy in his stronghold, as by organizing an elaborate system of counter-manœuvres. Thus because Walpole was for alliance with France, the Opposition was for alliance with Austria. Thus, when Walpole, though nominally the leader of the Whigs, became in everything but in name a Tory, the leaders of the Opposition, though they were for the most part Tories, became in everything but in name Whigs. When Walpole played the autocrat, the Opposition played the demagogue; Walpole harangued against factious incendiaries, and the Opposition harangued against Royal parasites.

But it was not on these points that the minority took their principal stand. It was no secret that to secure his majority Walpole practised corruption on a very large scale, and that to control Parliament he filled all places of honor and emolument with his creatures. We have not the smallest doubt that every member of the Opposition, with the exception, perhaps, of Barnard and Shippen, would, had he been in Walpole's place, have acted in precisely the same manner. But Walpole was in and the Opposition were out. To combat him with his own weapons was impossible. The Royal favor, boundless patronage, a venal Senate with ample means for purchasing its votes, venal constituencies with ample means for buying their electors, gave him an immense advantage over opponents whose only resources lay in eloquence and in the fortunes of private gentlemen. One course, and one course alone, was open to them. In such contests the ultimate appeal lies to the people. To the people, therefore, the Opposition determined to address themselves, and they prepared at the same time to endeavor to educate their judges. This was not difficult. The principles on which Walpole governed were, when interpreted by skilful rhetoricians, capable of being rendered peculiarly odious to a proud and high-spirited nation. It is one thing for a man to pocket a bribe, it is another thing for a man to feel himself a slave. No Englishman, however degraded, was insensible to the tradition of a great and splendid past, or would submit to see public morality systematically outraged, and the national honor sullied. No Englishman, however selfish, would consent, even at the price of material prosperity, to connive at tyranny, or to allow the slightest of his privileges to be tampered with. The old war-cries were still efficacious. The spirit which brought Strafford to the block and set the Deliverer on the throne still burned in the breasts of thousands. The King was unpopular, and was, like his predecessor, suspected of making the interests of England altogether subordinate to the interests of Hanover, and in this unpopularity Walpole soon found himself involved.

In 1730 the retirement of Townshend left Walpole in the possession of power more absolute than any English Minister had enjoyed since the days of the first two Stuarts. This soon became a fertile theme with his enemies. The invectives of Bolingbroke, Pulteney, and Amhurst increased every day in audacity and vehemence. Were the countrymen of Hampden and Sidney, they cried, to become the prey of a despotic parasite? Would the descendants of men who had vindicated with their blood the rights of Englishmen, consent, for a few guineas, to barter away the most sacred of all inheritances? Had Buckingham and Strafford been forgotten? Was the Court of Edward II. to be revived in the Court of George II.? Whose blood should not boil to see the benches of the House of Commons crowded with the puppets of a Royal minion, and the House of Lords teeming with the lackeys of a base upstart? While these themes, so admirably adapted to catch and inflame the multitude, continued to fill the pages of the *Craftsman* week after week, the Opposition were not idle within the walls of Parliament. Every measure which the Minister brought forward was traversed. Every scheme which could be devised for embarrassing him was essayed. They had already interpreted the Treaty of Hanover as a base and impolitic concession to the Throne and to the Electorate, and on this subject they continued, during many sessions, to harp. They then opposed, and on this occasion opposed with justice, the proposal for maintaining a large body of Hessian troops with English pay. Then they pretended that, in spite of the sinking fund, the public burdens had increased, and demanded an explanation. A loud and angry controversy ensued. They were beaten. Upon that they requested to know to what uses a large sum of money which had been charged for secret service had been applied. They were answered. Next they attacked the Government on the question of Gibraltar. The ministers had, they said, pledged the honor of the nation that that fortress should be ceded to Spain, and they assailed them for not keeping their promise. But the cession of that fortress would, they contended, be detrimental to the interest of England, and they assailed them for having made it; taunting them with falsehood on the one hand, and with treachery on the other. As soon as the Treaty of Seville had set this question at rest, they shifted their ground, and struck at Walpole on another side. They moved for leave to bring in a Bill which should disable all persons who had any pension, or any office held in trust for them from the Crown, from sitting in Parliament, and they proposed that every member should, on taking his seat, make oath that he enjoyed no such preferment. Defeated on this point by a skilful manœuvre on the part of Walpole, they raised a cry that the French were repairing the fortifications and harbor of Dunkirk. A long and singularly intemperate debate followed.*

---

* At this debate Montesquieu, then on a visit to England, was present, and has left in his "Notes sur l'Angleterre" a curious account of it. As the passage appears to have escaped the notice not only of Bolingbroke's biographers, but of Coxe and Lord Stanhope, we will transcribe it: "J'allais avant-hier au parlement à la chambre basse: on y traita de l'affaire de Dunkerque. Je n'ai jamais vu un si grand feu. La séance dura depuis une heure après midi jusqu'à trois heures après minuit. M. Walpole attaqua Bolingbroke de la façon la plus cruelle, et disait qu'il avait mené toute cette intrigue. Le Chevalier Wyndham le défendit. M. Walpole raconta en faveur de Bolingbroke l'histoire du paysan qui, passant avec sa femme sous un arbre, trouva qu'un homme pendu respirait encore. Il le détacha

But nothing illustrates more clearly the factious and vexatious spirit of these malcontents than their conduct with regard to the second Treaty of Vienna. During several years their chief cause of complaint against the foreign policy of Walpole had been its tendency to depress Austria and to exalt France. No such objection could now be urged. The second Treaty of Vienna adjusted the scales exactly as the Opposition had long contended that they should be adjusted. But no sooner was it concluded than it was assailed. It involved us, they said, in a meshwork of treaties and guarantees. It necessitated our interference as principals in any rupture which might take place among European Powers. And yet, as islanders, it was our interest to maintain a strictly neutral attitude with respect to Continental politics, and a strictly defensive attitude with regard to ourselves. With the maintenance of the balance of power, except in a purely subordinate capacity, we had nothing to do.*

But it was not till the spring of 1733 that the ascendency which the Opposition had by degrees been gaining over the public mind became fully manifest. In that year they succeeded in shaking the Government to its very foundations; in that year they all but succeeded in driving Walpole in ignominy from power. It is now generally allowed that the Excise scheme was one of the wisest and most equitable measures which ever emanated from a British financier. It infringed no right, it introduced no

et le porta chez lui: il revint. Ils trouvèrent le lendemain que cet homme leur avait volé leurs fourchettes. Ils dirent: il ne faut pas s'opposer au cours de la justice, il le faut rapporter où nous l'avons pris."

* See the *Craftsman*, Nos. 242, 248, 251; Coxe's "Memoirs of Sir Robert Walpole," vol. i., p. 346.

innovation. Its burden fell lightly, and it fell equally. There is not the smallest reason for supposing that Walpole contemplated extending its operation further than the duties on wine and tobacco. That, indeed, he expressly stated, not merely in his public speeches, but in private letters and in conversation. The benefits accruing from it would have been immense. It would have enabled the Government to check the frauds by which, in the tobacco trade alone, the revenue was annually robbed of half a million sterling. It would have enabled the Exchequer to dispense with the Land-tax. It would, by converting the duties on importation into duties on consumption, have been greatly to the advantage of the merchant importer. It would, as Walpole justly boasted, have tended to make London a free port, and, in consequence, one of the greatest centres of commerce in the world. It affected in no way the scale of prices either in the wholesale or retail markets. But the Opposition saw at a glance that it was a measure peculiarly susceptible of distortion, a measure which, in their controversy with the Minister, might, by dint of a little sophistry, be turned to great account. And to great account they turned it. Aggravating the prejudices which already existed against this mode of taxation, and boldly assuming that the proposed excise on wine and tobacco was the prelude to a general excise, they drew an appalling picture of what would, they said, in a few years be the condition of the English people. Food and raiment, all the necessities as well as all the luxuries of life, would be taxed. These taxes would be collected by armed officers who would constitute a standing army, and this odious body would be empowered to enter and ransack private houses. Trade would be ruined. Liberty would be at an end. The rights of a free people would be the sport of a tyrannical Monarch at the head of a tyrannical Ministry. Magna Charta would be repealed. The Bill of Rights would be a dead letter; and the House of Commons would be abolished. While this monstrous rhodomontade circulated among the vulgar, other arguments less extravagant, but scarcely less absurd, were addressed to politer politicians. In a few weeks the object of the Opposition had been gained. From the Peak to the Land's End, and from the Wrekin to the Humber, the whole country was in a blaze. Petitions came pouring in. The Press and the Pulpit teemed with philippics. Every street and every village resounded with cries of "No slavery, no excise, no wooden shoes." One fanatic swore that he would have Walpole's head. A turbulent mob forced their way into the Lobby and into the Court of Requests, and on the night on which the Bill passed, the First Minister was in imminent peril of encountering the fate of De Witt.* The measure became law, but the temper of the nation was such that, if the provisions of the Bill had been carried out, they could only have been carried out at the point of the bayonet, and Walpole was therefore reduced to the ignominious necessity of abandoning his scheme.† This blow he never recovered.

Elated by their triumph, the Opposition now moved for the repeal of the Septennial Act, a motion peculiarly adapted to embarrass the Government, and peculiarly calculated to please the mob. A debate ensued, distinguished even in those agitated times for its acrimony and intemperance.

* This has been contradicted, but see particularly Lord Hervey's "Memoirs," vol. i., pp. 200, 201.

† For the whole question of the Excise scheme, see the *Craftsman* from October 28, 1732, where it is first discussed, to August 4, 1733.

One episode in that debate was long remembered. The onslaught made by Wyndham on Walpole, and the reply in which Walpole, ignoring Wyndham, struck at Bolingbroke, are perhaps the finest specimens of vituperative oratory which have come down to us from times anterior to Burke. But the attempt failed; the Act remained unrepealed. Parliament was shortly afterwards dissolved, and Walpole, with a majority slightly impaired, weathered the elections, and in the following January resumed office for another seven years.

During the whole of the period of which we have been speaking, the period, that is to say, extending from the Parliament which met in January, 1728, to the Parliament which met in January, 1735, Bolingbroke was the soul and author of almost every movement on the part of the Opposition. It was Bolingbroke who pointed out in what way the affair of Gibraltar might be utilized. It was Bolingbroke who originated the outcry about Dunkirk. It was Bolingbroke who directed the attack on the Excise scheme. It was Bolingbroke who suggested the repeal of the Septennial Act. Popular report assigned to his dictation the ablest of Wyndham's speeches. So notorious, indeed, was the influence exercised by him on the councils of the Opposition, that Walpole constantly taunted them with being his mouthpieces, his creatures, and his tools. Nor was this all. With his pen he was indefatigable. His first contribution to the *Craftsman* appeared on the 27th of January, 1727. It was entitled "The Vision of Camelick," and is, under the disguise of an Eastern fable, a virulent attack on the despotism of Walpole, on the complete subserviency of the King to his unprincipled favorite, and on the venality of electors. At the beginning of the summer of 1730 he produced a singularly luminous and

powerful pamphlet—" The Case of Dunkirk Considered."*
In this pamphlet he discusses at length the negotiations
relative to the demolition of that harbor; demonstrates how
necessary it was to the interests of England that the stipulations made at Utrecht should be carried out; and not
merely taunts the Ministry with criminal negligence in per-
mitting the infringement of such stipulations, but attributes their conduct to a base desire to play into the hands
of France. With contemporary events these works ceased
to interest; but between August, 1730, and June, 1731,
there appeared in the *Craftsman*, under the signature of
"Humphrey Oldcastle," a series of essays which have long
survived the controversies which inspired them. These
were the "Remarks on the History of England." Bolingbroke here gives a bold and graphic sketch of English Constitutional history, from the Conquest to the meeting of
the Long Parliament. In the course of his work, he advances several ingenious theories which were not lost on
Hume and Hallam: his occasional reflections are suggestive and happy, and his pages teem with those acute observations which have, in the "Discorsi" of Machiavelli and in
the "Réflexions" of Montesquieu, delighted succeeding
generations of thoughtful men. But it is not as serious
contributions to political philosophy that these Essays
were intended to be judged; their didactic value was a
value purely accidental. The immediate purpose with
which they were written was not to trace the history of
Constitutional government, but to convey satire under the
form of analogue. Particular epochs, and particular incidents in the history of past times, become, in the hands of
their skilful delineator, counterparts of the history of the

* Reprinted in "A Collection of Political Tracts," published anony-
mously in 1748.

present: the Court of the Plantagenets, of the Tudors, of the Stuarts, reflects the Court of the House of Hanover; and the Ministers who invaded popular rights in the reign of Richard or Charles transform themselves into the Ministers who are invading these rights in the reign of George II. In the person of Wolsey and Buckingham, for example, he paints and assails Walpole. In the person of Elizabeth Woodville he draws Queen Caroline; in the person of Richard II. he depicts her husband. In his pictures of the reigns of Edward III. and Elizabeth he satirizes by contrast, as in his pictures of the reign of Richard II. he satirizes directly, the character, conduct, and Court of George II. The skill with which he contrives to convert the reign of Elizabeth into an analogue of the reign of Anne, and the reign of Elizabeth's contemptible successor into an analogue of the reigns of the two first Georges, is really wonderful. The virulence and audacity of these diatribes, which their author had the front to define as "a few inoffensive remarks on the nature of liberty and of faction," alarmed the Government, and were of immense service to the Opposition. Their sentiments delighted the vulgar, their inimitable style fascinated the polite.

It was soon known that Bolingbroke was the author. The incidents of his public life were still fresh in the memory of thousands, and, in the paper war which these Essays excited, his character was very severely handled. But against his polemical skill, his impudence, and his mendacity truth was powerless. The juster the charges advanced, the more ridiculous they seemed to become. The stronger the case against him, the more unanswerable appeared his apology. Examples of his unscrupulous dexterity in controversy are to be found in his "Twenty-fourth Letter" and in his "Final Answer to the *Craftsman's* Vindication," a pamphlet in which he reviews and defends those circumstances in his career which had justly exposed him to the taunts of his adversaries. In September of the following year he wrote three papers on the Policy of the Athenians, in which he drew a series of ingenious parallels between portions of Greek and portions of English history, on the same principle and with the same objects as the "Remarks on English History."*

The nation now began to show, by very unequivocal symptoms, that these writings had not been without effect. The popularity of Walpole visibly declined. His foreign and home policy were sharply criticised. Many who had up to this time pocketed their bribes and held their peace, grew moody and scrupulous. Young men talked republicanism, and old men grumbled. At last popular discontent became articulate. The tremendous storm, which convulsed the country during the period of the Excise Bill, gathered and burst. The Government tottered to its base, and before Walpole could recover himself his indefatigable opponent was again in the field. The "Dissertation upon Parties," commencing in October, 1733, and ending in December, 1734, is, with the exception of the "Letters of Junius," beyond question the finest series of compositions which the political controversies of the eighteenth century inspired. Nothing equal to them had ever appeared before, nothing superior to them has ever appeared since. Their diction is magnificent, their matter rich and various, their method admirable. Seldom have the baser passions caught with such exquisite skill

---

* These papers constitute Nos. 324, 325, and 326 of the *Craftsman*, and have been reprinted in the "Political Tracts." We may here take the opportunity of observing that the papers contributed by Bolingbroke to that periodical were marked "O."

the accents of their nobler sisters; seldom has satire, even in verse, assumed a garb so splendid. In a series of nineteen letters, preceded in their collected form by an ironical dedication to Walpole, he traces the history of the two great parties which, since the days of the Stuarts, had divided English politics; points out how, on the accession of William III., those two parties ceased to represent principles; how, since then, they had degenerated into mere factions; and how these factions would, but for the arts of men whose interest it was to keep them alive, have long since been extinguished. The whole work, under the disguise of a patriotic protest against misgovernment, against standing armies in time of peace, against corruption, against misappropriation of public money, against officious interference with foreign politics, is a malignant and ferocious attack on Walpole and on Walpole's coadjutors. But the spirit it breathes is so noble, the principles it advocates so exalted, that we seem, as we surrender ourselves to the charm of its eloquent rhetoric, to be listening to the voice of one not unworthy to be the prophet of Virtue and Liberty. The Dedication is superb. It is in the best vein of Chatham and Junius, but it is, in declamatory grandeur, superior to anything which has descended to us from Chatham, as it is, in polished invective, equal to anything which could be selected either from the Letters to Grafton or the Letters to Bedford. From a polemical point of view, the value of this work was inestimable. It not only dealt Walpole a series of blows which fell with fearful precision on those parts where he was most vulnerable, but it furnished his opponents with new elements of strength. The Opposition was composed, as we have seen, of advanced Tories, of moderate Tories, of a few Jacobites, of a large and discontented clique of Whigs; of bodies of men, that is to say, whose political creeds were entirely at variance, and whose sole bond of union was hostility to Walpole. These malcontents were therefore perpetually torn with schisms. Their alliance was radically and essentially unnatural. They were friends by accident, they were enemies on principle. A common feud held them together, and mutual feuds kept them apart. In these differences lay the security of Walpole, and to compose these differences was one of the chief objects of Bolingbroke's political writings. Hence arose his anxiety to obliterate party prejudice, hence his tirades against faction, hence those magnificent doctrines which were first promulgated in the "Dissertation upon Parties," and afterwards developed in the "Patriot King," doctrines which constituted the creed of the so-called Patriots, and which, as we shall presently see, were destined to exercise no small influence on political opinion during several generations.

But it is now time to contemplate Bolingbroke in another character. We enter his country-house at Dawley: the scene changes as if by magic; we are in a different world. The restless and acrid controversialist is transformed into the most delightful of social companions. The opponent of Walpole disappears in the friend of Pope and Swift. The coadjutor of Pulteney and Amhurst is lost in the generous and discriminating patron of wit and genius. We are no longer in the midst of men who have been indebted to history for a precarious existence in the annals of biography, but in the midst of men whose names are as familiar to us as the names of our own kindred. Tradition has, in truth, left us few pictures more charming than the life of Bolingbroke at Dawley. In this beautiful retreat, the site of which may still be discerned, he endeavored to per-

suade himself and his contemporaries that he had at last
attained what the sages of antiquity pronounced to be the
climax of human happiness; and, if happiness could consist
in what is external to the mind of those who court it,
Bolingbroke had assuredly every reason to congratulate
himself. He divided his time between his studies, his
friends, and the innocent recreations of country life. He
planted and beautified his grounds, he shouldered a prong
and assisted his haymakers. He subsisted on the plainest
fare. He amused himself with covering his summer-houses,
as he had done before at La Source, with texts from the
Latin Classics, and, to keep up the illusion, he contracted
with a painter to cover the walls of his entrance-hall with
pictures of rural implements. His correspondence—and
his correspondence at this period forms one of the most
pleasing portions of our epistolary literature—is that of a
man at peace with himself and at peace with fortune. So
studiously has he concealed the political schemes in which
he was, as we have already seen, simultaneously engaged,
that it would, we believe, be difficult to find in these letters
a single hint either of his manœuvres against Walpole,
or even of his connection with the *Craftsman*. How closely
he concealed his political writings is shown by the fact
that Swift, in a letter to Pope, dated May 12, 1735, did not
know that Bolingbroke had written the "Dissertation upon
Parties." It is, indeed, scarcely credible that, at a time
when his philippics against the Government had arrived
at their climax of intemperance and malignity, at a time
when he was straining every nerve for a place on the Opposition
benches, he could address Swift in a strain like
this:

"We are both in the decline of life, my dear Dean; we shall, of
course, grow every year more indifferent to it and to the affairs and

interests of a system out of which we are soon to go. The decay of passion strengthens philosophy, for passion may decay and stupidity not succeed. Is it a misfortune, think you, that I rise at this hour refreshed, serene, and calm? that the past, and even the present affairs of life, stand like objects at a distance from me, where I can keep off the disagreeables so as not to be strongly affected by them, and from whence I can draw the others nearer to me."

At Dawley Bolingbroke appears to have kept open house. On his arrival he had at once hastened to renew his acquaintance, not only with those who had shared with him the responsibilities of public life, but with those literary friends whose society was perhaps even more acceptable to him. Indifference to wit and genius had, in truth, never been among his faults. He had been always ready, even when party strife was raging most violently, to forget political differences in the nobler amenities of human intercourse. The generous hospitality, which he had before extended to Prior and Philipps, was now extended to those eminent men whose genius has cast a halo round the annals of the two first Georges. At Dawley, Arbuthnot forgot his ill-health and his onerous duties. There he poured out in careless discourse the fine wit, the delicate humor, the learning, the mellow wisdom, which have, in his correspondence and satires, been the delight of thousands. There Gay's artless laugh rang loudest. Hither, in 1726, with the manuscript of "Gulliver's Travels" in his pocket, came Swift; and hither, in the autumn of the same year, arrived a more illustrious guest. At Dawley Voltaire was, during his long sojourn among us, a frequent visitor. In Bolingbroke's library he studied our poetry, our science, and our philosophy, revised the proof-sheets of the "Henriade," sketched the finest of his tragedies, and learned to write our language with purity and vigor. In the draw-

ing-room at Dawley he was introduced to a society not
less brilliant than he had been accustomed to see assembled
in the Temple, for he was Bolingbroke's visitor during
those happy months in which for the last time Pope, Swift,
Arbuthnot, and Gay met together under the same roof.
Of Voltaire's more important obligations to his English
patron we have already spoken. He had himself so lively
a sense of what he owed to the philosopher of La Source
and Dawley, that he originally intended to inscribe the
"Henriade" to him. This intention was never carried out;
but on his return to Paris he dedicated to him, in very flattering terms, one of the most spirited of his tragedies.

But there was another friendship cemented at Dawley,
the effects of which will be appreciated as long as British
literature shall endure. The relations between Bolingbroke
and Pope form one of the most interesting episodes in the
literary history of the eighteenth century. They appear
to have been brought together for the first time by Swift,
either in the winter of 1713 or in the spring of 1714.
They were apparently on intimate terms when Bolingbroke
left England in 1715. On his return, in 1723, their acquaintance was renewed. When Bolingbroke, in the March
of 1725, established himself at Dawley, the two friends
became almost inseparable. The genius of Pope had at
that time arrived at maturity. His intellectual energy was
in its fullest vigor. The "Essay on Criticism" and the
"Rape of the Lock" had placed him at the head of living
English poets. The proceeds of his "Homer" had put
him beyond the reach of pecuniary embarrassment, and
had thus, by removing the most galling of all obstacles,
enabled him to compete for the most splendid of all prizes.
He was now busy with his "Miscellanies;" the "Miscellanies" led to the "Dunciad," and the "Dunciad" involved

him in feuds which unhinged his mind if they did not dwarf his powers. His temper, always irritable, grew every day more acrimonious. The baser emotions of his sensitive nature were in a continual state of malignant activity. To revenge himself on a rabble of scribblers, whose opinions were not worth the quills which inscribed them, and who, but for him, would have sunk below the soundings of antiquarianism, became the serious business of his life. His satire loaded with ephemeral scandal and noisome with filth, degenerated, in spite of its brilliant execution, into a mere Grub-street Chronicle. Indeed, it seemed at one time not unlikely that the most popular poet of the eighteenth century would encounter the fate of Regnier and Churchill. From this degradation he was rescued by Bolingbroke. By Bolingbroke his genius was directed to nobler aims. By Bolingbroke his poetry was inspired with loftier themes. It was he who raised him above the passions of the hour, and encouraged him to aspire to a place beside Lucretius and Horace. It was he who sketched the plan of that magnificent work, of which the "Essay on Man," the "Moral Essays," and the fourth book of the "Dunciad" are only fragments—a work which would, in all probability, had the health and energy of Pope been equal to the task, have been the finest didactic poem in the world.

The exact extent of Pope's obligations to Bolingbroke it is now impossible to ascertain. They were, in all likelihood, more considerable than any scrutiny, however minute, of what remains of the writings and correspondence of the two friends would reveal. For the influence which Bolingbroke exercised on his contemporaries was, as we have already observed in speaking of his relations with Voltaire, exercised for the most part, like that of the philosophers of old, in conversation. From the very first, the attitude of Pope towards his brilliant companion was that of a reverent disciple. From the very first, Bolingbroke's extraordinary powers of expression, his fiery energy, his haughty and aspiring spirit, his robust and capacious intellect, his wide and varied acquaintance both with the world of books and the world of men, his romantic history, his singularly fascinating manners, his magnificent presence, cast a spell over the delicate and sensitive poet. The first fruit of their intimacy was the "Essay on Man." That Pope owed much of the subject-matter of this poem to Bolingbroke is notorious. If we are to believe Lord Bathurst, he owed all. "Lord Bathurst," says Joseph Warton, "repeatedly assured me that he had read the whole scheme of the Essay in the handwriting of Bolingbroke, and drawn up in a series of propositions which Pope was to versify and illustrate." It is possible that this document may have perished among the papers which were, we know, destroyed by Pope a few days before his death. Mr. Mark Pattison, in his "Introduction to the Essay on Man," is inclined to identify the work to which Bathurst alluded with the manuscript of the "Fragments" or "Minutes of Essays," which occupy the fifth quarto volume of Bolingbroke's collected works. This is not probable. For we learn from a letter in Boswell's "Johnson,"* that Bathurst made the same statement on another occasion, in the presence of Mallet, and that Mallet himself drew attention to it as a singularly interesting piece of information which was altogether new to him. Now, as Mallet was the editor of Bolingbroke's works, and had himself printed these Minutes from Bolingbroke's own manuscript, it is clear

* See Boswell's "Life of Johnson," Croker's One Volume Edition, p. 635.

that the document to which Bathurst alluded could not have been identical with documents with which Mallet must of necessity have been familiar. The connection of the Minutes with the Essay — and the Minutes had, it should be remembered, been printed ten years before this conversation was held—is, moreover, so obvious that Bathurst, interested in everything that concerned Pope, could scarcely have failed to inspect them, or at all events to have been apprised of their contents. Had they been identical with the manuscript which he had seen on Pope's desk, the circumstance must at once have struck him, and he would have hastened to corroborate his assertion by pointing to the proof. Pope may therefore have received more assistance from Bolingbroke than the extant writings of Bolingbroke indicate. However this may be, the Minutes suffice to show that Pope received from his friend by far the greater portion of the material of the poem—the general outline, the main propositions, the reasoning by which these propositions are established, the ethics, the philosophy, several of the illustrations. Indeed he sometimes follows his master so closely that he copies his very words and phrases.* Bolingbroke was indefatigable in

* It is somewhat surprising that none of the commentators on the "Essay on Man" should have taken the trouble to point out to what extent Pope has availed himself of the "Minutes." The parallel passages, for example, collected by Warton and Wakefield, and reproduced by Mr. Elwin, by no means exhaust Pope's obligations. The germ, indeed, of almost every doctrine and of almost every idea in the Essay, more or less developed, will, on careful inspection, be found in them. Let the student turn, for example, to the following references, and compare them with the corresponding passages, which will at once suggest themselves, in Pope's poem. "Bolingbroke," vol. iii., pp. 384, 400, 401; vol. iv., pp. 1, 2, 3, 10, 11, 51-53, 159, 173, 316, 320, 324, 326, 327, 329, 366, 379, 388, 389, 391, 398; vol. v., pp. 9, 36,

stimulating Pope's genius. He was always at his side. He covered reams of paper with disquisitions intended for his guidance. He directed his studies; he held interminable conversations with him. While the "Essay on Man" was still incomplete, he hurried him on to the "Moral Essays," and while the "Moral Essays" were in progress he suggested the "Imitations of Horace." These attentions Pope returned with a devotion half pathetic, half ludicrous. The genius of his friend he had long regarded with superstitious awe. This awe, unimpaired by nearer communion, was now mingled with feelings of gratitude and friendship. His mind, naturally little prone either to credulity or illusion, became the prey of both. His reason, on ordinary occasions shrewd and penetrating, was completely subju-

37, 49, 55, 94, 95, 115. The passages describing the state of Nature; the origin of political society; the origin of civil society; of government; of religion; of the corruption of religion ("Essay," Epistle iii., pp. 146–318); the harmony of the universe and the scale of being (Epistle i., pp. 234–294); man's place in the creation (Epistle i., pp. 33–130); how man's imperfections are necessary for his happiness (Epistle i., pp. 190–232); the mutual dependence of men on each other (Epistle ii., pp. 240–260, and Epistle iii., pp. 308–318); the operation of self-love and reason (Epistle ii., pp. 53–100); of reason and instinct (Epistle iii., pp. 79–108); God's impartial care for his creatures (Epistle iii., pp. 21–48); the nature of human happiness (Epistle iv., pp. 77–372) —are all from Bolingbroke's sketches or suggestions. We cannot stop to enter further into this most interesting question, but we may notice that the famous quatrain which ends "And showed a Newton as we show an ape," was derived not from Palingenius, as all the commentators suppose, but from Bolingbroke. "Superior beings who look down on our intellectual system will not find, I persuade myself, so great a difference between a gascon petit-maitre and a monkey, whatever partiality we may have for our own species."—"Philosophical Works," vol. iv., p. 3. Bolingbroke, it may be added, appears to have derived it, in his turn, from a saying attributed to Heraclitus. See Plato's "Hippias Major," marg., p. 289.

gated. When he spoke of Bolingbroke, it was by no means unusual with him to employ language which ordinary men would never dream of applying to any but the Supreme Being. For the writings of his friend he predicted a splendid immortality. Indeed he observed more than once that his own title to a place in the memory of the world found its best security in his association with his patron. "My verses," he writes in one of his letters to Bolingbroke, "interspersed here and there in the noble work which you address to me, will have the same honor done them as those of Ennius in the philosophical treatises of Tully." So complete, indeed, was the ascendency which Bolingbroke had gained over him, that it would be difficult to find ten consecutive pages in his correspondence and poetry, between 1729 and 1744, in which a discerning eye could not detect traces of Bolingbroke's influence.

In the spring of 1735, to the surprise of all his friends, Bolingbroke suddenly quitted England. His motives for taking this step are involved in great obscurity. Whatever they may have been, it seems pretty clear that they were never explained to the satisfaction of those who were most intimate with him. It was conjectured by some that he was again in communication with the Pretender. It was conjectured by others that he had during his residence at Dawley been intriguing with foreign Ministers; that these intrigues, having come to the ears of the Government, had furnished them with a handle against the Opposition, and that the leaders of the Opposition had in consequence suggested the propriety of his ceasing to act with them. Grimoard is inclined to think that he had received a secret order from the King to leave the country.* Coxe and

* Essai Historique prefixed to the "Lettres Historiques,"vol. i., p. 160.

M. Rémusat attributed his exile to Walpole, who had, they make no doubt, obtained conclusive evidence of treasonable conduct. From his own correspondence all that can be gathered is this, that he did not leave England—we are quoting his own words—till some schemes were on the loom which made him one too many even to his most intimate associates; that he considered he had been treated with disingenuousness and ingratitude, that he had no longer any opportunity of being useful to his friends and his country, and that he had had some misunderstanding with Pulteney. "My part," he wrote to Wyndham, "is over, and he who remains on the stage after his part is over deserves to be hissed off." Our own impression is that he perplexed with mystery what really admits of a very simple interpretation. In leaving England he wished to figure as a patriot-martyr, voluntarily departing into honorable exile. His real motives were, we firmly believe, baffled ambition, ill-health, and pecuniary embarrassment. He was weary, he was disappointed. The results of the general election had just proved that he had nothing to expect from popular favor. The retirement of Lady Suffolk had recently deprived him of his only hope at Court. The Whig section of the Opposition were, in spite of his great services, regarding him with marked disfavor. He had recently brought down upon them two scathing philippics. Indeed, Pulteney had frankly told him that his presence served rather to injure than to benefit the common cause. Nor was this all. His expenditure at Dawley far exceeded his income. He was already involved in debt, and had been reduced to the ruinous expedient of having recourse to usurers, and to the disagreeable necessity of appealing to private friends. To the Marquis de Matignon, for example, he owed two thousand pounds, which had been advanced without security. That Pulteney attributed his departure to pecuniary difficulties is certain. Writing to Swift in November, 1735, he says: "You inquire after Bolingbroke, and when he will return from France. If he had listened to your admonitions and chidings about economy, he need never have gone there." In addition to this, his wife's health was bad, and his own was breaking, and a change to a milder climate was desirable. Such is, we venture to think, the solution of what Mr. Croker used to say was the most difficult problem in Bolingbroke's biography.

Angry with the Government, angry with the Opposition, Bolingbroke now resolved to take no further share in the controversies which were raging between them. He had, he said, fulfilled his duty; he had borne his share in the last struggle which would in all probability be made to preserve the Constitution; he feared nothing from those he had opposed; he asked nothing from those he had served. Till the end of the spring he was in Paris; at the beginning of the autumn we find him settled at Chantaloup, in Touraine. This delicious retreat had, Saint-Simon tells us, been built by Aubigny, the favorite of the Princess Orsini, who had herself superintended its erection. Here Bolingbroke at last found what he had during so many troubled years been affecting to seek. At Marcilly his studies were interrupted and his repose disturbed by obloquy. At La Source he had been on the rack of expectancy; at Dawley his life had been the prey of fierce extremes. Here there was little to tempt him from his books and his dogs. The firm alliance between Fleury and Walpole forbade any cabals with the Cabinet of Versailles. The Stuarts were no longer in France; his old allies were impotent or dead.

Under these favorable circumstances he determined to dedicate the rest of his life to the completion of two works, which he had long been meditating, and on which his fame was to rest. The first was to be a work which should establish metaphysical science on an entirely new basis. It was to embody in a regular system what he had hitherto communicated only in detached fragments. It was to define the limits of the Knowable, to strip metaphysics of jargon and empiricism, and to make them useful by making them intelligible. The other was to be a History of Europe, from the Treaty of the Pyrenees to the conclusion of the negotiations at Utrecht. Neither design was carried out; portions of both survive. His time was, however, well employed, for he produced during this period of his life the most popular of his writings. At the beginning of the winter of 1735 he began the "Letters on the Study of History." These Letters, eight in number, were addressed to Lord Cornbury, a young nobleman whose unblemished character and faultless taste elicited the most exquisite compliment which Pope ever paid. The work divides itself into two parts. The first five Letters point out that history, to be studied to advantage, must be studied philosophically; that its utility lies not, as pedants and antiquaries suppose, in the investigation of details and particulars, but in the lessons which it teaches, the hints which it gives. Its value is a practical value. It should enable us to anticipate action. It should teach us to profit from experiment. It should illustrate historical phenomena in their ultimate effects, and in their mutual relations; for in the brief span of our individual existence we can view events only in course of evolution, incomplete, isolated. Nothing can be more erroneous than to suppose that the chief end of historical study is to acquire information. Its true end is to mould and temper the character and the intellect. He then discusses the credibility of the early history of the Greeks and the Jews, concludes that the authorities for both are equally untrustworthy, and hurries on, after some desultory remarks on the falsification of testimony, to treat of the annalists of later times. The diction of these five Letters is copious and splendid. They abound in precepts to which the student of history may still turn with profit, and they are enriched with observations, always lively, often suggestive, and sometimes new. Their worst fault is a tendency to redundancy and vagueness, their principal deficiency lack of learning, their radical vice superficiality. In the last three Letters he sketches the course of events in Europe between the beginning of the sixteenth century and the end of Anne's reign. The eighth is an elaborate defence of the Treaty of Utrecht, and is composed with extraordinary energy and eloquence. It bears, indeed, little resemblance to a letter. It is a magnificent harangue, instinct with fire and passion. Excise a few paragraphs, substitute My Lords for My Lord, and the reader is perusing a masterpiece of parliamentary oratory. He has before him the relic for which Pitt and Brougham would have sacrificed the lost books of Livy; he has before him in everything but in title the speech of Bolingbroke. No one who peruses the work with any care could, we think, doubt this, and assuredly no one after perusing it would say that when tradition placed Bolingbroke at the head of contemporary orators tradition erred in its estimate of his powers. In our opinion it is, read as a speech, superior to any speech which has come down to us from those times.

While he was still busy with these works he addressed to his friend Lord Bathurst the "Letter on the true Use of Study and Retirement," a short treatise on the model of Seneca when Seneca is most tedious—a treatise in which all that is new is false and all that is true is trite.

Of a very different character was the "Letter on the Spirit of Patriotism." This majestic declamation was inscribed to Lord Lyttelton, who had recently become a conspicuous figure at Leicester House, and was the rising hope of that section of the Opposition whose political creed had been learned from the *Craftsman*. In none of his works are the peculiar beauties of Bolingbroke's diction more strikingly displayed. In none of his works do the graces of rhetoric and the graces of colloquy blend in more exquisite union. The passage in which he points out the responsibilities entailed on all who have inherited the right to a place in the councils of their country has often been deservedly admired. Not less spirited and brilliant is the picture of St. Stephen's under Walpole; and we are not sure that it would be possible to select from the pages of Burke anything finer than the dissertation on Eloquence.

Meanwhile the pleasures of retirement were beginning to pall on him. He continued, indeed, to assure his friends that, dead to the world, he was dead to all that concerned it; but his friends soon discovered that his sublime indifference coexisted with the keenest curiosity about public affairs. It was observed that though nothing was worth his attention nothing escaped it; and that though he continued to indulge in lofty jargon about Cleanthes and Zeno, he was in constant communication with the malcontents of Leicester House. The truth is, that the passion which had during forty years tortured his life still burned as fiercely as ever. Philosophy had left him where it found him; but political ambition had never for one instant relaxed its grasp. It had been his tyrant at twenty; it was destined to be his tyrant at seventy; it had filled his middle age with unrest and unhappiness; it was to fill his old age with bitterness and disappointment. At the end of June, 1738, he was in England. His hopes were high. His prospects had never looked so promising since the spring of 1723. The death of the Queen had removed one of the most influential and implacable of his opponents. The popularity of Walpole was waning. A portentous crisis in European affairs was approaching. The health of the King was precarious. The heir-apparent, at open war with his father and with his father's Ministers, was at the head of the Opposition. Every week that young and ardent band, on whose minds the doctrines of the "Dissertation on Parties" had made a deep impression, were gaining strength. Of these enthusiasts there was, with the exception of Pitt, scarcely any one who did at this time not regard Bolingbroke with superstitious reverence. The majority of them were, indeed, his acknowledged disciples. He was not, it is true, on cordial terms either with Pulteney or Carteret; but no man stood higher in the favor of the Prince of Wales, and on the Prince of Wales all eyes were now turning with eager interest.

It would, we believe, be impossible to find in the writings of those who have illustrated the private life of princes, from Suetonius to Mr. Greville, a character so completely despicable as that of Frederick Lewis. One who had for many years observed him narrowly, has told us that he was unable to detect the shadow of a virtue in him. His kindred regarded him with horror and disgust. He had even exhausted the forbearance and long-suffering of maternal love, and the fact that he had survived infancy was considered by both his parents to be the greatest calamity which had ever befallen them. Assuredly no man observed the infirmities of his fellow-creatures with a more indulgent eye than the elder Walpole; but Walpole could never speak of Frederick without a torrent of invectives. "He was," he said, "a poor, feeble, irresolute, false, lying, dishonest, contemptible wretch." In temper he belonged to that large class who are governed entirely by impulse, men of weak judgment and strong sensibilities. But with all the defects, he had none of the virtues which such people frequently display. The evil in his nature was, if we are to credit Hervey, without alloy. He exhibited a combination of vices such as rarely meet in the same person, and it was observed that in Frederick every vice assumed its most odious shape. He was a wastrel without a spark of generosity,* and a libertine without a grain of sentiment. When anger possessed him, its effect was not to produce the emotions which such a passion usually produces in our sex, but to excite emotions similar to those which a slight awakes in the breast of a superannuated coquette. He became charged with petty spite. He watched with patient malice for every opportunity of ignoble retaliation. His face wore smiles, his tongue dropped venom. In mendacity, poltroonery, and dirtiness he was not excelled either by his late secretary Bubb Dodington, or by his recent under-secretary Mallet. Even that part of his conduct in which traces of better things would seem at first sight to be discernible, will be found on nearer inspection to be of the same texture with the rest. He patronized literature because his father and his father's Minister despised it; he became a Patriot to fill his pockets; he supported popular liberty to vex his family. Ambition in its nobler forms was unintelligible to him. Of any capacity

* Horace Walpole ("Memoirs of George II.," vol. i., p. 77) tells us that "generosity was his best quality." Could contempt go further?

for the duties of public life he never, so far as we can discover, evinced a single symptom. His mind was jejune and feeble, his parts beneath contempt. Indeed, both nature and education had done their best to make this unhappy youth an object of pity to those who wished him well, and a subject for perpetual rejoicing to those who wished him ill.

Such was Frederick as he appeared to impartial observers, but such was not the Frederick of Bolingbroke and the Patriots. By them he was held up to public veneration as a being without blemish, by them he was proclaimed to be the Messias of a political millennium. Under his wise and beneficent sway, corruption, misgovernment, and faction were to disappear: in his person an ideal ruler was to be found at the head of an ideal Ministry; for the splendor of his character would be reflected on all who came in contact with him. Every week his levee at Norfolk House became more crowded; every day his vanity and insolence became more outrageous. At last his head was completely turned. He set his father openly at defiance. He appealed to the people. All this was the work of Bolingbroke. From the very first he had labored to widen the breach between Frederick and the King. It was he, indeed, who suggested the measure which made their breach public; it was he who now labored to make it irreparable. And his policy was obvious. It was to detach Frederick not only from Walpole and from Walpole's adherents, but from that section of the Opposition which was led by Pulteney and Carteret. If, on the event of the King's death, Pulteney and Carteret stood first in the estimation of the successor to the throne, Bolingbroke had, as he well knew, nothing to gain, for both those statesmen had long regarded him rather as a rival than as an ally. But if at that crisis he had succeeded in gaining the ascendency over Frederick, as he had already gained the ascendency over Frederick's counsellors, it required little sagacity to foretell that in a few weeks he would in all probability be at the head of affairs. He took care, therefore, to improve every advantage. He courted the Prince with unvaried assiduity, both in public and private. He descended to the grossest adulation. Indeed, his language and his conduct frequently bordered on the abject. To this period in his career is to be assigned the composition of the " Patriot King," a work written with the threefold purpose of exalting himself in the eyes of his young master, of making the Government odious in the eyes of the nation, and of furnishing the Patriots with a war-cry and a gospel.

Of all Bolingbroke's writings this treatise was the most popular. It was, on its publication in 1749, perused with avidity by readers of every class. Poets versified its sentiments and reflected its spirit. Allusions to it abound in the light literature of those times. On oratory and journalism its effect was in some degree similar to that which the Romance of Lyly had, a hundred and seventy years before, produced on prose diction during the latter years of Elizabeth. It created a new and peculiar dialect. To parley patriotism became an accomplishment as fashionable in political circles between 1749 and 1760 as to parley Euphuism had been in the society which surrounded the Great Queen between 1580 and 1600. The public ear was wearied with echoes of Bolingbroke's stately rhetoric. Scarcely a week passed without witnessing the appearance of some pamphlet in which his mannerisms, both of tone and expression, were copied with ludicrous fidelity. But it was not on style only that its influence was apparent. For some years it formed the manual of a large body of enthusiasts. From its pages George III. derived the articles of his political creed. On its precepts Bute modelled his conduct. It called into being the faction known to our fathers as the King's Friends. It undoubtedly contributed, and contributed in no small degree, to bring about that great revolution which transformed the Toryism of Filmer and Rochester into the Toryism of Johnson and Pitt.*

If this famous essay be regarded as a serious attempt to provide a remedy for the distempers under which the State was laboring, it is scarcely worth a moment's consideration. It is mere babble. Its proposals are too ridiculous to be discussed, its arguments too childish to be refuted. Where had the sublime and perfect being, whom Bolingbroke proposes to invest with sovereignty, any counterpart in human experience? How is the power of the Crown to be at once absolute in practice and limited in theory? How can Parliamentary Government possibly exist without parties, and

---

* It is curious to observe how exactly the political creed of Johnson coincides with the doctrines preached by Bolingbroke. "He asserted," writes Dr. Maxwell, in an account of some conversations he held with Johnson in 1770, "the legal and salutary prerogatives of the Crown, while he no less respected the Constitutional liberties of the people: Whiggism at the time of the Revolution, he said, was accompanied by certain principles: but latterly, as a mere party distinction under Walpole and the Pelhams, was no better than the politics of stock-jobbers and the religion of infidels. He detested the idea of governing by parliamentary corruption, and asserted that a Prince steadily and conspicuously pursuing the interests of his people could not fail of parliamentary concurrence. A Prince of ability might and should be the directing soul and spirit of his own Administration; in short, his own Minister, and not the mere head of a party; and then, and not till then, would the royal dignity be respected," etc. See the whole passage, Croker's "Boswell," royal octavo edition, p. 216.

when did parties ever listen to the voice of wisdom when wisdom opposed interest? Is it within the bounds of credibility that a king, who is potentially an absolute monarch, will consent to consider himself absolute only so long as he acts with the approbation of the national council, and that the moment the national council pronounces him to be guilty of error, he will confess that his prerogative is limited? How is the narrow spirit of party to transform itself into a diffusive spirit of public benevolence? These absurdities become, if possible, the more preposterous when we remember that the ruler contemplated by Bolingbroke was no other than his miserable disciple, Frederick Lewis —the more shameless when we remember that he had himself been the first to acknowledge that in a Constitution like ours the extinction of party would involve the extinction of popular liberty — the more monstrous when we know that he was at heart as cynical in his estimate of humanity as Swift and La Rochefoucault.

But if, as a didactic treatise, the "Patriot King" is a tissue of absurdities, as a party pamphlet it is a masterpiece. No flattery was, as Bolingbroke well knew, too gross for Frederick. No theories were too visionary for those hot-headed and inexperienced youths who were in the van of the Patriots, and to those fanatics Bolingbroke was particularly addressing himself. This was not, however, his only aim. Much of the work is, like the Utopia of More, satire under the guise of didactic fiction. The picture of Bolingbroke's political millennium is an oblique and powerful attack on Walpole's foreign and domestic policy. In depicting the character of his ideal monarch, he ridicules by implication the character of the reigning monarch. In elevating Frederick into a demigod, he degrades George into a dotard, and Walpole into a scheming knave; every allusion which reflects honor on Norfolk House is so contrived as to reflect infamy on the Court. Every reform which is to mark the new dispensation brands by allusion some abuse in the old. On the composition of the "Patriot King," Bolingbroke took more pains than was usual with him. It is perhaps, in point of execution, his most finished work. But style, though it will do much for a writer, will not do everything. Indeed, Bolingbroke's splendid diction frequently serves to exhibit in strong relief the crudity and shallowness of his matter, as jewels set off deformity. To the "Patriot King" he afterwards appended a "Dissertation on the State of Parties at the Accession of George I.," and this dissertation, if we except the unfinished "Reflections on the Present State of the Nation," written a few months afterwards, concludes his political writings.

He had now attained the object for which he had, during fourteen years, been incessantly laboring. The *Craftsman* had done its work. Bolingbroke had at last succeeded in making his enemy odious in every city and in every hamlet in Britain. He could hear the cries which he had set up—cries against corruption, cries against Ministerial tyranny and Royal impotence, cries against ignoble compromises with foreign powers, cries against standing armies, cries against the exportation of English wool, against Septennial Parliaments — echoing, savagely emphasized, from the lips of thousands. He had at last the satisfaction of seeing the Government tottering to its fall, the nation blind with fury, clamoring for war, clamoring for reform, clamoring for everything which could embarrass its rulers. He could see that the Patriots were now pressing onward to certain victory.

Before leaving England, at the beginning of the spring

of 1739, for his chateau at Argeville, he had suggested the famous secession of the Opposition which followed the debate on the convention with Spain, and during the next two years he appears to have been regularly consulted by Wyndham and by Wyndham's coadjutors. He affected, indeed, to be absorbed in metaphysics and history, but every page of his correspondence proves with what keenness and anxiety he was following the course of events in England. In February, 1742, the crash came. The Opposition triumphed. Walpole sent in his resignation, and all was anarchy. But Bolingbroke was again destined to be the sport of Fortune. He arrived in London just in time to find his worst fears realized, Carteret and Pulteney in coalition with Newcastle and Hardwicke, the prospects of the Patriots completely overcast, the Tories abandoned by their treacherous allies, and the Prince of Wales half reconciled with the King. So died his last hope. He had now, in his own melancholy phrase, to swallow down the dregs of life as calmly as he could; and little, indeed, but the dregs were left.

What remains to be told may be told in a few words. The death of his father relieved him from pecuniary embarrassment, and enabled him to settle down in comparative comfort at Battersea. But the infirmities of age, aggravated, perhaps, by early excesses, soon weighed heavily upon him. Every year found him more solitary. Of that brilliant society which had gathered round him at Dawley and at Twickenham scarcely one survived: Congreve, Gay, Arbuthnot, Lansdowne, all were gone. Swift was fast sinking into imbecility; Wyndham was no more. In May, 1744, he was summoned to Twickenham to weep over the wreck of that noble genius which had so often been dedicated to his glory, to close the eyes which for thirty years had never rested on him without veneration and love. And well, indeed, had it been if on that sad day the world had been called to mourn the master as well as the disciple. We should then have been spared one of the most melancholy incidents in literary annals. It is shocking to find that there are not wanting writers who attempt to justify Bolingbroke's subsequent conduct with regard to Pope. In our opinion, his conduct admits of no extenuation—in our opinion, a man of honor would never, even in self-defence and under the strongest provocation, have been guilty of such atrocity. The facts—and let the facts speak for themselves—are simply these: On the completion of the "Patriot King," Bolingbroke had forwarded the manuscript to Pope, requesting him to have a few copies printed, with a view to distributing them among private friends. A limited number of copies were accordingly printed and circulated; and so for a time the matter rested. But on the death of Pope it was discovered that, in addition to the copies for which he had accounted, he had ordered the printer to strike off fifteen hundred more. Of this, however, he had said nothing to Bolingbroke. That Pope, in thus acting, acted with disingenuousness must be admitted, but his disingenuousness on this occasion originated, we are convinced, from motives very creditable to him. It was notorious that he entertained exaggerated notions of Bolingbroke's merits as a writer. It is notorious that in conversation he frequently commented on his friend's indifference to literary distinction. In his letters he was constantly reminding him of the duties he owed both to contemporaries and to future ages. He had, for example, recently appealed to him in emphatic terms to publish both the "Essay on the Spirit of Patriotism" and the "Patriot King," but in vain. Afraid, therefore, that the precious treatise thus intrusted to him might, either by some sudden caprice on the part of the author, or by some carelessness on the part of the few who were privileged to possess it, be lost to the world, he determined to render the chance of such a catastrophe as remote as possible. He resolved to deal with Bolingbroke as Varius and Tucca dealt with Virgil—to save him in his own despite. Hence the surreptitious impression. It is remarkable that even to so ill-natured an observer as Horace Walpole, Pope's conduct at once presented itself in this light. Pope may, it is true, have acted in the mere wantonness of that spirit of trickery which entered so largely into his dealings with his fellow-men. But whatever may have been his object, it is perfectly clear now, and it must have been perfectly clear then, that he had no intention either of injuring Bolingbroke or of benefiting himself. Assuming, however, for a moment the existence of some less creditable motive, does the grave afford no immunity from insult? Was a single equivocal action sufficient to outweigh the devotion of a whole life? Had Bolingbroke no tenderness for the memory of one whose friendship had, for nearly a quarter of a century, been his chief solace in obloquy and misfortune, who had loved him with a love rarely found to exist between man and man, whose genius had elevated him above Memmius and Mæcenas; on whose dying face his tears had fallen? It is lamentable to be obliged to add that the motives which prompted Bolingbroke's libel were almost as derogatory to him as the libel itself. He had been annoyed at Pope's intimacy with Warburton. He had been still more irritated when he learned that Pope had appointed Warburton his editor. While this was rankling in his mind, the discovery relating to the "Patriot King" was made. On Pope's copy being inspected, it was found that he had inserted several alterations, had rearranged much of the subject-matter, and had in other ways presumed to tamper with the text. At this Bolingbroke's smouldering resentment burst into a flame. We very much question, however, whether rage would have carried him to such lengths had it not been aggravated by that bad man who was now always at his elbow.

Into Bolingbroke's relations with the cur Mallet we have no intention of entering. To the influence of that unprincipled adventurer and most detestable man is, we believe, in a large measure to be attributed almost everything which loaded his latter years with reproach—the assault on Pope, the unseemly controversy with Warburton, the determination to prepare for posthumous publication what he had not the courage to publish during life.*

* It is, we think, highly probable that the most obnoxious of Bolingbroke's writings would never have travelled beyond the circle of his private friends had it not been for the sordid cupidity of Mallet. Mallet, it is well known, anticipated enormous profits from the sale of his patron's works, and did all in his power to swell their bulk. It is dangerous to predicate anything of a man so inconsistent as Bolingbroke, but it is remarkable that he had several times expressed in the most emphatic terms his anxiety not to appear publicly among the assailants of the national faith. Indeed, he went so far as to caution Pope against heterodoxy. See his Letter to Swift, September 12, 1724; his Letter to Pope, "Works," quarto edition, vol. iii., p. 313, and again p. 330. See also "Marchmont Papers," vol. ii., p. 288, and Cooke's "Life," vol. ii., p. 252. It was said, also, that he had promised Lady Harlington that these works should never be published. See Cooke's "Life," vol. ii., p. 252. In a letter to Hardwicke (see Harris, "Life of Hardwicke," vol. ii., p. 112) he says that he "respected evangelical religion," as he "ought." The theory that he deceived Pope and Swift as to his real opinions is too absurd to be discussed. Is it likely that three such men as Bolingbroke, Pope,

Biography has few sadder pages to show than those which record the last days of Bolingbroke. From the Past he could derive no consolation, for he could look back on nothing but failure; in the Present his portion was pain, obloquy, and solitude. In the Future he saw only what the strongest mind cannot contemplate without apprehension, for his stern creed taught him to expect that the stroke which terminates suffering terminates being. A complication of disorders, soon to culminate in the most frightful malady to which man is subject, racked his body. His temper became irritable, even to ferocity. His noble intellect remained indeed unimpaired, but was clouded with misanthropy. He was at war with all classes, and all classes were at war with him. "The whole stock of moral evil"—such is his language to Lyttelton—"which severity of government, inveteracy of party resentments, negligence or treachery of relations and friends, could bring upon me seems to be at last exhausted."* Though he still aspired to direct the counsels of Frederick, he had the mortification of perceiving that he was an oracle whom few consulted, many ridiculed, and none heeded. Visitors to Battersea grew less and less frequent. Even his disciples began to fall off. "Je deviens tous les ans," he wrote in that language which had in happier days been so dear to him, "de plus en plus isolé dans ce monde." In March, 1750, the only tie which bound him to life was severed.

---

and Swift, would, in the freedom of familiar intercourse, discuss such topics with reserve? Is it likely that their opinions would materially differ. The truth probably is that Bolingbroke shrank, like Gibbon, from identifying himself with a clique whom he detested as a philosopher, as a statesman, and as a gentleman.

* Letter to Lyttelton, August 20, 1747. Phillimore's "Life of Lyttelton," vol. ii., p. 293.

His wife had long been ailing; for several weeks she had been on the point of death. The blow was, therefore, not unexpected, but when it came it came with terrible force, for he had loved her with a tenderness which seemed scarcely compatible with his cold and selfish nature. He laid her among his ancestors at Battersea, and he commended her virtues and accomplishments in an epitaph which is a model of graceful and dignified eulogy. He was not long in following her. For some time he had been troubled with a humor in his cheek. As it had caused him no inconvenience, he had paid little attention to it. But in the middle of 1751 it began to assume a malignant character, and at the end of August his physician pronounced it to be cancer. It was at first hoped that an operation might save him. He refused, however, to listen to those who were most competent to advise, and insisted on placing himself in the hands of a popular empiric. Unskilful treatment served only to aggravate his distemper. His sufferings were dreadful. He bore them with heroic fortitude, and he took his farewell of one of the few friends whom Fortune had spared him with sentiments not unworthy of that sublime religion which he had long rejected, and on which he was even then preparing to heap insult. "God who placed me here will do what he pleases with me hereafter, and he knows best what to do. May he bless you." These were the last recorded words of Bolingbroke. On the 12th of December, 1751, he was no more.

A little more than two years after Bolingbroke's death, his literary executor, Mallet, gave to the world in five stately quartos his literary and philosophical works. With most of the former the public were already acquainted. Of the latter they knew nothing. To the latter, therefore, all readers at once turned. Their first emotion was eager curiosity, their second astonishment and anger. Never before had an Englishman of Bolingbroke's parts and genius appeared among the assailants of the national faith. The whole country was in a ferment. The obnoxious works were denounced from the pulpit. The Grand Jury of Westminster presented them as a nuisance. The Press teemed with pamphlets. Warburton attacked them with characteristic vigor and acrimony; and Warburton was at no long interval succeeded by Leland. Nor was it by theologians only that the task of refutation was undertaken. Poor Henry Fielding, then fast sinking under a complication of diseases, commenced an elaborate reply, a fragment of which may still be found in his works, a fragment which seems to indicate that the prince of English novelists might, had he so willed it, have held no mean place among philosophical controversialists.

The writings which caused so much consternation among our forefathers have long since passed into oblivion. In our day they are rarely consulted even by the curious. Nor is this surprising. They satisfy no need, they solve no problem, they furnish little entertainment. What was worth preserving in them has been presented in a far more attractive shape by Pope. What was most daring in them is embalmed in the wit and grace of Voltaire. We shall therefore despatch them without much ceremony. Their object was threefold. It was to demolish theological and philosophical dogma, to purify philosophy from mysticism, and "to reconstruct on an entirely new basis the science of metaphysics." Bolingbroke's qualifications for the work of demolition consist of boundless fertility of invective, a very imperfect acquaintance with the works which he undertakes to condemn, and a degree of technical ignorance which is sometimes almost incredible. The writings on which he is most severe are the Old Testament, the Epistles of St. Paul, and the Platonic Dialogues. The first he pronounces, without any circumlocution, to be a farrago of gross and palpable falsehoods: in the second he discerns only the jargon of a fanatical visionary, perplexed himself, and perplexing everything he discusses. To Plato he can never even allude without a torrent of abuse. He is the father of philosophical lying, a mad theologian, a bombastic poet, the master of metaphysical pneumatics. Having thus disposed of those whom he regards as the earliest sources of Error, he next proceeds to deal, and to deal in a similar spirit, with their followers — with "superstitious liars" like Cyprian, with "vile fellows" like Eusebius, with "chimerical quacks" like Leibnitz, with "nonsensical paraphrasers of jargon" like Cudworth, with "orthodox bullies" like Tillotson, with "empty bullies" like Clarke, with "foul-mouthed pedants" like Warburton. To say that Bolingbroke has in all cases failed in his attacks would be to give a very imperfect idea of his character as a controversialist. The truth is that he knew, as a rule, little or nothing of what he professes to confute. It is obvious that he has frequently not even taken the trouble to turn to the works on which he passes sentence. What he knows of the philosophy of antiquity is what he has picked up from Cudworth and Stanley. What he knows of modern speculation is what he has derived from Bayle, Rapin, and Thomassin. Of the relative value of authority he appears to have no conception. The trash which has descended to us under the name of Orpheus is in his eyes as authentic as the History of the Peloponnesian War. He speaks with the same ignorant contempt of the statements of writers like Josephus, and of the statements of writers like

Herodotus and Diodorus. He classes Plato with Plotinus, and Aristotle with Iamblicus.

But however ludicrously he fails in point of knowledge, he fails, if possible, still more ludicrously when he attempts to reason. His logic is the logic of a woman in anger. He is not merely inconsistent, but suicidal. What he asserts with ferocious vehemence at one moment, he denies with ferocious vehemence the next. What is assumed as undeniably true at the beginning of a section is assumed to be undeniably false at the end of it. We will give one or two samples. One of his principal arguments against the authenticity of the Mosaic Writings is the *à priori* argument that, as man has no need of a revelation, no revelation has been conceded; and this argument he has been at great pains to establish. In the Essays he tells us that a revelation has undoubtedly been granted, and that this revelation is to be found in the Gospels. In the Letter on Tillotson's Sermon he informs us that one of the strongest presumptions against the veracity of Moses is the fact that none of his assertions are supported by collateral testimony. In the Essays he tells us that the Pentateuch "contains traditions of very great antiquity, some of which were preserved and propagated by other nations as well as the Israelites, and by other historians as well as Moses." Of Christianity he sometimes appears as the apologist, and sometimes as the opponent. In one Essay it is the authentic message of the Almighty, in another it is bastard Platonism. In the Minutes it is "a continued lesson of the strictest morality;" in the Essays it is the offspring of deliberate deceit. In the "Letter to Ponilly" he rejects, he says, any revelation which is not confirmed by miraculous evidence, because it lacks authority. In the "Letters to Pope" he rejects, he says, a revelation which is accompanied by miraculous evidence, because it shocks his reason.

Such is Bolingbroke's philosophy on its aggressive side, the side on which it is at once most offensive and most impotent. In the construction of his own system—we are speaking merely as critics—he has, it must be admitted, been more successful. The main features of that system are familiar to us from the poem of Pope. Pope, however, only followed his friend's theories so far as they were consistent with orthodox belief. Bolingbroke carried them much further. His philosophy, extricated from the rank and tangled jungle of the Essays and Minutes, may be briefly summarized: That there lives and works, self-existent and indivisible, One God; that the world is His creation; that all we can discern of His nature and His attributes is what we can deduce from the economy of the Universe; that what we can thus deduce is the quality of infinite wisdom coincident with infinite benevolence, both operating not by particular but by general laws; that any attempt to analyze His attributes further is blasphemy and presumption; that the Voice of God spoke neither in the thunders of Sinai nor from the lips of Prophets, but speaks only, and will continue to speak only, in the Harmony of the Universe; that one of the most striking proofs of that harmony lies in a sort of fundamental connection between the idea of God and the reason of man, and that it is this bond which ennobles morality into something more than a conventional code; that man's faculties are, like his body, adapted only for the practical functions of existence; that all his knowledge is derived from sensation and reflection, and that, though he is the crown of created beings, he has no connection with Divinity. There are, he contends, no grounds for supposing either that the soul is immortal, or that there is a world beyond the tomb, for everything tends to prove that the soul is woven of the same perishable material as the body, and a future state is not only logically improbable but essentially superfluous. Man's life is in itself complete; virtue constitutes, as a rule, its own reward, vice constitutes, as a rule, its own punishment. Where inequalities exist, they exist only in appearance. Whatever is, is right; but whatever is must be contemplated, not in its bearings on individuals, but as an integral portion of the vast and exquisite mechanism of the Great Whole. It will be at once perceived that this was not new, and that Bolingbroke, though he aspired to the glory of an original thinker, laid under contribution not only the philosophy* of antiquity and the writings of contemporary Deists, but the speculations of Locke, Shaftesbury, Leibnitz, Wollaston, Clarke, and Archbishop King.

This portion of his philosophic works is, to do him justice, not without merit. His reasoning is, it is true, more specious than solid, more skilful than persuasive: frequently contradictory, still more frequently inconclusive. But what he states he usually states with force, with perspicuity, and with eloquence. His illustrations are often singularly happy, his theories suggestive, his reflections shrewd and ingenious. We could point to fragments in which noble ideas are embodied in noble language; we could point to paragraphs as fine as anything in Cicero or Jere-

---

* The most sensible and the only valuable part of the Bolingbrokian Philosophy is in truth little more than an expansion of the well-known passage in the De Legibus: ὧν ἓν καὶ τὸ σόν, ὦ σχέτλιε, μόριον εἰς τὸ πᾶν ξυντείνει βλέπον ἀεὶ καίπερ πάνσμικρον ὄν· σὲ δὲ λέληθε περὶ τοῦτο αὐτὸ ὡς γίνεσις ἕνεκα ἐκείνου γίγνεται πᾶσα, ὅπως ᾖ ἡ τῷ τοῦ παντὸς βίῳ ὑπάρχουσα εὐδαίμων οὐσία, οὐχ ἕνεκα σοῦ γιγνομένη, σὺ δὲ ἕνεκα ἐκείνου· πᾶς γὰρ ἰατρὸς ἔντεχνος δημιουργὸς παντὸς μὲν ἕνεκα πάντα ἐργάζεται, πρὸς τὸ κοινῇ ξυντεῖνον βέλτιστον, μέρος μὴν ἕνεκα ὅλου καὶ οὐχ ὅλον μέρους ἕνεκα ἀπεργάζεται.—" *Plato De Legibus,* lib. x., p. 903.

my Taylor. But they are rare and far between; they are oases in a wilderness of unmethodical arrangement, of prolix digressions, of endless repetitions.

We must now take our leave of this brilliant but most unhappy man, the glory and the shame both of our history and of our literature. If in the course of our narrative we have commented with severity on his many errors, we would fain, in parting with him, remember only his nobler traits. We would do justice to his splendid and versatile genius; to his manly and capacious intellect; to his majestic eloquence; to the vastness and grandeur of his aspirations; to his invincible spirit; to his superhuman energy; to his instinctive sympathy with the exalted and the beautiful. We would think of him as the discriminating patron of philosophy, of science, and of literature. We would dwell on his superiority to those base passions which are too often found among men of letters, on his entire freedom from everything paltry and sordid, on that ambition which had no taint of envy; on that pride which never degenerated into vanity. With all his blemishes, he is a magnificent figure; with all his failures, he left the world in his debt. As we close with mingled feelings of wonder and pity, of admiration and sorrow, the checkered story of his life, we are insensibly reminded of the solemn words in which the Abbot passes sentence on Manfred:

> "This should have been a noble creature! He
> Hath all the energy which would have made
> A goodly frame of glorious elements,
> Had they been wisely mingled; as it is,
> It is an awful chaos—light and darkness,
> And mind and dust, and passions and high thoughts,
> Mixed and contending without end or order,
> All dormant or destructive. He will perish."

VOLTAIRE IN ENGLAND.

SUMMARY.

PART I.

Voltaire's stay in England, an unwritten chapter in his biography, p. 191, 192—Date of his arrival, p. 193, 194—First impressions, p. 196—The friends he makes in England: Bubb Dodington, Sir Everard Falkener, p. 196-198—Interview with Pope, p. 200, 201—Reverses of fortune: family afflictions, p. 202, 203—At Eastbury, meets Young, p. 205, 206—His views on men and manners, p. 206-208—Lady Hervey: Voltaire's English verses, p. 209—His double-dealing in politics, p. 210-212—His effusiveness as a critic, p. 212—Studies of English life, p. 212-215—Visit to France, p. 216.

PART II.

Scrap-book of Voltaire: a clew to his familiarity with English life, p. 216-218—His study of Newton's works, of Locke's, of Bacon's and Berkeley's, p. 218, 219—Warm sympathy with the Free-thought movement, as inaugurated by Collins and Woolston, p. 220—His literary productions in the English language, p. 220-224—Preparations for the publication of the "Henriade," p. 224-226—Issue of the work: its immense success, p. 226-228—Piratical publishers, p. 228, 229—Domestic troubles, p. 230—Alterations of the manuscript, p. 231—Comments of the Press, p. 231, 232—Untoward incident: Voltaire's clever escape, p. 233—British national self-complacency strikingly illustrated, p. 233, 234.

PART III.

Voltaire's different literary undertakings from April, 1728, until March, 1729, p. 234-236—His growing familiarity with English literature, p. 236-238—His indebtedness to English Men of Letters, p. 238-241—Retrospect at the close of his stay in England, p. 240—His respect for the English, p. 242—Calumnious statements circulated as to the cause of his departure from England, p. 243—Last interview with Pope, p. 244—Voltaire's return to France, p. 245.

VOLTAIRE IN ENGLAND.

SECTION I.
JUNE, 1726—NOVEMBER, 1727.

The residence of Voltaire in England is an unwritten chapter in the literary history of the eighteenth century. And yet, assuredly, few episodes in that history are so well worth attentive consideration. In his own opinion it was the turning-point of his career. In the opinion of Condorcet it was fraught with consequences of momentous importance to Europe and to humanity. What is certain is that it left its traces on almost everything which he subsequently produced, either as the professed disciple and interpreter of English teachers, or as an independent inquirer. It penetrated his life. "Dès ce moment," says Condorcet, "Voltaire se sentit appelé à détruire les préjugés de toute espèce, dont son pays était l'esclave." Its influence extended even to his poetry and to his criticism, to his work as a historian and to his work as an essayist. Nor is this all. The circumstances under which he sought our protection; his strange experiences among us; his relations with Pope, Swift, and Bolingbroke, with the Court, with our aristocracy, with the people; the zeal and energy with which he studied our manners, our government, our science, our history, our literature; his courageous attempts to distinguish himself as a writer in English—all combine to form one of the most interesting passages in his singularly interesting career.

But, unfortunately, no portion of Voltaire's biography is involved in greater obscurity. "On ignore," writes Charles Rémusat, "à peu près quelle fut sa vie en Angleterre. Ces deux années sont une lacune dans son histoire. C'est un point de sa biographie qui mériterait des recherches." Carlyle, who attempted in the third volume of his "Frederick the Great" to throw some light on it, abandoned the task in impatient despair. Mere inanity and darkness visible—such are his expressions—reign, in all Voltaire's biographies, over this period of his life. "Seek not to know it," he exclaims; "no man has inquired into it, probably no competent man ever will."*

It happened, however, that at the very time Carlyle was thus expressing himself, a very competent man was engaged on the task. The researches of Desnoiresterres succeeded in dispersing a portion at least of the obscurity which hung over Voltaire's movements during these mysterious years. He took immense pains to supply the deficiencies of preceding biographers. Judging rightly that all that could now be recovered could be recovered only in scattered fragments, he diligently collected such information as lay dispersed in Voltaire's own correspondence and writings, and in the correspondence and writings of those with whom his illustrious countryman had, when in England, been brought into contact. Much has, it is true, escaped him; much which he has collected he has not, perhaps, turned to the best account; but it is due to him—the fullest and the most satisfactory of Voltaire's biographers—to say that his chapter, "Voltaire et la Société Anglaise," must form the basis of all future inquiries into this most interesting subject. To higher praise he is not, we

* Carlyle's own account is full of errors, some of them evincing almost incredible carelessness.

think, entitled. Some of Desnoiresterres's deficiencies are supplied by Mr. Parton, whose "Life of Voltaire" appeared in two goodly octavos in 1881. Mr. Parton has made one or two unimportant additions to what was already known, but he has, we are sorry to find, done little more. We gratefully acknowledge our obligations both to Desnoiresterres and to Mr. Parton. But these obligations are slight.

The first point to be settled is the exact date of his arrival in England, and that date can, we think, be determined with some certainty. On May the 2d (N. S.), 1726, an order arrived for his release from the Bastile, on the understanding that he would quit France and betake himself, as he had offered to do, to England. On May the 6th he was, as his letter to Madame de Ferriole proves, at Calais;* and at Calais he remained for some days, the guest of his friend Dunoquet, the treasurer of the troops. How long he remained at Calais we cannot say, as no documents have as yet been discovered which throw light on his movements between the 6th of May and the beginning of June. From his letter to Madame de Ferriole it certainly appears that he had no immediate intention of embarking. He asks her to send him news and to give him instructions, and tells her that he is waiting to receive them. In all probability he continued at Calais, not as the biographers assert, for four days, but for nearly five weeks—that is to say, from the 6th of May to the 8th or 9th of June. He tells us himself that he disembarked near Greenwich, and it is clear from the passage which follows that he landed on the day of Greenwich Fair. That fair was invariably held on Whit-Monday, and Whit-Monday fell in 1726 on May the 30th (o. s.). Now a reference to the *Daily Courant* for May the 30th shows that a mail arrived from

---

* And see the "Letter to A. M*** Mélanges," vol. i., p. 17.

France on Sunday the 29th, which would be, of course, according to the new style, June 10th. Supposing, therefore, that his visit at Calais was protracted to five weeks after his letter to Madame de Ferriole—and there is, as we have shown, no reason for supposing that it was not—the time would exactly tally. That he should have remained on board till Monday morning need excite no surprise. But there is other evidence in favor of this date. In the remarkable passage in which he describes what he saw on landing, he tells us that the vessels in the river had spread their sails (déployé leurs voiles) to do honor to the King and Queen,* and he particularly notices the splendid liveries worn by the King's menials. We turn to the *London Gazette* for Monday, May the 30th, and we find that on that day the King's birthday, the rejoicings for which had been deferred from the preceding Saturday, was "celebrated with the usual demonstrations of public joy;" and in the *British Gazetteer* for Saturday, May the 21st, we read that "great preparations are making for celebrating the King's birthday," and that "the King's menial servants are to be new clothed on that occasion." We believe, then, that Voltaire first set foot in England on Whit-Monday, May the 30th, 1726.

On the voyage he had been the prey of melancholy thoughts. He drew, in the bitterness of his soul, a parallel between his own position and the position in which his favorite hero once stood. And his feelings found expression in verse—

"Je ne dois pas être plus fortuné
Que le héros célébré sur ma vielle.

---

* In adding the name of the Queen he was of course mistaken, as she was in confinement.

Il fut proscrit, persécuté, damné
Par les dévots et leur douce séquelle.
En Angleterre il trouva du secours,
J'en vais chercher." *

But on landing he soon recovered his cheerfulness, and throwing himself, in a transport of joy, on the earth, he reverently saluted it.† Many of his countrymen have described their first impressions of the land of Shakespeare and Newton, but to none of them has it ever presented itself as it presented itself to the fascinated eye of Voltaire. Everything combined to fill the young exile with delight and admiration. Though his health was delicate, he was in exuberant spirits. It was a cloudless day in the loveliest month of the English year. A soft wind from the west—we are borrowing his own glowing description—tempered the rays of the hot spring sun, and disposed the heart to joy. The Thames, rolling full and rapid, was in all its glory; and in all their glory, too, were the stately trees which have now disappeared, but which then fringed the river-banks on both sides for many miles. Nor was it nature only that was keeping carnival. It was the anniversary of the Great Fair, and it was the anniversary of the King's birthday. The river between Greenwich and London was one unbroken pageant. Farther than the eye could see stretched, with every sail crowded, two lines of merchant-ships drawn up to salute the royal barge, which, preceded by boats with bands of music, and followed by wherries rowed by men in gorgeous liveries, floated slowly past. Everywhere he could discern the signs of prosper-

---

* Quoted in the "Historical Memoirs" of the author of "The Henriade" (1778), where the writer speaks of having seen these verses in a letter in Voltaire's own handwriting, addressed to M. Dumas d'Aigueberc. † Duvernet, "Vie de Voltaire," p. 64.

ity and freedom. Loyal acclamations rent the air, and Voltaire observed with interest that a nation of freemen was a nation of dutiful subjects.

From the river he turned to the park, and, curious to see English society in all its phases, he spent the afternoon in observing what was going on. He wandered up and down the park, questioning such holiday-makers as could understand him, about the races, and the arrangements for the races. He admired the skill with which the young women managed their horses, and was greatly struck with the freshness and beauty of their complexions, the neatness of their dress, and the graceful vivacity of their movements. In the course of his rambles he accidentally met some English merchants to whom he had letters of introduction. By them he was treated with great courtesy and kindness. They lent him a horse, they provided him with refreshments, and they placed him where both the park and the river could be seen to most advantage. While he was enjoying the fine view from the hill, he perceived near him a Danish courier who had, like himself, just arrived in England. The man's face, says Voltaire, was radiant with joy; he believed himself to be in a paradise where the women were always beautiful and animated, where the sky was always clear, and where no one thought of anything but pleasure. "And I," he adds, "was even more enchanted than the Dane."*

The same evening he was in London, in all probability the guest of Bolingbroke. His acquaintance with that distinguished man had begun at La Source in the winter of 1721. Their acquaintance had soon ripened into intimacy, and though since then their personal intercourse had been interrupted, they had interchanged letters. At

* "Letter to A. M*** Mélanges," vol. i., p. 17 *sqq*.

that time Bolingbroke was an exile; he had recently obtained a pardon, and was now settled in England, where he divided his time between his town-house in Pall Mall and his country-house at Dawley. The friendship of Bolingbroke would have been a sufficient passport to the most brilliant literary circles in London, but as the connection of Bolingbroke lay principally among the Tories, the young adventurer had taken the precaution to secure a protector among the Whigs. The name of Bubb Dodington is now a synonyme for all that is vilest and most contemptible in the trade of politics, but at the time of which we are writing his few virtues were more prominent than his many vices. His literary accomplishments, his immense wealth, and his generous though not very discriminating patronage of men of letters, had deservedly given him a high place among the Mæcenases of his age. At his palace in Dorsetshire he loved to assemble the wits and poets of the Opposition, the most distinguished of whom were Thomson and Young—the one still busy with his Seasons, the other slowly elaborating his brilliant Satires. For his introduction to Dodington he was indebted to the English Ambassador at Paris, Horace Walpole the elder, who had, at the instigation of the Count de Morville, written a letter recommending him to the patronage of Dodington. How fully he availed himself of these and other influential friends is proved by the fact that when he quitted England in 1729 there was scarcely a single person of distinction, either in letters or politics, with whom he was not personally acquainted. But his most intimate associate was an opulent English merchant who resided at Wandsworth, and whose name was Everard Falkener. He had become acquainted with him in Paris, and had promised, should opportunity offer, to visit him in England.* Falkener's house he seems to have regarded as his home, and of Falkener himself he always speaks in terms of affection and gratitude. He dedicated "Zaïre" to him; he regularly corresponded with him; and to the end of his life he loved to recall the happy days spent under his good friend's hospitable roof at Wandsworth. Many years afterwards, when he wished to express his sense of the kindness he had received from King Stanislaus, he described him "as a kind of Falkener." Of Falkener few particulars have survived. We know from Voltaire that he was subsequently appointed Ambassador to Constantinople, that he held some appointment in Flanders, and that he was knighted. We gather from other sources that he became secretary to the Duke of Cumberland, and that he was one of the witnesses called on the trial of Simon Lord Lovat, in 1747. To this it may be added that he became, towards the end of George the Second's reign, one of the postmasters-general; that in 1747† he married a daughter of General Churchill; and that he died at Bath, November 16, 1758.‡ That Voltaire should have delighted in his society is not surprising, for though we know little of Falkener's character, we know enough to understand its charm. "I am here"—so runs a passage in one of his letters, quoted by Voltaire in his remarks upon Pascal—"just as you left me, neither merrier nor sadder, nor richer nor poorer; enjoying perfect health, having everything that renders life agreeable, without love, without avarice, without ambition, and without envy; and, as long as all that lasts, I shall call myself a very happy man." §

* Goldsmith's "Life of Voltaire," Miscellaneous Works, vol. iv., p. 20. † *Gentleman's Magazine* for February, 1747.
‡ *Gentleman's Magazine* for November, 1758.
§ "Œuvres Complètes," Beuchot, vol. xxxviii., p. 46.

To what extent Voltaire was acquainted with the English language on his arrival at Greenwich it is impossible to say. We can find no traces of his having been engaged in studying it before his retirement subsequent to the caning he received from the Chevalier de Rohan, at the beginning of February, 1726. If this was the case, what he knew of our language was what he had been able to pick up in about three months. His progress must have been unusually rapid, for he had not only made himself understood at Greenwich Fair, but on the following day he had mingled familiarly with the company at the coffee-houses. It is of course possible that the conversation had, on these occasions, been carried on in his native language. Then, as now, large numbers of French refugees had found a home in London. They had their own places of worship; they had their own coffee-houses, the principal being the "Rainbow," in Marylebone, and there was quite a colony of them at Wandsworth. Then, as now, almost all educated Englishmen were conversant with the language of Racine and Molière. Regularly as each season came round a Parisian company appeared. At Court it was the usual mode of communication. By 1728 its attainment was held to be so essential a part of education that in the October of that year a journal was started, the professed object of which was to facilitate the study of it.* Indeed, wherever he went he would encounter his countrymen, or Londoners who could converse with him in the language of his countrymen. In Bolingbroke's house he would probably hear little else, for Lady Bolingbroke scarcely ever ventured to express herself in English; and of Falkener's proficiency in French we have abundant proof. But

* See the *Flying Post* or *Weekly Medley*, the first number of which appeared on October 8, 1728.

among the cultivated Englishmen of that day there was one remarkable exception, and that was unfortunately in the case of a man with whom Voltaire was most anxious to exchange ideas. "Pope," wrote Voltaire many years afterwards, "could hardly read French, and spoke not one syllable of our language."* Voltaire's desire to meet Pope had no doubt been sharpened by the flattering remarks which Pope had, two years before, made about the "Henriade," or, as it was then entitled, "La Ligue." A copy of the poem had been forwarded to him from France by Bolingbroke, and to oblige Bolingbroke he had managed to spell it out. The perusal had given him, he said, a very favorable idea of the author, whom he pronounced to be "a bigot, but no heretic; one who knows authority and national sanctions without prejudice to truth and charity; in a word, one worthy of that share of friendship and intimacy with which you honor him."† These complimentary remarks Bolingbroke had, it seems, conveyed to Voltaire, and a correspondence appears to have ensued between the two poets, though no traces of that correspondence are now to be found.‡ Of his first interview with Pope three accounts are now extant. The first is that given by Owen Ruffhead, the substance of which is repeated by Johnson in his life of Pope; the second is that given by Goldsmith, and the third is that given by Duvernet. It will be well, perhaps, to let each authority tell his own story.

"Mr. Pope," writes Owen Ruffhead, "told one of his most intimate friends that the poet Voltaire had got some recommendation to him when he came to England, and that the first time he saw him was at

---

* See Spence's "Anecdotes" (Singer, 8vo.), p. 204, *note*.
† Letter to Bolingbroke, dated April 9, 1724.
‡ See Pope's letter to Caryl, dated December 25, 1725.

Twickenham, where he kept him to dinner. Mrs. Pope, a most excellent woman, was then alive, and observing that this stranger, who appeared to be entirely emaciated, had no stomach, she expressed her concern for his want of appetite, on which Voltaire gave her so indelicate and brutal an account of the occasion of his disorder, contracted in Italy, that the poor lady was obliged immediately to rise from the table. When Mr. Pope related that, his friend asked him how he could forbear ordering his servant John to thrust Voltaire head and shoulders out of his house? He replied that there was more of ignorance in this conduct than a purposed affront; that Voltaire came into England, as other foreigners do, on a prepossession that not only all religion, but all common decency of morals, was lost among us."—*Life of Pope*, 4to, p. 156.

Next comes Goldsmith:

"M. Voltaire has often told his friends that he never observed in himself such a succession of opposite passions as he experienced upon his first interview with Mr. Pope. When he first entered the room and perceived our poor, melancholy poet, naturally deformed, and wasted as he was with sickness and study, he could not help regarding him with the utmost compassion; but when Pope began to speak and to reason upon moral obligations, and dress the most delicate sentiments in the most charming diction, Voltaire's pity began to be changed into admiration, and at last even into envy. It is not uncommon with him to assert that no man ever pleased him so much in serious conversation, nor any whose sentiments mended so much upon recollection."—*Life of Voltaire*, Miscellaneous Works, vol. iv., p. 24.

It is difficult to reconcile these accounts with the narrative of Duvernet, who, as he almost certainly had his information from Thiériot, is an authority of great weight:

"Dans leur première entrevue ils furent fort embarrassés. Pope s'exprimait très péniblement en Français, et Voltaire n'étant point accoutumé aux sifflements de la langue Anglaise ne pourrait se faire entendre. Il se retira dans un village et ne rentra dans Londres que lorsqu'il eut acquis une grande facilité à s'exprimer en Anglais."

This seems to us by far the most probable account. It is certain that Voltaire devoted himself with great assiduity to the systematic study of English, shortly after his arrival among us. He provided himself with a regular teacher, who probably assisted him not only in the composition of his letters, which he now regularly wrote in English, but in the composition of his two famous essays.* He obtained an introduction to Colley Cibber, and regularly attended the theatres, following the play in a printed copy.† His studies were, however, interrupted by his suddenly leaving England for France—an expedition attended with considerable peril, and conducted with the utmost secrecy. The particulars of this journey are involved in great obscurity. That he undertook it with the object of inducing the Chevalier de Rohan to give him an opportunity of avenging his wounded honor—that for some time, at least, he remained concealed in Paris, not venturing to have an interview with any friend or with any relative—is clear from his letter to Thiériot, dated August 12, 1726. That he was at Wandsworth again, almost immediately afterwards, is proved by a letter to Mademoiselle Bessières, dated October the 15th, in which he speaks of himself as having been there for two months.

He arrived in England in a state of abject depression, and this depression was aggravated by ill-health and the cross accidents of fortune. He had brought with him a bill of exchange of the value of 20,000 francs, and this bill—as he was not in immediate need of money—he had neglected to present. On presenting it to the man on whom it had been drawn—one D'Acosta, a Jew—D'Acosta informed him that three days before he had become

---

* "La Voltairomanie," pp. 46, 47.
† Chetwood's "History of the Stage," p. 46.

bankrupt; and the money was lost. Voltaire's misfortune, however, happening to reach the ears of the King, the King good-naturedly sent him a sum which has been variously estimated, but which probably amounted to a hundred guineas, and so relieved him from pressing embarrassment. But what affected him most was the news of the death of his sister. This threw him into an agony of grief. There is nothing in the whole range of Voltaire's voluminous correspondence so touching as the letter in which his feelings on this sad occasion found vent. It was addressed to Mademoiselle Bessières, the lady who had sent the intelligence. It is dated "Wandsworth, October 15, 1726." He describes himself as acquainted only with the sorrows of life; he is dead, he says, to everything but the affection he owes to his correspondent. He alludes bitterly to the "retraite ignorée" from which he writes; and he says it would have been far better, both for his relatives and himself, had death removed him instead of his sister. "Les amertumes et les souffrances"—so run his gloomy reflections—"qui en ont marqué presque tous les jours ont été souvent mon ouvrage. Je sens la peu que je vaux; mes faiblesses me font pitié et mes fautes me font horreur." On the following day he wrote in a similar strain to Madame de Bernières. He was in deep distress, too, at the cruelty and injustice with which he had been treated by his brother; and to this distress he subsequently gave passionate utterance in a letter to Thiériot.* But neither depression nor sorrow ever held long dominion over that buoyant and volatile spirit. On the very day on which he was thus mournfully expressing himself to Madame de Bernières, he was, in another letter, dilating with

* See letter dated "Wandsworth, June 14, 1727," "Œuvres Complètes" (ed. 1880), vol. xxxiii., p. 172.

enthusiasm on the beauties of Pope's poetry. This we learn from a very interesting fragment preserved by Warburton in his notes to the "Epistle to Arbuthnot." As the fragment appears to have escaped the notice of all Voltaire's editors and biographers, and as it proves the very high opinion he entertained of Pope's genius, we will quote a portion of it:

"I look upon his poem called the 'Essay on Criticism' as superior to the 'Art of Poetry' of Horace, and his 'Rape of the Lock' is, in my opinion, above the 'Lutrin' of Despreaux. I never saw so amiable an imagination, so gentle graces, so great variety, so much wit, and so refined knowledge of the world, as in this little performance."

It would be interesting to know if this manuscript letter, which Warburton described as being before him when he wrote, is now in existence. It was dated October 15, 1726.*

Of his movements during the autumn of 1726 we know nothing. The probability is that he was engaged in close study, and saw little society. He instructs his correspondents in France to direct their letters to the care of Lord Bolingbroke; but he was evidently not in personal communication with Bolingbroke, or with any member of the Twickenham circle. This is proved by the fact that he knew nothing of the serious accident by which Pope nearly lost his life until two months after it had happened, as his letter to Pope, dated November the 16th, shows. Another letter,† too—a letter undated, but evidently belonging to this period and written in English—addressed to John Brinsden, Bolingbroke's secretary, points to the same conclusion. Very little, however, of the following year was

---

* Warburton's "Pope" (octavo edition), vol. iv., p. 40.
† Preserved in Colet's "Relics of Literature," p. 70.

spent in retirement, for we find traces of him in many places. His attenuated figure and eager, haggard face grew familiar to the frequenters of fashionable society. He passed three months at the seat of Lord Peterborough, where he became intimate with Swift,* who was a fellow-visitor. At Bubb Dodington's mansion, at Eastbury, he met Young, who had not as yet taken orders, but was seeking fortune as a hanger-on at great houses. It was a curious chance which brought together the future author of the "Night Thoughts" and the future author of "La Pucelle;" it was a still more curious circumstance that they should have formed a friendship which remained unbroken, when the one had become the most rigid of Christian divines, and the other the most daring of anti-Christian propagandists. Many years afterwards Young dedicated to him in very flattering terms one of the most pleasing of his minor poems—the Sea Piece.

At Eastbury occurred a well-known incident. A discussion had arisen as to the merits of "Paradise Lost." Young spoke in praise of his favorite poet; Voltaire, who had as little sympathy with Milton as he had with Æschylus and Dante, objected to the episode of Sin and Death, contending that as they were abstractions, it was absurd to assign them offices proper only to concrete beings. These objections he enforced with his usual eloquence and sarcastic wit. The parallel between the hungry monster of Milton, "grinning horrible its ghastly smile," and the meagre form of the speaker—his thin face lighted up, as it always was in conversation, with that peculiar sardonic

* See a very interesting extract from a MS. journal kept by a Major Broome, who visited Voltaire in 1765, and who heard this and other particulars from Voltaire himself. It is printed in "Notes and Queries" (first series), vol. x., p. 403.

smile familiar to us from his portraits—was irresistible. And Young closed the argument with an epigram (we quote Herbert Croft's version):

> "You are so witty, profligate, and thin,
> At once we think thee Milton, Death, and Sin."

It appears, however, from Young's poem, in which he plainly alludes to this conversation, that he succeeded in impressing on his friendly opponent "that Milton's blindness lay not in his song"—

> "On Dorset downs when Milton's page,
> With Sin and Death provoked thy rage,
> Thy rage provok'd, who sooth'd with gentle rhymes?
> Who kindly couch'd the censure's eye,
> And gave thee clearly to descry
> Sound judgment giving law to fancy strong?
> Who half inclin'd thee to confess,
> Nor could thy modesty do less,
> That Milton's blindness lay not in his song?"

A letter written about this time to a friend in France, dated by the editors—but dated, we suspect, wrongly—1726, is a sufficient proof that the young exile was no longer either discontented or unhappy. "You who are a perfect Briton"—thus the letter runs—"should cross the Channel and come to us. I assure you that a man of your temper would not dislike a country where one obeys to (*sic*) the laws only, and to one's whims. Reason is free here, and walks her own way. Hypochondriacs are especially welcome. No manner of living appears strange. We have men who walk six miles a day for their health, feed upon roots, never taste flesh, wear a coat in winter thinner than your ladies do in the hottest days."*

* "Pièces Inédites de Voltaire." Paris, 1820.

In March he was present at the funeral of Sir Isaac Newton. It was a spectacle which made a profound impression on him, and he ever afterwards delighted to recall how he had once been the denizen of a country in which the first officers of the State contended for the honor of supporting the pall of a man whose sole distinction had lain in intellectual eminence. How differently, he thought, would the author of the "Principia" have fared in Paris. He subsequently made the acquaintance of the philosopher's niece, Mrs. Conduit, and of the physician and surgeon who attended him in his last moments; from them he learned many interesting particulars. It is perhaps worth mentioning that we owe to Voltaire the famous story of the falling apple,* and the preservation of the reply which Newton is said to have given to the person who asked him how he had discovered the laws of the universe.

In the course of this year he met Gay, who showed him the "Beggar's Opera" before it appeared on the stage:† and it was probably in the course of this year that he paid his memorable visit to Congreve. His admiration of the greatest of our comic poets is sufficiently indicated in the "Lettres Philosophiques," and that admiration he lost no time in personally expressing. But Congreve, whose temper was probably not improved by gout and blindness, and who was irritated, perhaps, by the ebullience of his young admirer, affected to regard literary distinction as a trifle. "I beg," he said, "that you will look upon me, not as an author, but as a gentleman." "If," replied Voltaire, dis-

---

* "Lettres Philosophiques XV.," and "Éléments de la Philosophie de Newton," Partie III., chap. iii., where he says that he had heard the story from M. Conduit.

† MS. letter written by a Major Broome, who visited Voltaire in 1765: printed in "Notes and Queries" (first series), vol. x., p. 403.

gusted with his foppery, "you had had the misfortune to be simply a gentleman, I should not have troubled myself to wait upon you." To Congreve he owed, we suspect, his introduction to the Dowager Duchess of Marlborough, who not only communicated to him some interesting particulars which he afterwards wove into his "Siècle de Louis XIV." and into his "History of Charles XII.," but is said to have solicited his assistance in drawing up her memoirs. This task he at first consented to undertake. The Duchess laid the papers before him, and issued her instructions. Finding, however, that he was to write not as unbiassed historical justice required, but as her Grace's capricious prejudices dictated, he ventured to expostulate. Upon that her manner suddenly changed. Flying into a passion, she snatched the paper from him, muttering, "I thought the man had sense; but I find him, at bottom, either a fool or a philosopher." The story is told by Goldsmith;* it would be interesting to know on what authority.

Another story, resting, it is true, on no very satisfactory testimony, but in itself so intrinsically probable that we are inclined to believe it genuine, is related by Desnoiresterres. Voltaire, hearing that the Duchess was engaged in preparing her memoirs for publication, ventured to ask if he might be permitted to glance at the manuscript. "You must wait a little," she said, "for I am revising it;" coolly observing that the conduct of the Government had so disgusted her that she had determined to recast the character of Queen Anne, "as I have," she added, "since these creatures have been our rulers, come to love her again." Pope's Atossa was assuredly no caricature, and a better commentary on it it would be impossible to find.

* "Life of Voltaire," Miscellaneous Works, vol. iv., p. 25.

Like most of his countrymen, Voltaire appears to have been greatly struck with the beauty of the English women, and about this time he became acquainted with one whose charms have been more frequently celebrated than those of any other woman of that age. Voltaire was one of the thousand adorers of Molly Lepel, then the wife of Lord Hervey. To her he addressed a copy of verses which are interesting, as being the only verses now extant composed by him in English. Their intrinsic merit is not, it must be admitted, of a high order, but as a literary curiosity they will bear repetition—

> "Hervey, would you know the passion
> You have kindled in my breast?
> Trifling is the inclination
> That by words can be express'd.

> "In my silence see the lover—
> True love is best by silence known;
> In my eyes you'll best discover
> All the power of your own."

A curious fortune attended these verses. They were subsequently transcribed and addressed to a lady named Laura Harley—the wife of a London merchant—by one of her gallants, and they formed a part of the evidence on which her husband grounded his claim for a divorce.* This has misled Mr. Parton, who supposes that Voltaire wrote them, not in honor of Lady Hervey, but in honor of poor Mr. Harley's erring wife. That they awoke no jealousy in Lord Hervey is proved by Voltaire's letter to Thiériot, dated April, 1732, and by a letter he addressed

---

* This circumstance is mentioned by Châteauneuf in his "Les Divorces Anglais," vol. i., pp. xxxv., xxxvi. "Notions Preliminaires," and is discussed by Desnoiresterres, "La Jeunesse de Voltaire," p. 387.

to Hervey himself in 1740. But the beautiful wife of Lord Hervey was not the only lady distinguished by the admiration of Voltaire. He has spoken in rapturous terms of the graces and accomplishments of Lady Bolingbroke, for whom he finds a place in his "Siècle de Louis XIV.;" and an unpublished letter in the British Museum shows that he had paid assiduous court to Lady Sundon, who had evidently not been insensible to his flattery.*

And now we come to a very curious story, a story which is related in detail by Ruffhead, and has been repeated by Johnson. It had long been suspected by Pope and Bolingbroke that Voltaire was playing a double part; in other words, that he had formed a secret alliance with the Court party, and was acting as their spy. Their suspicion was soon confirmed. In February, 1727, appeared the third of a series of letters in which the character and policy of Walpole were very severely handled. The letter was written with unusual energy and skill; it attracted much attention, and Walpole's friends were anxious to discover the author. While it was still the theme of conversation Voltaire came to Twickenham, and asked Pope if he could tell him who wrote it. Pope, seeing his object, and wishing to prove him, informed him in the strictest confidence that he was himself the author of it, "and," he added, "I trust to your honor as a gentleman, Mr. Voltaire, that you will communicate this secret to no living soul." The letter had really been written by Bolingbroke, and bore in truth no traces of Pope's style; but the next day every one at Court was speaking of it as Pope's composition, and Voltaire's treachery was manifest. To this Bolingbroke apparently alludes in a letter to Swift (May the 18th, 1727): "I would have you insinuate that the only reason Walpole

* Brit. Mus. Add. MSS., 20,105.

can have to ascribe them (*i.e.*, the occasional letters just alluded to) to a particular person is the authority of one of his spies, who wriggles himself into the company of those who neither love, esteem, nor fear the Minister, that he may report, not what he hears, since no man speaks with any freedom before him, but what he guesses." Conduct so scandalous as this ought not to be lightly imputed to any man, and it would be satisfactory to know that Voltaire had either been traduced or misrepresented. It is not likely, however, that the story was invented by Warburton, from whom Ruffhead almost certainly obtained it, and there is, moreover, strong presumptive evidence in its favor. Voltaire had undoubtedly been meddling with the matter, for in a letter to Thiériot, dated May 27, 1727, he says: "Do not talk of the Occasional Writer. Do not say that it is not of my Lord Bolingbroke. Do not say that it is a wretched performance. You cannot be judge." It is certain that he twice received money from the Court; it is certain that he visited Walpole, and that he sought every opportunity to ingratiate himself with the King and with the King's friends. It is clear that neither Pope nor any member of Pope's circle had much confidence in him. Bolingbroke has indeed expressly declared that he believed him capable of double-dealing and insincerity,* and what Bolingbroke observed in him was observed also by Young.† Nor was such conduct at all out of keeping with the general tenor of Voltaire's behavior during his residence among us. Throughout, his aims were purely selfish, and to attain his ends he resorted to means which no man of an honest and independent spirit would have stooped to use.

* See his letter to Madame de Ferriole, dated December, 1725; "Lettres Historiques," vol. iii., p. 274.
† Spence's "Anecdotes," p. 285.

It would perhaps be unduly harsh to describe him as a parasite and a sycophant; but it is nevertheless true that he too often figures in a character closely bordering on both. His correspondence — and his conversation no doubt resembled his correspondence — is almost sickening. His compliments are so fulsome, his flattery so exaggerated, that they might excusably be mistaken for elaborate irony. He seems to be always on his knees. There was scarcely a distinguished man then living in England who had not been the object of this nauseous homage. He pours it indiscriminately on Pope, Swift, Gay, Clarke, on half the Cabinet and on half the peerage. In a man of this character falsehood and hypocrisy are of the very essence of his composition. There is nothing, however base, to which he will not stoop; there is no law in the code of social honor which he is not capable of violating.* The fact that he continued to remain on friendly terms with Pope and Bolingbroke can scarcely be alleged as a proof of his innocence, for neither Pope nor Bolingbroke would, for such an offence, be likely to quarrel with a man in a position so peculiar as that of Voltaire. His flattery was pleasant, and his flattery, as they well knew, might some day be worth having. No injuries are so readily overlooked as those which affect neither men's purses nor men's vanity. Another disagreeable trait in Voltaire's social character was the gross impropriety of his conversation, even in the presence of those whose age and sex should have been sufficient protection from such annoyance. In one of his visits to Pope his talk was, as has been already mentioned, so offensive that it absolutely drove Mrs. Pope out of the room.†

---

* For an illustration of Voltaire's duplicity and meanness in social life, see Horace Walpole's "Short Notes of my Life."

† Johnson's "Life of Pope," Ruffhead's "Life of Pope."

Meanwhile he was diligently collecting materials which were afterwards embodied in his "Lettres Philosophiques," his "Dictionnaire Philosophique," his "Siècle de Louis XIV.," and his "Histoire de Charles XII." First he investigated the history and tenets of the Quakers. With this object he sought the acquaintance of Andrew Pitt, "one of the most eminent Quakers in England, who having traded thirty years, had the wisdom to prescribe limits to his fortune and desires and settled in a little solitude at Hampstead."* And it was in this solitude at Hampstead that Voltaire visited him, dining with him twice. He attended, also, a Quaker's meeting, of which he gives a very amusing account, near the Monument. The substance of his conversation with Pitt, supplemented by his own independent study of Quaker literature, he has embodied in the article on Quakers in the "Philosophical Dictionary" and in the first four "Philosophical Letters." He investigated the various religious sects into which English Protestantism had divided itself, and to these schisms he somewhat paradoxically ascribes the harmony and contentment reigning in the religious world of England. "If," he observes, "only one religion were allowed in England, the government would very possibly become arbitrary; if there were but two, the people would cut one another's throats; but as there are such a multitude, they all live happy and in peace." He studied the economy of the Established Church, and the habits and character of the clergy. Our commerce, our finance, and our government each engaged his attention, and on each he has commented with his usual superficial cleverness. Three things he observed with especial pleasure, because they contrasted so strongly with

* See obituary notice of Pitt in the London *Daily Post* for April, 1736.

what he had been accustomed to witness in France. He found himself for the first time in his life in the midst of a free people, a people who lived unshackled save by laws which they had themselves enacted; a people who, enjoying the inestimable privilege of a free Press, were, in the phrase of Tacitus, at liberty to think what they pleased and to publish what they thought. He beheld a splendid and powerful aristocracy, not, as in Paris, standing contemptuously aloof from science and letters, but themselves not unfrequently eager candidates for literary and scientific distinction. The names of many of these noble authors he has recorded, and they are, he adds, more glorious for their works than for their titles. With not less pleasure he beheld the honorable rank assigned in English society to a class who were in the Faubourg St. Germain regarded with disdain. Voltaire was perhaps the first writer of eminence in Europe who had the courage to vindicate the dignity of trade. He relates with pride how, when the Earl of Oxford held the reins of Great Britain in his hands, his younger brother was a factor at Aleppo; how, when Lord Townshend was directing the councils of his Sovereign in the Painted Chamber, one of his nearest relatives was soliciting custom in a counting-house in the City. He draws a sarcastic parallel between a "seigneur, powdered, in the tip of the mode, who knows exactly what o'clock the King rises and goes to bed, and who gives himself airs of grandeur and state at the same time that he is acting the slave in the antechamber of a Prime-minister," and a merchant who enriches his country, despatches orders from his counting-house to Surat and Grand Cairo, and contributes to the felicity of the world.*

* See the remarkable passage at the end of the tenth letter in the "Lettres Philosophiques."

But nothing impressed him so deeply as the homage paid, and paid by all classes, to intellectual eminence. Parts and genius were, he observed, a sure passport not, as in France, to the barren wreath of the Academy, but to affluence and popularity. By his pen Addison had risen to one of the highest offices of the State. A few graceful poems had made the fortunes of Stepney, Prior, Gay, Parnell, Tickell, and Ambrose Philipps. By his Essays Steele had won a Commissionership of Stamps and a place in Parliament. A single comedy had made Congreve independent for life. Newton was Master of the Mint, and Locke had been a Commissioner of Appeals. He records with pride that the portrait of Walpole was to be seen only in his own closet, but that the portraits of Pope were to be seen in half the great houses in England. "Go," he says, "into Westminster Abbey, and you find that what raises the admiration of the spectator is not the mausoleums of the English Kings, but the monuments which the gratitude of the nation has erected to perpetuate the memory of those illustrious men who contributed to its glory." He thought bitterly how in his own country he had seen Crébillon on the verge of perishing by hunger, and the son of Racine on the last stage of abject destitution. When, too, on his return to France, he saw the body of poor Adrienne Lecouvreur refused the last rites of religion, and buried with the burial of a dog, "because she was an actress," his thoughts wandered to the generous and large-hearted citizens who laid the coffin of Anne Oldfield beside the coffins of their kings and of their heroes.

> "O rivale d'Athène, O Londres! heureuse terre,
> Ainsi que les tyrans, vous avez su chasser
> Les préjugés honteux qui vous livraient la guerre.
> C'est là qu'on sait tout dire et tout récompenser.

> Nul art n'est méprisé, tout succès a sa gloire.
> Le vainqueur de Tallard, le fils de la victoire,
> Le sublime Dryden, et le sage Addison,
> Et la charmante Oldfield, et l'immortel Newton
>   Ont part au temple de mémoire,
> Et Lecouvreur à Londre aurait eu des tombeaux
> Parmi les beaux-esprits, les rois et les héros.
> Quiconque a des talents à Londre est un grand homme."
>   *La Mort de Mlle. Lecouvreur.*

In January, 1727, he had the honor to be introduced to the King, who received him very graciously.* At the end of June he obtained permission from the French Government to visit Paris, but it was on the understanding that he was not to remain there for more than three months, counting from the day of his arrival. If that time was exceeded, it was exceeded at his peril. Of the particulars of this visit nothing is known. It is even doubtful whether he undertook it. If it was undertaken it was, like the former visit, kept a profound secret, even from his most intimate friends.†

SECTION II.

NOVEMBER, 1727—MARCH, 1728.

AMONG the Ashburnham MSS.‡ there is a curious relic of Voltaire's residence in England. It is the Common-

---

* *British Journal*, January 28, 1726–27, where a special paragraph is inserted to commemorate this interview.

† Desnoiresterres asserts that Voltaire did not avail himself of the permission given, but remained in England, and this is certainly borne out, not only by the absence of any proof of his absence from England, but by Voltaire's own letter to Thiériot, absurdly dated by the editors 1753, properly to be dated end of 1728, or spring of 1729.

‡ Barrois, 653. For permission to inspect these most curious notes I am indebted to the courtesy and kindness of Lord Ashburnham.

place-book in which he entered from time to time such things as struck him, either in his reading or in what he heard in conversation. The memoranda, which are interspersed with extracts from Italian and Latin poets, are in English and French, and they range from traditionary witticisms of Rochester, often grossly indecent, and from equally indecorous anecdotes and verses picked up no doubt in taverns and coffee-houses, to notes evidently intended for the dedication to "Brutus," the "Life of Charles XII.," and the "Letters Philosophiques," and to fragments of original poems and translations. They unfortunately throw no light on his personal life, beyond communicating the not very important fact that he kept a footman.

The variety and extent of Voltaire's English studies are, considering his comparatively short residence in this country, and his numerous occupations during that residence, amazing. He surveyed us on all sides, and his survey was not confined to the living world before him; it extended back to the world of the past, for, as his writings prove, he was versed both in our antiquities and in our history. But the subjects which most interested him were, as was natural, philosophy and polite letters. In philosophy two great movements were at this time passing over England; the one was in a scientific, the other in a theological or metaphysical direction; the one emanated from Bacon and Newton, the other from that school of deists which, originating with Herbert and Hobbes, had found its modern exponents in Tyndal, Toland, Collins, and Woolston. His guides in these studies were Bolingbroke and Dr. Samuel Clarke. Of all Newton's disciples, Clarke was the most generally accomplished. In theology, in metaphysics, in natural science, in mathematics, and in pure scholarship, he was almost equally distinguished. He had lived on terms of close intimacy with Newton, whose "Optics" he had translated into Latin. He was as minutely versed in the writings of Bacon and Locke as in the writings of Descartes and Leibnitz; and of the learned controversies of his time there was scarcely one in which he had not taken a leading part. With this eminent man Voltaire first came into contact in the autumn of 1726. At that time their conversation turned principally on metaphysics. Voltaire was fascinated by the boldness of Clarke's views, and blindly followed him. In his own expressive phrase, "Clarke sautait dans l'abîme, et j'osai l'y suivre." But he soon recovered himself, and was on firm ground again.

His acquaintance with Clarke probably led to his acquaintance with another distinguished disciple of Newton. This was Dr. Henry Pemberton. Pemberton was then busy preparing for the press the first popular exposition of Newton's system, a work which appeared in 1728 under the title of "A View of Sir Isaac Newton's Philosophy." It is clear that Voltaire had seen this work either in proof or in manuscript. For in a letter to Thiériot, dated some months before the treatise was published, he speaks of it in a manner which implies that he had inspected it. It was most likely under Pemberton's auspices that he commenced the study of the "Principia" and "Optics" which he afterwards resumed more seriously at Cirey. That the work was of immense service to him in his Newtonian studies is certain. Indeed his own account of the Newtonian philosophy in the "Lettres Philosophiques," and in the "Eléments de la Philosophie de Newton," is in a large measure based on Pemberton's exegesis.

From Newton, whose "Metaphysics" disgusted him, he proceeded to Locke. Locke's "Essay" he perused and reperused with delight. It became his philosophical gospel. In his writings and in his conversation he scarcely ever alluded to it except in terms of almost extravagant eulogy; and to Locke he remained loyal to the last. "For thirty years," he writes in a letter dated July, 1768, "I have been persecuted by a crowd of fanatics because I said that Locke is the Hercules of Metaphysics, who has fixed the boundaries of the human mind."* His acquaintance with Bacon was probably slight, and what he knew of his Latin works was, we suspect, what he had picked up in conversation from Bolingbroke and Clarke. No man who had read the "Novum Organum " would speak of it as Voltaire speaks of it in his Twelfth Letter. But Bacon's English writings, the "Essays," that is to say, and the History of Henry VII., he had certainly consulted. He appears also to have turned over the works of Hobbes and Cudworth. Berkeley he knew personally, and though he was, he said, willing to profess himself one of that great philosopher's admirers, he was not inclined to become one of his disciples. How carefully he had read "Alciphron" is proved by his letter to Andrew Pitt.† Nor did his indefatigable curiosity rest here. He took a lively interest in natural science, and was acquainted with several members of the Royal Society, and particularly with the venerable President, Sir Hans Sloane, to whom he presented a copy of the English Essays.‡ Of that society he was

---

* See the very interesting letter to Horace Walpole printed in the appendix to the "Historical Memoirs of the Author of the Henriade."

† This interesting letter, written in English, is printed in Leonard Howard's "Collection of Letters," p. 604. Howard's character was not above suspicion, but there seems no reason for questioning the genuineness of this letter, the original of which was, he says, in the hands of one of his friends.

‡ See the copy with the autograph inscription in the British Museum.

some years after elected a Fellow, as the archives of the Society still testify.*

But what most engaged his attention was the controversy then raging between the opponents and the apologists of Christianity. It was now at its height. Upward of two years had passed since Anthony Collins had published his "Discourse on the Grounds and Reasons of the Christian Religion." No work of that kind had made so deep an impression on the public mind. It had been denounced from the pulpit; it had elicited innumerable replies from the press. Other works of a similar kind succeeded, each in its turn aggravating the controversy. In 1727 appeared, dedicated to the Bishop of London, the first of Woolston's "Six Discourses on the Miracles of Christ," a work which brought into the field the most distinguished ecclesiastics then living. We believe that Voltaire owed infinitely more to Bolingbroke than to all the other English deists put together, but how carefully he had followed the course of this controversy is obvious from innumerable passages in his subsequent writings. Of Woolston, in particular, he always speaks with great respect, and he has, in an article in the "Dictionnaire Philosophique," given a long and appreciative account of the labors of that courageous freethinker. Nor was his admiration confined to mere eulogy, for when, three years later, Woolston was imprisoned and fined for his heterodox opinions, Voltaire at once wrote off from France voluntarily to be responsible for a third of the sum required.†

In the winter of 1727 he published a little volume, which is not only among the curiosities, but among the

---

* He was elected a Fellow on November 3, 1743.—*Archives of the Royal Society.*

† Duvernet, "Vie de Voltaire," p. 72.

marvels of literature. It contained two essays. The first was entitled "An Essay upon the Civil Wars in France," the other, "An Essay upon Epic Poetry." Both these essays are composed in English—not in such English as we should expect to find written by one who had acquired the language, but in such English as would in truth have reflected no discredit on Dryden or Swift. If we remember that at the time when he accomplished this feat he had only been eighteen months in England, and that he was, as he informs us in the preface, writing in a language which he was scarcely able to follow in conversation, his achievement may be fairly pronounced to be without parallel in linguistic triumphs.* As the work is neither generally known nor very accessible, we will transcribe a short extract from each discourse. The first essay is an historical sketch of the civil troubles in France between the accession of Francis the Second and the reconciliation of Henry the Fourth with the Church of Rome. The character and position of the Protestants are thus described:

"The Protestants began then to grow numerous, and to be conscious of their strength. The superstition, the dull, ignorant knavery of the monks, the overgrown power of Rome, men's passions for novelty, the ambition of Luther and Calvin, the policy of many princes—all these had given rise and countenance to this sect, free indeed from superstition, but running as headlong towards anarchy as the Church of Rome towards tyranny. The Protestants had been unmercifully persecuted in France, but it is the ordinary effect of persecution to make proselytes. Their sect increased every day amid the scaffolds and tortures. Condé, Coligni, the two brothers of Coligni, all their adherents, all who were opposed by the Guises, turned Protestants at once.

---

* He told Martin Sherlock that he was never able to pronounce the English language perfectly, but that his ear was sensitively alive to the harmony of the language and the poetry.—*Letters from an English Traveller* (Letter xxv.).

They united their griefs, their vengeance, and their interests together, so that a revolution both in the State and in religion was at hand."

The second essay, which is a dissertation on Epic Poetry, and a review of the principal epic poems of antiquity and of modern Europe, is a piece not unworthy of a place beside the best of Dryden's prefaces. The remarks on Virgil, Lucan, and Tasso are admirable, and the critique on "Paradise Lost," which is described as "the noblest work which human imagination hath ever attempted," gives us a higher idea of Voltaire's critical powers than any of his French writings. For the account of Camoens he is said to have been indebted to Colonel Martin Bladen. "I remember," says Warton, in his notes on the "Dunciad" "that Collins the poet told me that [his uncle] Bladen had given to Voltaire all that account of Camoens inserted in his Essay on the Epic Poets, and that Voltaire seemed before entirely ignorant of the name and character of Camoens."* Indeed the whole treatise well deserves attentive study. The purity, vigor, and elegance of the style will be at once evident from the following extract, which is, we may add, a fair average sample:

"The greatest part of the critics have filched the rules of epic poetry from the books of Homer, according to the custom, or rather to the weakness, of men who mistake commonly the beginning of an art for the principles of the art itself, and are apt to believe that everything must be by its own nature what it was when contrived at first. But

---

* Warton's "Pope," vol. v., p. 284. Though Warton has in this passage confused Martin Bladen, the translator of "Cæsar's Commentaries," with Edmund Bladen, who was Collins's uncle, there is no reason for doubting the substantial truth of what he reports. That Colonel Martin Bladen had some special acquaintance with Spanish and Portuguese seems certain, from the fact that in 1717 he was offered the Envoyship Extraordinary to the Court of Spain, and that in his will he leaves legacies to Dr. de Arboleda and Josias Luberdo.

as Homer wrote two poems of a quite different nature, and as the 'Æneid' of Virgil partakes of the 'Iliad' and of the 'Odyssey,' the commentators were forced to establish different rules to reconcile Homer with himself, and other new rules again to make Virgil agree with Homer, just as the astronomers labored under the necessity of adding to or taking from their systems, and of bringing in concentric and eccentric circles, as they discovered new motions in the heavens. The ignorance of the ancients was excusable, and their search after the unfathomable system of nature was to be commended, because it is certain that nature hath its own principles, unvariable and unerring, and as worthy of our search as remote from our conceptions. But it is not with the inventions of art as with the works of nature."

If Voltaire was able after a few months' residence in London to produce such prose as this, it is not too much to say that he might with time and practice have taken his place among our national classics. With the exceptions of De Lolme and Blanco White, it may be doubted whether any writer to whom English was an acquired language has achieved so perfect a mastery over it. It is, however, not improbable that he obtained more assistance in composing these essays than his vanity would allow him to own. The Abbé Desfontaines asserts, indeed, that the Essay on Epic Poetry was composed in French, and that it was then translated into English under the superintendence of Voltaire's "maître de langue."* But the testimony of that mean and malignant man carries little weight, and if it had not been partially, at least, confirmed by Spence we should have left it unnoticed. What Spence says is this: " Voltaire consulted Dr. Young about his essay in English, and begged him to correct any gross faults he might find in it. The doctor set very honestly to work, marked the passages most liable to censure, and when he went to explain himself about them, Voltaire could not avoid burst-

* "La Voltairomanie," p. 46.

ing out a-laughing in his face." The reason of this ill-timed merriment it is not very easy to see: the anecdote is, perhaps, imperfectly reported. But in spite of Desfontaines and Spence, there can be no doubt that the Essays are what they pretend to be, the genuine work of Voltaire. We have only to turn to his English correspondence at this period to see that he was quite equal to their production. The little book was favorably received. In the following year a second edition was called for, a third followed at no long interval, and in 1731 it reached a fourth; a Discourse on Tragedy, which is merely a translation of the French "Discours sur la Tragédie" prefixed to Brutus, being added. And it long held its own. Its popularity is sufficiently attested by the fact that in 1760 it was reprinted at Dublin, with a short notice attributed, but attributed erroneously, to Swift, who had of course been long dead.

Voltaire was not the man to waste his energy on the production of a mere *tour de force*. The volume had an immediate practical object. That object was to prepare the public for the appearance of the "Henriade," which was now receiving the finishing touches, and was almost ready for the printer. It was probably to facilitate its publication that he removed about this time (end of 1727) from Wandsworth to London, where he resided, as the superscriptions of two of his letters show, in Maiden Lane, Covent Garden, at the sign of the White Peruke. Nor is Maiden Lane the only part of London associated with Voltaire during this period. It would seem that Billiter Square is entitled to the honor of having once numbered him among its occupants. This we gather from an undated letter addressed to John Brinsden, Bolingbroke's confidential secretary,* in which Brinsden is directed to ad-

* Preserved in Colet's "Relics of Literature," p. 70.

dress his reply to Mr. Cavalier, Belitery (*sic*) Square, by the Royal Exchange, a request which Voltaire would scarcely have made had he not been residing there. In Billiter Square, which is described by a contemporary topographer as "a very handsome, open, and airy place, with good new brick buildings," he would be within a few paces of his agents, Messrs. Simon & Benczet.

Of the many letters which were doubtless written by him at this time, some have been preserved. One is addressed to Swift, to whom he had a few months before given a letter of introduction to the Count de Morville. He sends him a copy of the Essays, professes himself a great admirer of his writings, informs him that the "Henriade" is almost ready, and asks him to exert his interest to procure subscribers in Ireland. In another letter he solicits the patronage of the Earl of Oxford, informing him of the distinguished part which one of his ancestors plays in the "Henriade," alluding to his own personal acquaintance with Achilles de Harley, and importuning the earl to grant him the favor of an interview.* With Thiériot, on whom he relied to push the poem in France, he regularly corresponded. Meanwhile popular curiosity was stimulated by successive advertisements in the newspapers, and in January, 1728, an elaborate puff appeared in the columns of the leading literary periodical: "We hope every day," so runs the notice, "to see Mr. De Voltaire's 'Henriade.' He has greatly raised the expectations of the curious by a beautiful Essay he lately published upon the Civil Wars of France, which is the subject of his poem, and upon the Epic Poets, from Homer down to Milton. As this gentleman seems to be thoroughly acquainted with all the best poets, both an-

* Unprinted letter among the manuscripts at Longleat, for a copy of which I am indebted to the kindness of the librarian.

cient and modern, and judges so well of their beauties and
faults, we have reason to hope that the 'Henriade' will be
a finished performance, and as he writes with uncommon
elegance and force in English, though he has been but eighteen months in this country, we expect to find in his poem
all that beauty and strength of which his native language
is capable."*

All through the summer and winter of 1727 he was
hard at work on the manuscript or the proofs.† But this
was not the only task he had in hand. He was busy with
his "Essai sur la Poésie Epique," which is not, he is careful to explain, a translation of his English essay, but an
independent work, a work of which the English essay was
to be regarded as the preliminary sketch.‡ It was afterwards prefixed to the "Henriade." A comparative study
of the two will show with what skill he adapts himself,
even as a critic, to the countrymen of Boileau and Racine
on the one hand, and to the countrymen of Milton and
Addison on the other.

At last the "Henriade" was ready. It was first announced, in a succession of advertisements, that it would
appear in February (1728); it was then announced in a
second succession of advertisements that it would appear
in March, and in March it was published. The subscribers
had at first been alarmingly slow in coming forward; but
when the day of publication arrived the names on the subscription list amounted to three hundred and forty-four;
and among the subscribers were the King, the Queen, and
the heads of almost all the noble families connected with
the Court. In its first form the poem had been dedicated

* "Present State of the Republic of Letters," vol. i., p. 88.
† Letter to Thiériot, dated August, 1728.
‡ See his English letter to Thiériot, dated 14th of June, 1727.

to Louis XV. That dedication was now cancelled, and a dedication, written in flowing English, to Queen Caroline was substituted. Descartes, said the poet, had inscribed his "Principles" to the Princess Palatine Elizabeth, not because she was a princess, but because of all his readers she understood him best; he too, without presuming to compare himself to Descartes, had ventured to lay his work at the feet of a queen who was not only a patroness of all arts and sciences, but the best judge of them also. "He reminded her that an English Queen, the great Elizabeth, had been the protectress of Henry IV., and by whom," he asked, "can the memory of Henry be so well protected as by one who so much resembles Elizabeth in her personal virtues?" The Queen was not insensible of the honor which had been paid her, and the fortunate poet received a substantial mark of the royal gratitude. It is not easy to determine the exact sum. Voltaire himself states it to have been two thousand crowns (*écus*), which would, supposing he means English crowns, have been equivalent to five hundred pounds sterling. Baculard says it was "six mille livres."[*] Nor was this all. The King honored him with his intimacy, and invited him to his private supper parties.[†] Goldsmith adds, but adds erroneously, that the Queen presented him with her portrait. A portrait of Queen Caroline Voltaire certainly possessed, but it was a medallion, and it came to him, not from the Queen herself, but through the hands of the Countess de la Lippe from the Queen of Prussia.[‡] The poem succeeded beyond his most sanguine expectation. Every

---

[*] Préface d'une édition des Œuvres de M. de Voltaire, Longchamp et Wagnière, vol. ii., p. 492.

[†] *Ibid.*, same page.

[‡] Voltaire, "Correspondance Générale," July 22d, 1728.

copy of the quarto impression was disposed of before the day of publication. In the octavo form, three editions were exhausted in less than three weeks, "and this I attribute," he says in a letter to a friend, "entirely to the happy choice of the subject, and not to the merit of the poem itself." Owing to the carelessness of Thiériot, he lost the subscription money due to him from France, but the sum realized in England was undoubtedly considerable. It has been variously estimated: Nicolardot, in his "Menage et Finances de Voltaire," calculates it to have been ten thousand francs; and that is the lowest computation. Baculard asserts that from the quarto edition (*edition imprimée par souscriptions*) alone the poet cleared ten thousand crowns. Perhaps we should not be far wrong if we estimated the sum, including the money received from George II., at two thousand pounds sterling. Whatever it was, it formed the nucleus of the most princely fortune ever yet amassed by a man of letters.* The publication of the "Henriade" involved Voltaire in a very disagreeable controversy with two of his countrymen. He had out of pure kindness given permission to one Coderc, a publisher in Little Newport Street, near Leicester Fields, to print an edition of the poem for his own benefit; of this permission Coderc made an assignment to another publisher named Prévost. Accordingly in March, 1728, almost immediately after the appearance of the authentic editions, appeared in the *Daily Post* an announcement of a new issue of the "Henriade." It was printed—so it was stated—with the author's privilege, and to the advertisement a postscript was added to the effect that the poem now appeared for the first time

---

* Carlyle ("Life of Frederick," vol. iii., p. 220) computes Voltaire's annual income during his latter years to have been, according to the money value of the present day, about £20,000.

uncastrated and in its integrity. All that Prévost had really done was to substitute six bad verses, taken from the poem in its earlier form, for six good verses in the later recension. Voltaire, justly annoyed at this audacious stratagem on the part of a piratical bookseller, at once replied by inserting a counter advertisement both in the *Daily Post* and in the *Daily Journal:* "This is to give notice that I never gave any privilege to Prévost, but I was betrayed into such kindness for one Coderc as to grant him leave of printing my book for his own benefit, provided he should sell none before mine had been delivered. It is a thing unheard of that a bookseller dares to sell my own work in another manner than I have printed it and call my own edition castrated. The truth of the matter is that he has printed six bad and insignificant low lines, which were not mine, printed in a former edition of 'La Ligue,' and in the room of which there are six others a great deal bolder and stronger in the Henriade."* To this Prévost replied in the columns of the same paper, defending the course he had taken, and flatly contradicting what Voltaire asserted. The two notices continued to appear in the advertisement sheet of the *Daily Post* till the end of March. There can be no doubt that this controversy was of great service in advertising the poem. Indeed we are half inclined to suspect that the whole thing was got up by Voltaire for that purpose. He certainly bore Prévost no ill-will afterwards.† The money realized from the sale of the "Henriade" was the more acceptable as it was sorely needed. For upwards of a year he had

---

* *Daily Post*, March 21, 1728.

† For the controversy, see advertisement sheets of the *Daily Post* from March 21st to March 30th, and of the *Daily Journal* of same date.

been in straightened circumstances. To live in society was then an expensive luxury, and the expenses were greatly swelled by the fees which the servants of the aristocracy were permitted to levy on their masters' guests. At no house in London did the abuse reach a higher pitch than at Lord Chesterfield's; and Voltaire, who dined there once, was so annoyed at the imposition, that, on Chesterfield asking him to repeat his visit, he declined, sarcastically adding that his lordship's ordinary was too dear.* His wretched health had, moreover, necessitated medical attendance and thus had added greatly to his expenses. As early as February, 1727, we find him complaining of these difficulties to Thiériot: "Vous savez peut-être que les banqueroutes sans ressource que j'ai essuyées en Angleterre" (an allusion of course to his mishap with Acosta), "le retranchement de mes rentes, la perte de mes pensions, et les dépenses que m'ont coûtées les maladies dont j'ai été accablé ici, m'ont réduit à un état bien dur."† He was now enabled to relieve the necessities of his unfortunate fellow-countrymen, many of whom were assisted by him when he was in London, particularly one St. Hyacinthe.‡

When the poem was passing through the press a curious incident occurred. A proof-sheet of the first page had by some accident found its way into the hands of one Dadichy, a Smyrniote Greek, who was at that time residing as an interpreter in London, and who appears to have been a scholar of some pretensions. The poem then opened, not with the simple ringing verses with which it now opens,

* John Taylor's "Memoirs," vol. i., p. 330.
† "Correspondance Générale," 1727.
‡ Duvernet, p. 72.

but with a series of verses of which the first couplet may serve as a specimen:

> "Je chante les combats et ce roi généreux,
> Qui força les Français à devenir heureux."

The man whose taste had been formed on purer models was justly offended by this obscure and forced epigram. He made his way to Voltaire's residence, and abruptly announcing himself as the "countryman of Homer," proceeded to inform him that Homer never opened his poems with strokes of wit and enigmas. Voltaire had the good sense to take the hint given him by his eccentric visitor, and the lines were altered into the lines with which all the world is familiar.*

We have not, after a careful search, been able to find any notice or critique of the "Henriade" in journals then current in London. But before the year was out there appeared in an edition, published by a firm in Russell Street, Covent Garden, some remarks which are, no doubt, a fair indication of the impression made by the poem on the mind of contemporary England. The writer, who writes in French, begins by observing that as a rule he cares little for French poetry, it lacks energy, and it is monotonous, but in the "Henriade" he discerns qualities which he has not discerned elsewhere in the verse of Frenchmen; it is various, brilliant, and forcible. But he is, he says, at a loss to understand how a poet whose conception of the deity is so wise and noble could have selected for his hero a character so contemptible as Henri Quatre, who was not merely a Papist but a Papist "par lâche intérest."† He

---

* For this anecdote see "Henriade," Variantes du Chant Premier.

† "La Henriade de Mr. de Voltaire." Seconde édition revûe, corrigée et augmentée de remarques critiques sur cet ouvrage. A Londres chez Woodman et Lyon, dans Russel Street, Covent Garden, 1728.

is angry that Voltaire should, throughout the poem, lean so decidedly to the side of Popery; he is still more angry that he should have placed on the same footing Popery and Protestantism, for the essence of Popery is intolerance, and the essence of Protestantism is enlightened toleration. "You arrived in our island," he goes on to say, "with a book against our religion, and we received you with open arms, our king and our queen presented you with money. I wonder," he continues, "how an Englishman who introduced himself to Cardinal Fleury with an attack on Popery would be likely to fare." He concludes by hoping that Voltaire will continue to reside in England, and he exhorts him to prepare "une nouvelle édition moins Papiste de la 'Henriade.'" This critique purported to be the work of an English nobleman. It was in reality the work of a French refugee named Faget. Voltaire was greatly amused at his being taken for a Catholic propagandist.* "You will see," he writes in a letter to a friend in France, "by some annotations tacked to my book, and fathered upon an English lord, that I am here a confessor of Catholic religion." To this criticism he made no reply during his residence in England, but on its reappearance under another title in an edition of the "Henriade" printed at the Hague he answered it.

It was probably during his sojourn either in Maiden

---

* And it is not less amusing to us to find him thus writing to Père Porée: "Surtout, mon révérend père, je vous supplie instamment de vouloir m'instruire si j'ai parlé de la religion comme je le dois; car, s'il y a sur cet article quelques expressions qui vous déplaisent ne doutez pas que je ne les corrige à la première édition que l'on pourra faire encore de mon poëme. T'ambitionne votre estime non seulement comme auteur mais comme Chrétien."—*Correspondance Générale*, Année 1728.

Lane or in Billiter Square that his adroitness and fluent mastery over our language saved him from what might otherwise have been an unpleasant adventure. He chanced one day to be strolling along the streets when his peculiar appearance attracted attention. A crowd collected, and some ribald fellow began with jeers and hoots to taunt him with being a Frenchman. Nothing is so easily excited as the passions of a rabble, and the passions of a rabble, when their victim is defenceless, rarely exhaust themselves in words. The miscreants were already preparing to pelt him with mud, and mud would no doubt have been followed with missiles of a more formidable kind. But Voltaire was equal to the crisis. Boldly confronting his assailants, he mounted on a stone which happened to be at hand, and began an oration of which the first sentence only has been preserved. "Brave Englishmen!" he cried, "am I not sufficiently unhappy in not having been born among you?" How he proceeded we know not, but his harangue was, if we are to believe Wagnière, so effective that the crowd was not merely appeased, but eager to carry him on their shoulders in triumph to his lodgings.* This was not the only occasion on which he experienced the rudeness with which the vulgar were in those days accustomed to treat his countrymen. He happened to be taking the air on the river when one of the men in charge of the boat, perceiving that his passenger was a Frenchman, began to boast of the superior privileges enjoyed by English subjects; he belonged, he said, not to a land of slaves but to a land of freemen. Warming with his theme, the fellow concluded his offensive remarks by exclaiming with an oath that he would rather be a boatman on the Thames than an archbishop in France. The sequel of the

* Longchamp and Wagnière, vol. i., p. 23.

story is amusing. Within a few hours the man had been seized by a press-gang, and next day Voltaire saw him at the window of a prison with his legs manacled and his hand stretched through the bars, craving alms. "What think you now of a French archbishop?" he cried. "Ah, sir!" replied the captive, "the abominable government have forced me away from my wife and children to serve in a king's ship, and have thrown me into prison and chained my feet for fear I should escape before the ship sails." A French gentleman who was with Voltaire at the time owned that he felt a malicious pleasure at seeing that the English, who were so fond of taunting their neighbors with servitude, were in truth quite as much slaves themselves. "But I," adds Voltaire in one of those noble reflections which so often flash across his pages, "felt a sentiment more humane: I was grieved to think that there was so little liberty on the earth."*

It appears from Atterbury's "Correspondence," that about the time the "Henriade" was published Voltaire had also published an ode written in English, but of that ode, after a most careful search, we have been able to find no trace.†

SECTION III.

APRIL, 1728—MARCH, 1729.

As soon as the "Henriade" was off his hands he applied himself steadily to his History of Charles XII. In the composition of this delightful biography, which he ap-

---

* See for the whole story his Letter to M***, "Œuvres Complètes" (Beuchot), vol. xxxviii., p. 22.

† See Atterbury's "Correspondence," vol. iv., p. 114. Nicholls (see his note) was equally unsuccessful.

pears to have begun as early as 1727, he was greatly assisted by Von Fabrice. Few men then living knew more of the public and private life of the great Swede than Fabrice, and what he knew he liberally communicated. Much useful information was derived from Bolingbroke and the Dowager Duchess of Marlborough. But Charles XII. was not the only work with which he was occupied. He began, prompted by Bolingbroke and inspired by Shakespeare and Lee, the tragedy of "Brutus," the first act of which he sketched in English prose. We give a short specimen of the original draught, which the reader may find it interesting to compare with the corresponding passage in the French text as it now stands. It is the speech of Brutus in the second scene of the first act:

"*Brutus.* Allege not ties: his (Tarquin's) crimes have broken them all. The gods themselves, whom he has offended, have declared against him. Which of our rights has he not trod upon? True, we have sworn to be his subjects, but we have not sworn to be his slaves. You say you've seen our Senate, in humble suppliance, pay him their vows. Even he himself has sworn to be our father, and make the people happy in his guidance. Broken from his oaths, we are let loose from ours. Since he has transgressed our laws, his is the rebellion. Rome is free from guilt."

This tragedy, which he completed on his return to Paris, he dedicated to Bolingbroke. Mr. Parton in his list of Voltaire's writings enters among them an edition of "Brutus," published in London in 1727. Of that edition after a laborious search we can find no trace. It was certainly unknown to Desnoiresterres, to Benchot, and to all the editors; and—what is, we think, final—there is no mention of it in the exhaustive bibliography of Voltaire, just published by M. Georges Bengesco. Mr. Parton has, we suspect, been misled by an ambiguous paragraph at the end of the preface to the fourth edition of the "Essay on Epic Poetry."

At Wandsworth, or possibly in London, he sketched also another tragedy, a tragedy which was not, however, completed till 1734. This was "La Mort de César," suggested, as we need scarcely say, by the masterpiece of Shakespeare.* Meanwhile (end of 1728) he was engaged in the composition of those charming letters which were afterwards published in English under the title of "Letters concerning the English Nation," and in French under the title of "Lettres Philosophiques." They were addressed to his friend Thiériot, and under Thiériot's auspices (par les soins de Thiériot) were translated into English. The publication of the English translation preceded the publication of the French original. The first French editions appeared in 1734, but two editions had appeared in English during the preceding year, one printed in London, and the other in Dublin. But the indefatigable energy of Voltaire did not exhaust itself in study and composition. It appears from Duvernet, that he attempted to open a permanent French theatre in London, and with this object he induced a company of Parisian actors to come over; but the project met with so little encouragement that he was forced to abandon it, and the company went back almost immediately to Paris.†

In the midst of these multifarious pursuits he had found time to peruse almost everything of note both in our poetry and in our prose. He began with Shakespeare, whose principal dramas he studied with minute attention, analyzing the structure, the characterization, the diction. His criticisms on Shakespeare are, it is true, seldom cited except to be laughed at, but the defects of these criticisms

---

* See "Œuvres Complètes" (edit. 1877), vol. ii., note.
† Duvernet, p. 72.

originated neither from ignorance nor from inattention. His real opinion of Shakespeare is not to be gathered from the "Des Théâtres Anglais" and from the "Lettres à l'Académie," but from the "Lettres Philosophiques" and from the admirable letter to Horace Walpole.* The influence of Shakespeare on Voltaire's own tragedies is very perceptible, and the extent of that influence will be at once apparent if we compare the plays produced before his visit to England with the plays produced on his return to France, if we compare "Œdipe," "Artémise," and "Marianne," with "Brutus," "Eryphile," and "Zaïre." "Brutus" and "La Mort de César" flowed not more certainly from Julius Cæsar than "Zaïre" from "Othello;" while reminiscences of "Hamlet" are unmistakable both in "Eryphile" and in "Sémiramis." The first three acts of "Julius Cæsar" he subsequently translated into French, and he has in the "Lettres Philosophiques" given an admirable version of the famous soliloquy in "Hamlet." Milton he studied, as his "Essay on Epic Poetry" and his article on the Épopée† prove, with similar diligence. He had, in addition to "Paradise Lost," read "Paradise Regained" and "Samson Agonistes," neither of which he thought of much value. He was well acquainted with the poems, the dramas, and the essays of Dryden, and with the writings of Dryden's contemporaries. Garth's‡ "Dispensary" he carefully studied, and places above the "Lutrin." Even such inferior poets as Oldham, Roscommon, Dorset, Sheffield, Halifax, and Rochester had not escaped his curious eye. Rochester, indeed, he pronounced to be a poet of great genius; he puts his satires on a level with those of

* Dated Ferney, July, 1768. "Correspondance Générale," vol. xiv.
† "Dictionnaire Philosophique," article "Épopée."
‡ *Ibid.*, article "Burlesque."

Boileau, and in one of the "Philosophical Letters" (the twenty-first) he turns a portion of the satire on Man into French heroics. With the poems of Denham he was greatly pleased; and of Waller, whose "Elegy on the Death of Cromwell" he has translated into French verse, he speaks in terms of enthusiastic admiration, ranking him above Voiture, and observing that "his serious compositions exhibit a strength and vigor which could not have been expected from the softness and fluency of his other pieces." He read Otway, whom singularly enough he underrated, and of whose "Orphan" he has, in his "Appel a Toutes les Nations," given a sarcastic analysis. He was acquainted with Lee's tragedies, and he enjoyed the comedies of Wycherley, Vanbrugh, and Congreve, on which he has left many just and interesting observations. Indeed he did Vanbrugh the honor to steal from him many of the incidents, most of the characters, and the whole of the underplot of the "Relapse." It is singular that the French editors who are careful to point out that "Le Comte de Boursouffle Comédie Bouffe" is merely a recast of "L'Échange Comédie en trois actes," should have omitted to notice that both of them are simply Vanbrugh's play in a French dress.

But nothing illustrates his mastery over our language and his power of entering into the spirit of our literature, even when that literature is most esoteric, so strikingly as his remarks on "Hudibras." "I never found," he says, "so much wit in any single book as that. It is 'Don Quixote' and the 'Satire Ménippée' blended together." Of the opening lines he has, in the "Lettres Philosophiques," given a French version, reproducing with extraordinary felicity both the metre and the spirit. With not less pleasure he perused the poems of Prior. In the "Philosophical Dictionary" he devotes an article to him, and in another article he pauses to draw attention to the merits of "Alma." With the essays and poems of Addison, whom he pronounces to be the best critic as well as the best writer of his age, he was well acquainted.* His "Allegories" he has imitated;† his "Campaign" he took as the model for "Fontenoy;" from his criticism on Milton he has borrowed; and his "Cato" he placed at the head of English tragedies. Indeed, he has gone so far as to say that the principal character in that drama is the "greatest that was ever brought upon any stage." His observations upon the defects of the play are less open to question, and prove that if he had the bad taste to prefer Addison to Shakespeare, he was sufficiently acquainted with the history of our drama to be able to point out in what way the appearance of "Cato" marked an era in its development. To the genius of Swift he paid enthusiastic homage. He owed, he said, to Swift's writings the love he bore to the English language. He considered him immeasurably superior to Rabelais; and he was so delighted with "Gulliver's Travels" that he encouraged his friend Thiériot to undertake a translation of them into French, judiciously advising him, however, to confine his efforts to the first part. His own "Micromégas" is largely indebted to "Gulliver." Nor did his nice and discriminating appreciation end here. Voltaire was the first critic who drew attention to the peculiar merits of Swift's verses.‡

With the poems and tragedies of Thomson he was, as a

---

* For his remarks on Cato, see "Dictionnaire Philosophique," article "Addison," where he gives a French version of Cato's Soliloquy.

† See particularly the Vision in section ii. of the article on "Religion" in the "Philosophical Dictionary."

‡ "Lettres Philosophiques," xxii.; see, too, "Lettres, A. S. A. M^{or} Le Prince Mélanges," v. 489.

very interesting letter to George, Lord Lyttelton, shows,* thoroughly conversant. "I was acquainted," so runs the letter, which is written in English and is dated Paris, May 17, 1750 (N.S.), "with Mr. Thomson when I stayed in England. I discovered in him a great genius and a great simplicity. I liked in him the poet and the true philosopher, I mean the lover of mankind. I think that without a good stock of such a philosophy a poet is just above a fiddler who amuses our ears and cannot go to our soul. I am not surprised your nation has done more justice to Mr. Thomson's 'Seasons' than to his dramatic performances." As this letter is an interesting specimen of Voltaire's composition nearly twenty years after he had left us, our readers may perhaps like to see more of it. We will, therefore, transcribe a few paragraphs. He is accounting for the comparative indifference with which the English public regarded Thomson's tragedies.

"There is one kind of poetry of which the judicious readers and the men of taste are the proper judges. There is another kind, that depends on the vulgar great or small; tragedy and comedy are of these last species; they must be suited to the turn of mind and proportioned to their taste. Your nation two hundred years since is used to a wild scene, to a crowd of tumultuous events, to an emphatical poetry mixed with low and comical expressions, to a lively representation of bloody deeds, to a kind of horror which seems often barbarous and childish, all faults which never sullied the Greek, the Roman, and the French stage. And give me leave to say that the taste of your politest countrymen differs not much in point of tragedy from the taste of the mob at bear-gardens. 'Tis true we have too much of action, and the perfection of this art should consist in a due mixture of the French taste and the English energy.... Mr. Thomson's tragedies seem to me wisely intricated and elegantly writ. They

---

* This letter is among the archives at Hagley, and I am indebted for a copy of it to the great kindness of Lord Lyttelton.

want, perhaps, some fire, and it may be that his heroes are neither moving nor busy enough, but taking him all in all, methinks he has the highest claims to the greatest esteem."

The poetry of Pope he read and reread with an admiration which occasionally expresses itself in hyperbole. The "Essays on Criticism" he preferred both to the masterpiece of Horace and to the "Art Poétique" of Boileau; the "Rape of the Lock" he considered the best mock heroic poem in existence; and the "Essay on Man," which appeared about five years after he had returned to France, he describes as "the most beautiful didactic poem—the most useful—the most sublime—that has ever been written in any language."*

It would be interesting to trace the influence of Pope's poetry upon Voltaire's. We can here only pause to point out that the "Temple du Goût" was undoubtedly suggested by the "Dunciad," that the "Le Désastre de Lisbonne" and the "Discourse en vers sur l'Homme" bear the impress of the "Essay on Man," and that "La Roi Naturelle" was certainly modelled on it.

At the beginning of 1729 he prepared to quit England for his native country. There was now, indeed, nothing to detain him. He had published the "Henriade;" he had completed his collections for the "Lettres Philosophiques;" he had collected materials for the "Siècle de Louis XIV.," and for the "History of Charles XII.;" he had made what friends he cared to make; he had seen all he wished to see; and, what was of equal importance to him, he had made money. But it would be doing him great injustice

---

* See, too, "Parallèle d'Horace, de Boileau, et de Pope," where he says of the Essay, "Jamais vers ne formèrent tant de grandes idées en si peu de paroles."—*Mélanges*, vol. iii., p. 224. See, too, "Lettres Philosophiques," xxii.

to suppose that the only ties which bound him to England were ties of self-interest. He had become sincerely attached to the country and to the people. "Had I not been obliged," he said in a letter to Thiériot, "to look after my affairs in France, depend upon it I would have spent the rest of my days in London." And again, many years afterwards, he wrote in a letter to his friend Keate: "Had I not fixed the seat of my retreat in the free corner of Geneva I would certainly live in the free corner of England. I have been for thirty years the disciple of your ways of thinking."* The kindness and hospitality which he received he never forgot, and he took every opportunity of repaying it. To be an Englishman was always a certain passport to his courteous consideration. When, in 1776, Martin Sherlock visited him at Ferney he found the old man, then in his eighty-third year, still full of his visit to England. He had had the garden laid out in the English fashion; the books with which he was surrounded were the English classics, the subject to which he persistently directed the conversation was the English nation.†

His departure from England is said to have been hastened by a quarrel with his bookseller, Prévost; and a story was afterwards circulated by Desfontaines, that, previous to his departure, he was severely cudgelled by an infuriated member of the trade—for what reason, and under what circumstances, is not recorded.‡ However this may be, it seems clear that he had either done or said something which had made him enemies: there was certainly an im-

---

* Voltaire to Keate, January 16, 1760, British Mus. Addit. MSS. 30,991.

† "Letters from an English Traveller" (Letter xxiv.).

‡ See "La Voltairomanie," p. 37, and cf. Desnoiresterres, "La Jeunesse de Voltaire," p. 397.

pression in the minds of some that he quitted England under a cloud. In a notice of the "History of Charles XII." in the *Gentleman's Magazine* for May, 1732, the writer asserts that "Mr. Voltaire enriched himself with our contributions and behaved so ill that he was refused admittance into those noblemen's and gentlemen's families in which he had been received with great favor and distinction. He left England full of resentment, and wrote the King of Sweden's Life to abuse this nation and the Hanoverian family." The latter statement is, as we need scarcely say, quite untrue; the former statement is as plainly a gross exaggeration. A very disgraceful story connected with his departure from England appeared some years later in the columns of the same periodical.* It is there stated that Peterborough, wishing to have a certain work written, had commissioned Voltaire, then his guest, to do it, and had supplied him from time to time with the money necessary to defray the expenses of publication. But these sums, instead of paying them over to the publisher, who had, on the strength of the first instalment, put a portion of the work into type, Voltaire appropriated to his own use. He then proceeded to play a double game. He told the publisher, who for want of funds had stopped the press, that Peterborough would advance nothing further till the book was out. To Peterborough, on the other hand, he accounted for the delay in publication by attributing it to the dilatoriness of the publisher. At last the publisher, justly considering that he had been treated very hardly, determined to apply to Peterborough himself. With this object he had an interview with him at Parson's Green. All was explained. The earl, so far from

---

* See a letter to the editor of the *Gentleman's Magazine*, vol. lxvii., part ii., p. 820 *sqq.*, signed E. L. B., in the number for October, 1797.

being guilty of the injustice and meanness attributed to him by Voltaire, had regularly advanced the money required, as Voltaire had regularly retained it. Peterborough's rage knew no bounds. He drew his sword and rushed at his treacherous guest, who happened to come up in the course of the interview, and it was only by a precipitate flight that Voltaire escaped mortal injury. That night he concealed himself in a neighboring village. Next day he returned to London, and almost immediately afterwards he left England for the Continent. This story no one would wish to believe, and there is happily strong reason for doubting its truth. In the first place, it did not appear till nearly seventy years after the supposed event. It is related by an anonymous writer, on anonymous authority, and it appears in a letter obviously animated with the most violent hostility to Voltaire. Nor is there, so far as we know, any allusion to it elsewhere.

Before setting out he went down to Twickenham, to have a final interview with Pope. "I am come," he said, "to bid farewell to a man who never treated me seriously from the first hour of my acquaintance with him to the present moment." To this Pope—who, as soon as Voltaire's back was turned, acknowledged the justice of the remark—probably replied with evasive politeness, or with an emphatic assurance to the contrary; for it is certain that in none of Voltaire's subsequent writings are there any indications either of unfriendliness or ill-will towards him. And it is equally certain that, had he quitted Pope under the impression that he had been ill-treated by him, his vengeance would have been sure, prompt, and signal.*

* The authority for this is Owen Ruffhead ("Life of Pope," p. 165), who almost certainly had the anecdote, which was communicated by Pope himself, from Warburton.

The exact date of Voltaire's departure from England we have not been able to discover. We may, however, conjecture with some certainty that it took place during the second or third week in March, 1729 (N. S.). In a letter to Thiériot, dated—but without the month—1729, he says that he hopes to be in Paris about the 15th of March. In another letter to Thiériot, dated the 10th of March, 1729, he writes, "In all likelihood I shall stay at Saint-Germain, and there I intend to arrive before the 15th. On the 25th of March he was certainly at Saint-Germain.* It is probable, then, that he left England between the 10th and the 20th of March, 1729 (N. S.). The time, therefore, spent by Voltaire in England was, deducting a month for his short visit to France in the summer of 1726, about two years and eight months, and not, as Carlyle and others erroneously assert, two years.

* In his Correspondence (vol. i. of the last edition of the "Œuvres Complètes") there is a letter to Thiériot, dated from Saint-Germain-en-Laye, March 2, 1729, a date which, as the letter of March 10th proves, is certainly erroneous.

NOTE.

" We owe to Voltaire the famous story of the falling apple."— Page 207.

THE history of the preservation of this anecdote is interesting, and it may be well perhaps for me to justify what is asserted in the text, that we owe its preservation to Voltaire. It is not, so far as I can discover, to be found in any publication antecedent to the "Lettres sur les Anglais." It is not mentioned by Newton's friend Whiston in his "Sir Isaac Newton's Mathematical Philosophy More Easily Demonstrated," published in 1716. Nor is it mentioned by Fontenelle in his Eloge of Newton delivered in 1727, and inserted in the following year in the "Histoire de l'Académie des Sciences," nor in the "Life of Sir Isaac Newton," published in London in 1728. It is not recorded by Henry Pemberton in his "View of Newton's Philosophy," 1728, though Pemberton does record that Newton was sitting in a garden when the first notion of his great theory occurred to him. Pemberton's words are, " The first thoughts which gave rise to his 'Principia' he had when he retired from Cambridge in 1666 on account of the Plague. As he sat alone in a garden, he fell into a speculation on the power of gravity." It would seem, too, that the story was not known to Newton's intimate friend, Dr. Stukely, for Stukely says nothing about it in his long letter to Dr. Mead (printed in Turner's Collections for the History of Grantham), written just after the philosopher's death, and containing many particulars about Newton's life and studies. But it was apparently known to Martin Folkes, then Fellow, and subsequently President of the Royal Society, and by him communicated to Robert Green, who in his "Miscellanea Quædam Philosophica," appended to his "Principles of the Philosophy of the Expansive and Constructive Forces," published in 1727, thus obscurely, or rather enigmatically, alludes to it (p. 972): "Quæ sententia—*i. e.*, the doctrine of gravitation—originem duxit, uti omnis, ut fertur, cognitio nostra, a pomo; id quod accepi ab ingeniosissimo at doctissimo viro . . . Martino Folkes Armigero Regiæ vero Societatis socio meritissimo." But it was first recorded in the form in which Voltaire gives it by John Conduit, a very intimate friend of Newton, and the husband of his niece, who in 1727 drew up a number of notes containing particulars of Newton's life for the use of Fontenelle, then engaged in preparing his Eloge. Fontenelle, however, made no use of the anecdote, and Conduit's notes remained in manuscript till 1806, when they were printed by Edmund Turner in his Collections for the History of Grantham (p. 160). Conduit's words are, "In the year 1665, when he retired to his own estate on account of the Plague, he first thought of his system of gravitation, which he did upon observing an apple fall from a tree." Voltaire's first account is in the fifteenth of the "Lettres sur les Anglais," published in 1733 or possibly earlier, and it runs thus: "S'étant retiré en 1666 à la campagne près de Cambridge, un jour qu'il se promenait dans son jardin et qu'il voyait des fruits tomber d'un arbre, il se laissa aller à une méditation profonde sur cette pesanteur, dont tous les philosophes ont cherché si longtemps la cause en vain." Relating the anecdote afterwards in his "Eléments de la Philosophie de Newton," part iii., chap. iii., he gives his authority: "Un jour en l'année 1666 Newton retira à la campagne, et voyant tomber des fruits d'un arbre, *à ce que m'a conté sa nièce Madame Conduit*, se laissa aller," etc. It is satisfactory, therefore, to know that the anecdote rests on the best authority, that, namely, of Newton's favorite disciple and of the niece who lived with him, as it is interesting to know that Voltaire was the first to give it to the world.

INDEX.

ABRANTES, Duke of, announces succession to Spanish monarchy, 29.
Addison, Joseph, Voltaire's opinion of, 239.
Akenside, Mark, his indebtedness to Bolingbroke, 15; writes against Walpole, 137.
Alari, correspondence with Bolingbroke, 9.
Amhurst, Nicholas, his abilities and antecedents, 137; Editor of *Craftsman*, 138.
Anne, Queen, her accession to the throne, 34; dislike to Godolphin and to his Ministry, 40; discourtesy to Godolphin, 45; opens Parliament, 69; is only conditionally averse to the Pretender, 70, 71; has an apoplectic fit, 74; dies, 76.
Arbuthnot, Dr., writes for peace being signed, 57.
Arouet, François (*vide* Voltaire).
Atterbury, Francis, writes for peace being signed, 57; is in favor of appealing to nation and declaring open war with Hanover, 81; meets Bolingbroke when going into exile, 121.
Aubigny, designer of château Chantaloup, 165.

BACON (Lord Verulam): Voltaire's knowledge of his writings, 219.
Bathurst, Lord: "Letter on the true use of Study and Retirement," by Bolingbroke, addressed to, 167.
Beaufort, Duke of, congratulating Queen Anne, 47.
Bengesco, George, bibliographer of Voltaire, 235.
Berkeley, Dr. George, Voltaire's opinion of, 219.
Berndorf, Count, favorite of King George II., 122.
Bernières, Madame de, Voltaire's letter to, 203.
Berwick, Marshal: interview with Bolingbroke at Paris, 90; testimony in Bolingbroke's favor, 106.
Bessières, Mademoiselle, Voltaire's letter to, 202, 203.
Bladen, Colonel Martin, furnishes Voltaire with information regarding Camoens, 222.
Blaithwayte, Mr., resigns office as Secretary of War, 37.
Bolingbroke, Lord Viscount, characteristics of, 6-14; as an orator, 13-61; his influence on English literature, 14; on foreign literature, 15; on politics of his time, *ib.*; ancestry and lineage, 16; birth at Battersea, 18; early education, 18, 19; honorary doctor, Oxford, 20; familiarity with classics, 20, 21; riotous youth, 21-23; erotic poetry, 23; Continental tour, 23, 24; stay in Paris, connec-

tion with English embassy, 24; indifferent poetry, *ib.*; early profligacy, 25; marries Frances Winchescombe, 26; enters Parliament, 27; guiding motives 32; assists Hodges in bringing in bill for further Security of Protestant Succession, 34; introduces bill against Occasional Conformity, 37; sits on Commission against Halifax, *ib.*; opposes Robert Walpole, *ib.*; Secretary of War, 38; owing to Marlborough's influence, *ib.*; is a party to Harley's intrigues while holding office under Godolphin, 40; resigns his seat in Cabinet, 41; devotes himself to literary pursuits, 42; is appointed Secretary of State for Northern Department, 46; his prospects as such, 47; his policy and double-dealing, 48; publishes a pamphlet inscribed "A Letter to the *Examiner*," 49; rises into eminence and aims at Premiership, 56; intrigues with France with a view of concluding peace, *ib.*; virtually directs affairs and creates twelve new peers, 60; preliminaries of Treaty of Utrecht, 61; abandons Allies to vengeance of Louis XIV., 62; is created Viscount of Bolingbroke, *ib.*; his growing aversion to Oxford, 63; his being sent on a mission to France, *ib.*; his triumphant reception there, *ib.*; is betrayed by an adventuress, 64; by his damaged reputation, *ib.*; superseded by the Earl of Dartmouth, *ib.*; resumes his duties as Secretary of State and signs peace of Utrecht, 65; keeping his treachery to the Allies, 66; public feeling growing against him, 68; determines to seize the reins of Government, 71; his prospects to that effect, 72; draws up the Schism bill, *ib.*; his growing antagonism to Oxford, *ib.*; feasts the chiefs of the Whig party, 73; gives friendly assurance to Gaultier, 74; difficulties of his position, *ib.*; collapse of his schemes, 75; his position at death of Queen Anne, 81; his policy in consequence of this event, 81, 82; offers his services to the Elector, 81-83; dismissed from his post as Secretary of State, 84; is refused admittance to the King, *ib.*; moves an amended address in defence of his late policy, 85; is being charged by Walpole, 86; flees the country and retires to France, 87; letter to his father and to Lord Lansdowne, 88; inconsistency of his explanations, 89; puts himself into communication with the English embassy at Paris, 90; opens secret negotiations with the Pretender, *ib.*; retires to Dauphine, *ib.*; outlawed, 93; allies himself with the Jacobites and becomes their leader, 95; his interview with the Pretender, 96; proceeds to Paris, 97; endeavors to form a Jacobite ministry, *ib.*; but finds his efforts unavailing, 99; sets about organizing Jacobite movement both in England and abroad, 100, 101; meets with reverses and disappointments, 103-107; calumniated by the Jacobite clique, 106; accused by the Earl of Mar, and by Ormond, 107; is rudely dismissed from his post by the Chevalier, *ib.*; is being sounded by Lord Stair, 108; expresses his desire to be pardoned and to return to England, 108; mingles in the social life of French aristocracy, 109; engages in literary pursuits, 110; writes the "Reflections on Exile" and the "Letter to Sir William Wyndham," *ib.*; accused of crimes towards the Jacobite party in the "Letter from Avignon," 111; meets with the Marquise de Villette,

113; marries her at Aix-la-Chapelle, 114; speculates in the Mississippi scheme, *ib.*; removes with his wife to La Source, *ib.*; studies at La Source, 114, 115; "Letters to Pouilly," a "Treatise on the Limits of Human Knowledge," the "Reflections on Innate Moral Principles," etc., 115; reputation of Archbishop Tillotson, *ib.*; conversational powers, 116; intercourse with Voltaire, *ib.*; influence on Voltaire, 117; solicits the intervention of Du Bois and of the Duke of Orleans, 120; interview with Lord Polwarth, 121; return to England, *ib.*; meets Atterbury going into exile, *ib.*; arrives in London, *ib.*; endeavors to secure the reversal of his Bill of Attainder, 121-125; starts for Aix-la-Chapelle, but meets with no success, 123; proceeds to Paris and finds himself in dilemma, 124; offers his mediation at the French court to Walpole, 125; returns to La Source, 126; is restored to his civil rights, 127; his double life, *ib.*; influence on contemporary politics, 131, 132; his exasperation against Walpole and causes of same, 136; is organizing the Opposition against the Walpole Government, *ib.*; starts the journal, the *Craftsman*, 138; publishes in same, under the title the "Occasional Writer," three papers against Walpole, *ib.*; at the same time is intriguing at the Court, 139; solicits an interview with the King, 140; but is unsuccessful, *ib.*; factious opposition to the Walpole Government, 142-144; determines to appeal to the people, 144; inflaming the populace against Walpole, 145; directing all the movements of the Opposition, 150; contributes the "Vision of Camelick" to the *Craftsman*, *ib.*; publishes in same "The Case of Dunkirk considered," 151; "Remarks on the History of England," *ib.*; is creating a deep impression on the public mind, 152; writes on "The Policy of the Athenians," 153; publishes his "Dissertation upon Parties," *ib.*; writes with a view of obliterating party prejudice, 155; is engaged in beautifying his country residence at Dawley, 156; letter to Swift, *ib.*; his hospitality to English friends and to Voltaire, 157; his friendship with Pope, 158; influence on Pope, 162, 163; leaves England, 163; reason therefor, 164, 165; resides first in Paris, 165; afterwards in Touraine, *ib.*; begins the "Letters on the Study of History," 166; writes the "Letter on the Spirit of Patriotism," 167; returns to England, 169; stands high in the favor of the Prince of Wales, *ib.*; assiduously courts him, 171; his motive for doing so, *ib.*; writes the "Patriot King," and thereby greatly influences the younger school of politicians, 172-175; writes the "Dissertation on the State of Parties at the accession of George I.," 175; also the "Reflections on the Present State of the Nation," *ib.*; leaves England again for France, *ib.*; returns to find himself baffled, 176; his treachery to Pope, 177, 178; his misanthropy, 180; his waning influence, *ib.*; death of his wife, 181; his isolation and growing illness, *ib.*; his death, *ib.*; review of his philosophical works, 182-187; summary of his character, 187.

Bothmar, Count, protests against the peace being signed, 57; circulates a report with a view of throwing the Tories off the track, 83; favorite of George I., 122.

Bourbon, Duke of, assumes the reins of Government in France, 124.
Boyle, Mr., resigns his seat in the Cabinet, 46.
Brinsden, John, Bolingbroke's Secretary, 204.
Brooke, Henry, his literary indebtedness to Bolingbroke, 15.
Broome, Major, his acquaintance with Voltaire, 205, *foot-note*.
Burgess, Daniel, tutor of Bolingbroke, 19.
Burke, Edmund, his literary indebtedness to Bolingbroke, 14.
Burnet, Gilbert, his opinion of Harley, 55; writes against the peace being signed, 57; his prognostication to the Queen, *ib*.
Bute, Marquis of, influenced by the "Patriot King," 173.
Butler, Samuel, his "Hudibras" eulogized by Voltaire, 238; Versions from, *ib.*
Buys (Dutch ambassador) protests against the peace being signed, 56.

CAMOENS, Luis de, Voltaire's criticism of, 222.
Canella, Salvatore, bearing testimony to the influence of Bolingbroke's writings on Italian literature, 15.
Carlyle, Thomas, his hopelessness as to gathering information about Voltaire's stay in England, 192; his errors, *ib.*, *foot-note.*
Caroline, Queen, thwarts the plans of the Opposition, 142; Dedication of "Henriade" to, 227.
Carteret, Lord, instrumental in obtaining a pardon for Bolingbroke, 121; his influence at Court and in Government circles, 122; his power declining, 123; is in coalition with Newcastle and Hardwicke, 176.
Catalans shamefully abandoned by Bolingbroke, 67.
Charles, Archduke of Austria, eventual successor to Spanish monarchy, 29.
Châteauneuf (author of "Les Divorces Anglais"), 209.
Chesterfield, Lord, opinion of, on Bolingbroke, 7; opinion of Bolingbroke's elocutionary powers, 118; satrapian habits at the house of, not suiting Voltaire, 230.
Chetwood, "History of Stage" quoted, 202.
Christie, W. D., 11.
Churchill, Charles, his literary indebtedness to Bolingbroke, 15.
Cibber, Colley, 202.
Clarke, Samuel, denounced by Bolingbroke, 183; highly appreciated by Voltaire, 217.
Coderc, Piracy of the "Henriade," 228.
Colet, "Relics of Literature" quoted, 204, 224.
Collins, Anthony, 220.
Collins, William, his indebtedness to Bolingbroke, 15; gives evidence as to Col. Martin Bladen, 222.
Condorcet, his opinion on Voltaire's stay in England, 191.
Conduit, John, 246, *note.*
Conduit, Mrs., 207.
Congreve, William, his acquaintance with Voltaire, 207, 208.
Cooke, Wingrove, author of a biography of Bolingbroke, 4; *id.* of a "History of Parties," *ib.*; is not sufficiently aware of the in-

fluence Bolingbroke had on the intellectual activity of his age, 79, 80.
Cornbury, Lord: "Letters on the Study of History," addressed to, by Bolingbroke, 166.
Couvreur, Adrienne de, 215.
Cowper, Earl of, declines to enter Harley's Ministry, 46; reads the King's speech, 85.
Coxe, Archdeacon, testifies to Bolingbroke's skill in plodding, 125; author of "Memoirs of Horatio Lord Walpole," 126; reason he assigns for the sudden departure of Bolingbroke from England, 163.
Cudworth, Ralph, denounced by Bolingbroke, 183; studied by Voltaire, 219.
Cyprian, Saint, denounced by Bolingbroke, 183.

DADICHY suggests an alteration of the opening lines of the "Henriade" to Voltaire, 231.
Darlington, Countess of, 122.
Dartmouth, Earl of, supersedes Bolingbroke, 64.
Davenant, Charles, solicited by Harley, 49.
De Foe, Daniel, 14; supports Harley, 49.
Denham, Sir John, 238.
Desfontaines, Abbé, libels on Voltaire, 223.
Desnoiresterres, his diligent inquiries respecting Voltaire's stay in England, 192, 193.
Dodington, Bubb, Secretary of Frederick Lewis, Prince of Wales, 170; is a Mæcenas of men of letters and friend of Voltaire, 197.
Dryden, John, his influence on English literature, 14; first acquaintance with Bolingbroke, 23; opinion passed on, by Voltaire, 237.
Du Bois solicited by Bolingbroke to secure him a pardon, 120.
Dunoquet, host of Voltaire at Calais, 193.
Dunton, John, writes against the Peace of Utrecht, 57.
Duvernet, biographer of Voltaire, 236.

EUSEBIUS denounced by Bolingbroke, 183.

FALKENER, Sir Everard, intercourse with Voltaire, 197; his career, character, and death, 198.
Fenton, Elijah, patronized by Bolingbroke, 7.
Ferriole, Madame de, correspondence with Voltaire, 193, 211.
Fielding, Henry, prepares to refute Bolingbroke's philosophical writings, 182.

GALLAS, DE, is being forbidden the Court, 57.
Galway, Earl of, supported by the Whigs, 52.
Gaultier, Abbé, his interview with Bolingbroke, 74.
Gay, John, his acquaintance with Voltaire, 207.
George I. landing at Greenwich, 84; espouses the cause of the Whigs, 85; grants an interview to Bolingbroke, 140; departs for Hanover, and dies there, 141.

Gibbon, Edward, his literary indebtedness to Bolingbroke, 14.
Gloucester, Duke of, death of, 29.
Glover, Richard, his literary indebtedness to Bolingbroke, 15.
Godolphin, Earl of, first Lord of the Treasury, 30; character and antecedents of, 35; policy of, 36; his downfall, 42; review of his administration, and deserving traits of same, 42, 43; reasons of its collapse, 44.
Goldsmith, Oliver, biography of Bolingbroke, 4; his literary indebtedness to Bolingbroke, 14; his statement about the publication of the "Henriade," 227.
Green, Robert, quoted, 246, *note*.
Greg, scandal of, 41.
Grimoard, General, author of "Essai Historique," 4; reasons which he assigns for sudden departure of Bolingbroke from England, 163.
Guiscard, Antoine de, character and antecedents of, 53; acquaintance with St. John, 54; stabs Harley in a surreptitious assault, *ib.*; motives therefor, 55.

Halifax, Earl of, declines to enter Harley's ministry, 46.
Hanmer, Sir T., author of the Representation, 61; moves an adjournment of the consideration of Walpole's report, 93.
Harcourt, Sir Simon, is ignored by the King, 84.
Hardwicke, Earl of, his correspondence with Bolingbroke, 9.
Harley, Robert (*vide* Oxford, Earl of).
Harley, Thomas, his arrest, 91.
Hurlington, Lady, promise given by Bolingbroke to, 179, *foot-note*.
Hedges, Sir Thomas, appointed Secretary of State, 30; removed from Ministry, 39.
Hervey, Lady, poetry dedicated to, by Voltaire, 209.
Hervey, Lord, his Memoirs, 149, *foot-note;* friendship with Voltaire, 209.
Hill, Aaron, opinion passed on by Bolingbroke, 7.
Hobbes, Thomas, studied by Voltaire, 219.
Hooker, Richard, his influence on English literature, 14.
Howard, Leonard, 219.
Howard, Mrs., favorite of the Prince of Wales, 139; powerless to assist Bolingbroke after the death of the King, 142.
Hume, David, his indebtedness to Bolingbroke, 14.

Isocrates, 11.

James II., death at Saint Germain, 33.
James the Pretender, character of, 94; his interview with Bolingbroke, 95; dallies at St. Malo, 105; hurries off to Scotland, *ib.*; dismisses Bolingbroke, 107.
Jersey, Earl of, retirement from Secretaryship of State (1700), 30; resigns his seat in the Ministry (*anno* 1702), 37.
Johnson, Dr. Samuel, conformity of his political opinions with those of Bolingbroke, 173.
Junius, his literary indebtedness to Bolingbroke, 14.

KEATE, George, 242.
Kendal, Duchess of, her animosity against Walpole, 139; is patronizing Bolingbroke, *ib.*

LANSDOWNE, Lord, written to by Bolingbroke, 88.
Leibnitz, G. W. de, denounced by Bolingbroke, 183.
Lepel, Molly, *vide* Hervey, Lady.
Lewis, Erasmus, letter to Swift, anent Bolingbroke's fitness for the post of Prime-minister, 74.
Lewis, Frederick (Prince of Wales), at open war with his father, 169; his character and temper, 169, 170; half-reconciled with the King, 176.
Locke, John, Voltaire's admiration for, 218, 219.
Louis XIV. (King of France), sympathy with the Jacobite cause, 99; his death, 102.
Lovat, Simon Lord, 198.
Lyttelton, Lord, "Letter on the Spirit of Patriotism" inscribed to, by Bolingbroke, 168.

MACAULAY, Lord, his literary indebtedness to Bolingbroke, 14.
Macknight, Thomas, author of Life of Bolingbroke, 4, 5; not sufficiently aware of the influence Bolingbroke had on the intellectual activity of his age, 79, 80.
Mallet, David, biographer of Bolingbroke, 3; under-secretary of Frederick Lewis (Prince of Wales), 170; his mercenary and unscrupulous conduct towards him, 179.
Manton, Dr., author of a hundred and ninety sermons on the 119th psalm, 19.
Mar, Earl of, receives instructions from Bolingbroke, 104; but has already anticipated them, *ib.;* accuses Bolingbroke of incapacity and negligence, 107.
Marlborough, Duchess of, opinion held by, of Robert Harley, 31; is forbidden the Court, 52; is sought after by Voltaire, 208; who is invited to draw up her Memoirs, *ib.*
Marlborough, Duke of, 8; military operations on the Meuse, 35; assists Bolingbroke, 38; opposed to Sacheverel's impeachment, 43; his inordinate ambition, 45; arrives in England, 52; interviews with Bolingbroke, *ib.;* arrives from the Hague and takes counsel with the Chiefs of the Opposition, 57; delivers impressive speech in Parliament, 58, 59; is removed from command, 60; joins the Jacobite movement, 101.
Masham, Mrs., her influence on Queen Anne, 44; becomes a favorite at Court, 52.
Matignon, Marquis de, advances money to Bolingbroke, 164.
Mesnager, arranges preliminaries of peace, 58; his suite engages in a contest with the suite of Van Rechtheren, Holland, 64.
Milton, John, not sufficiently appreciated by Voltaire, 205, 206; diligently perused by Voltaire, 237.
Montague, Earl of, attack on, 28.

Montesquieu, De, his literary indebtedness to Bolingbroke, 15; gives account of debate in Parliament, *i.e.*, Dunkerque fortifications, 146.
Morgan, accessary to Bolingbroke's escape from England, 87.
Morville, Count de, recommends Voltaire to Horace Walpole the elder, 197.

NEWTON, Sir Isaac, his death commented on by Voltaire, 207; Voltaire's anecdotes of, *ib.*; the falling apple, 246, *note*.
Nicolerdot, Estimate of Voltaire's gain by the "Henriade," 228.
Nottingham, Earl of, disagrees with his Ministerial colleagues, 37; hands in his resignation, *ib.*; consents to move resolution against peace, 57; does so in Parliament, 58.

Oldfield, Anne, 215.
Oldmixon, John, writes against peace being signed, 57.
Orford, Earl of, inquiry into the administration of, 28.
Orleans, Duke of, Regent of France, undecided attitude in Jacobite movement, 103; is solicited by Bolingbroke for pardon by English Government, 120; death, 124.
Ormond, Duke of, ignored by King, 84; deserts his post as lieutenant Jacobite movement, 102; sails for Devonshire, 104.
Orsini, Princess, supervising construction château Chantaloup, 165.
Otway, Thomas, 238.
Oxford, Earl of, antecedents, physique, characteristics, 30, 31; is appointed Lord Treasurer (?) in Godolphin's Ministry, 37; his intrigues while holding office, 40; is removed from office, 41; influences Queen Anne against the Whigs, 44; is appointed Chancellor of the Exchequer, 45; hires the Press, 49; is confronted by the feeling of the extreme Tories, 53; falls ill, *ib.*; is wounded by Antoine de Guiscard's dastardly assault, 54; reaps the benefit of it through enhanced popularity and royal favor, 55; organizes a committee to inquire into expenditure of Godolphin Ministry, *ib.*; withdraws seals of State from Bolingbroke and confers them on Earl of Dartmouth, 64; becomes more and more irresolute, 69; is removed from office, 73; is openly insulted by King, 84.

PARTON, biographer of Voltaire, 193; erroneously attributes to Voltaire an English edition of Brutus, 235.
Patrick, Dr., author of "Mensa Mystica," 18.
Pelham, Henry, quoted, 141.
Pemberton, Dr. Henry, Voltaire's acquaintance with, 218; assists Voltaire in studying Newton, *ib.*
Peterborough, Earl, supported by Tories, 52; host of Voltaire, 205; Voltaire's treachery to, 243, 244.
Philip, King of Spain, claims right of succession to the throne of France, 102.
Philips, John, poet and student of Christ Church, 20.
Pitt, William, opinion of, on Bolingbroke's eloquence, 8; literary indebtedness to Bolingbroke, 14.

Pitt, Andrew, the Quaker, Voltaire's acquaintance with, 213.
Platen, Countess of, favorite at Court, 122.
Polwarth, Lord, solicited by Bolingbroke with view of obtaining pardon, 121.
Pope, Alexander, correspondence with Bolingbroke, 9; perfidious treatment at the hand of Bolingbroke, *ib.*; his literary indebtedness to Bolingbroke, 15; his attachment to Bolingbroke, 158, and stimulus he received from him, 159; difficulty to fix the amount of indebtedness he owed to Bolingbroke, 160–162; his unbounded admiration of Bolingbroke, 162, 163; ungratefully dealt with by Bolingbroke, 177; reasons therefor, 178, 179; his acquaintance sought after by Voltaire, 200, 201; decoys and exposes him, 210; Voltaire's opinion of, 241; last interview with Voltaire, 244.
Porée, Père, Voltaire's letter to, 232.
Port, Adam de, ancestor of Bolingbroke, 16.
Prior, Matthew, correspondence with Bolingbroke, 9; writes from Paris complaining, 65; believed by Bolingbroke to have turned State's evidence against him, 86; is arrested, 90; Voltaire's opinion of, 238.
Pulteney, Daniel, his antecedents and character, 133.
Pulteney, William, his antecedents, character, and talents, 134, 135; his hostility to Walpole, how caused, 135; bluntly deprecates further co-operation of Bolingbroke, 164; writes to Swift anent Bolingbroke's sudden departure from England, 165; is in coalition with Newcastle and Hardwicke, 176.

RABY, Lord, letter from Bolingbroke to, 65, *foot-note*.
Rechtheren, his suite engages in a contest with the suite of Mesnager, France, 64.
Rémusat, De, author of a study on Bolingbroke, 5; confounds the "Letter to Sir William Wyndham" with the "Letter to Wyndham," 111; reason he assigns for Bolingbroke's sudden departure from England, 164; uncertainty concerning Voltaire's stay in England, 192.
Ridpath, George, writes against the peace being signed, 57.
Rochester, Earl of, resigns his seat in the Ministry, 37; succeeds Somers as President of the Council, 46; heads the Opposition to Harley, 53; his death, 55.
Roscommon, Earl of, Voltaire reads his poems, 237.
Ruffhead, Owen, relates incident relative to Pope, 200; also 244, *foot-note*.

SACHEVEREL, Dr., impeachment of, by Godolphin, 43; reasons of same, *ib.*
Schaub, Sir Luke, English Ambassador at Paris, creature of Bolingbroke, 122; is at loggerheads with the partisans of Walpole, 124.
Seymour, Earl of, resigns his seat in Ministry, 37.
Shakespeare, William, Voltaire's indebtedness to, 235, 236; his real opinion of, 236, 237.

Sherlock, Rev. Martin, quoted, 221, 242.

Shrewsbury, Duke of, secedes from the Tory party, 75; supports the motion in defence of the Bolingbroke Ministry, 86; joins the Jacobite movement, 101.

Somers, Earl of, disapproves of Sacheverel's impeachment, 43; disapproves of Bolingbroke's being declared an outlaw, 93.

Somerset, Duchess of, becomes a favorite at Court, 52.

Somerset, Duke of, is dismissed from office, 60.

Spence, Rev. Joseph, quoted, 200; *foot-note*, 211, 223.

St. John, Henry, *vide* Bolingbroke.

St. John, Henry, the elder, marries Mary, second daughter Earl of Warwick, 17; commits murder and seriously jeopardizes his life, *ib.*; dies at Battersea, 176.

St. John, John, member of the Council of Nine, 16.

St. John, Oliver, is appointed Lord Deputy of Ireland and created a baronet of Tregoze, 16.

St. John, Walter, marries Joanna, daughter of the Chief-justice, 16; founds the school at Battersea, 17.

Stair, Lord, interview with Bolingbroke, 90; demands surrender of Jacobite flotilla, 104; receives instructions to sound Bolingbroke, 108; does not commit himself to any pledge about Bolingbroke's pardon, 109.

Stanhope, Earl of, accuses Bolingbroke of having distrained State papers, 86; declines to accede to Hanmer's motion, 93; keeps Bolingbroke in expectancy *re* his pardon, 109.

Steele, Richard, attempts made by Harley to subvert him prove unsuccessful, 50; writes against the peace being signed, 57.

Suffolk, Lady, retires from Court, 164.

Sunderland, Earl of, is appointed Lord Treasurer by Godolphin, 39; disliked by Queen Anne, 40; keeps Bolingbroke in expectancy *re* his pardon, 109.

Sundon, Lady, 210.

Swift, Jonathan, his description of Bolingbroke's character, 6; correspondence with Bolingbroke, 9; and causes of rupture, *ib.*; his influence on English literature, 14; impression on, created by Lady Bolingbroke, 26; puts his pen at the service of the Harley Ministry and edits the *Examiner*, 50; his eminent fitness for the post, 50, 51; writes for the peace being signed, 57; prognosticates a felon's fate to the Earl of Oxford and to himself, 59; endeavors to interpose between Bolingbroke and Oxford, 72; writes to Peterborough about state of public affairs, 73; is fast sinking into imbecility, 176; his previous acquaintance with Voltaire, 205; his being written to by Voltaire, 225; and is much admired by him, 239.

TANKERVILLE, Lord, is appointed Lord Privy Seal, 30.

Taylor, Jeremy, 14.

Taylor, John, 230.

Thiériot, correspondence with Voltaire, 203, 211, 218, 225, 230, 236;

is encouraged by Voltaire to undertake the translation of Swift's "Gulliver's Travels," 239 ; correspondence with Voltaire, 245.
Thomson, James, his literary indebtedness to Bolingbroke, 15 ; is highly thought of by Voltaire, 239.
Tillotson, Archbishop, written against by Bolingbroke, 115 ; denounced by Bolingbroke, 183.
Torcy, De, not the superior of Bolingbroke, 8.
Townshend, Lord, is voted enemy to his country, 60 ; is instrumental in obtaining a pardon for Bolingbroke, 120 ; retires from the Cabinet, 145.

VALLIÈRE and Bara, affair of, 41.
Vanbrugh, Sir John, Voltaire's plagiarism from, 238.
Villiere, Marquis de, intrigues for a dukedom, 126, *foot-note*.
Villiers, Second Duke of Buckingham, points of resemblance with Bolingbroke, 12.
Villette, Marquise de, her antecedents, attractions, acquaintance with Bolingbroke, 113 ; marriage at Aix-la-Chapelle, 114 ; goes to London to plead her case in a lawsuit, and is successful, 126, 127 ; her death, 181.
Voltaire, François Arouet de, his indebtedness to Bolingbroke attested by Condorcet, 15 ; first acquaintance with Bolingbroke at La Source, 116 ; feelings of respect and veneration entertained by, towards Bolingbroke, 118 ; peculiarity of influence of Bolingbroke on Voltaire, 119–121 ; his release from the Bastile, 193 ; stay at Calais, *ib.* ; disembarks at Greenwich, *ib.* ; impressions during his voyage, 194 ; first impressions on setting foot on English soil, 194–196 ; arrival in London, 196 ; and is a guest at Bolingbroke's house, *ib.* ; is recommended to Bubb Dodington, 197 ; previously was caned by the Chevalier de Rohan, 199 ; devotes himself to learning the English language, *ib.* ; makes the acquaintance of Pope, 200 ; awkward incident happening at this interview, 201 ; leaves England for France and returns again, 202 ; his disappointment in money affairs and family afflictions, 202, 203 ; his correspondence with French friends, 203, 204 ; his opinion of Pope, 204 ; his opinion of Milton, 205 ; his views on English habits and customs, 206 ; is present at the funeral of Sir Isaac Newton, and comments thereon, 207 ; is invited to draw up the Memoirs of the Duchess of Marlborough, 208 ; his opinion of the beauty of English women, 209 ; dedicates a poem to Lady Hervey, *ib.* ; acts as a political emissary to the Court of St. James, 210 ; is decoyed and exposed by Pope, *ib.* ; endeavors to ingratiate himself with the Court and with Walpole, 211 ; and is looked down upon by Bolingbroke and friends, *ib.* ; his fulsome flattery and indecent conversation, 212 ; is collecting materials for his new works, 213 ; comments on the religious life of England, *ib.* ; notes the differences between English and French social life and the advantages of the former, 214–216 ; his scrap-book, 217 ; has the works of Sir Isaac Newton explained to him by Dr. Clarke, 217 ; makes the acquaintance of Dr. Pember-

ton, 218; becomes familiar with the works of Locke, of Bacon, of Hobbes, and of Cudworth, 218, 219; studies Berkeley, 219; identifies himself with the movement originated by Collins and Woolston, 220; and assists Woolston financially, *ib.*; publishes two essays in the English language, 220–222; goes to reside in Maiden Lane and in Billiter Square, 224; solicits the patronage of the Earl of Oxford, 225; is being highly spoken of by English press, 225, 226; publishes " Henriade," 226; dedicates it to Queen Caroline, 227; and is highly successful with sale, 227, 228; is robbed by piratical booksellers, 228, 229; but realizes, nevertheless, a handsome reward, 228; domestic trouble and indifferent health, 230; alters opening lines of "Henriade," 231; sharply criticised in a French pamphlet, *ib.*; meets with a mishap, but cleverly extricates himself, 232, 233; undertakes his " History of Charles XII.," also " Brutus," 234, 235; prepares a tragedy, " La Mort de César" and the " Lettres Philosophiques," 235, 236; proposes to open a French theatre in London, 236; studies the works of Shakespeare, and is inspired by them, *ib.*; peruses the works of all the classical, and a great many of the minor, poets and prose writers of England, 236–240; prepares for return to France, 241; grateful remembrance borne by him to England, 242; disparaging stories circulated about the causes of his departure, 243, 244; leaves England, 245; anecdote of Newton's apple, 246, *note*.

WALLER, Edmund, opinion passed on by Voltaire, 238.
Walpole (Horace the elder) gives a letter of introduction to Voltaire for Bubb Dodington, 197.
Walpole, Sir Robert, his college studies at Eton, 19; opposed to Sacheverel's impeachment, 43; is imprisoned in the Tower, 60; speaks in opposition to, and charges Bolingbroke with faithlessness to his King, 86; directs a Commission of Inquiry, 90; and brings in a Bill of Attainder against Bolingbroke, 93; declines to accede to Hanmer's motion, *ib.*; meets Bolingbroke's overtures with a blunt rebuff and with a warning, 123; paralyzes Bolingbroke's offer of mediatorship at the French Court, 125; is strenuously opposed to restore Bolingbroke to his civil rights, 126; at last forced to do so by the King, 127; replies to the " Occasional Writer" of the journal, the *Craftsman*, 138; advises the King to grant Bolingbroke an interview, 139; is becoming alarmed, *ib.*; passes through a critical period after the death of the King, 141; maliciously attacked by the Opposition, 145–150; is attacked by Sir William Wyndham, 150; resumes office for another seven years, *ib.*; is becoming unpopular, 153; alliance with Cardinal Fleury, 165; resigns his Ministry, 176.
Walsingham, Lady, her animosity against Walpole, 140.
Whitefield, George, 7.
William, Prince of Orange, difficult position of, 27; proroguing Parliament, 33; arrived in London and remodels the Ministry, 34; his death, *ib*.

Wilmot, Earl of Rochester, the prototype of youthful libertines, 22.
Winchescombe, Frances, daughter of Sir Henry W., marriage of, with Henry St. John, 26; her affection towards him and subsequent estrangement, *ib.;* her death, 113.
Wright, Sir Nathan, resigns his seat in Ministry, 37.
Wyndham, Sir William, his correspondence with Bolingbroke, 60; warrant made out for his arrest, 103; letters to, from Bolingbroke, 110, 111; his position as leader of the Hanoverian Tories, 136; attacks Walpole in Parliament, 150; receives letter from Bolingbroke explaining his sudden departure from England, 164.

Young, Edward, the poet, his acquaintance with Voltaire, 205; dedicated one of his poems to him, *ib.;* author of an epigram on Voltaire, 206; assists him in revising manuscript of his English essays, 223.

THE END.

www.ingramcontent.com/pod-product-compliance
Lightning Source LLC
Chambersburg PA
CBHW031949230426
43672CB00010B/2105